797,885 Books

are available to read at

Forgotten Books

www.ForgottenBooks.com

Forgotten Books' App
Available for mobile, tablet & eReader

ISBN 978-1-331-00913-9
PIBN 10132980

This book is a reproduction of an important historical work. Forgotten Books uses state-of-the-art technology to digitally reconstruct the work, preserving the original format whilst repairing imperfections present in the aged copy. In rare cases, an imperfection in the original, such as a blemish or missing page, may be replicated in our edition. We do, however, repair the vast majority of imperfections successfully; any imperfections that remain are intentionally left to preserve the state of such historical works.

Forgotten Books is a registered trademark of FB &c Ltd.
Copyright © 2017 FB &c Ltd.
FB &c Ltd, Dalton House, 60 Windsor Avenue, London, SW19 2RR.
Company number 08720141. Registered in England and Wales.

For support please visit www.forgottenbooks.com

1 MONTH OF FREE READING

at

www.ForgottenBooks.com

By purchasing this book you are eligible for one month membership to ForgottenBooks.com, giving you unlimited access to our entire collection of over 700,000 titles via our web site and mobile apps.

To claim your free month visit:
www.forgottenbooks.com/free132980

* Offer is valid for 45 days from date of purchase. Terms and conditions apply.

English
Français
Deutsche
Italiano
Español
Português

www.forgottenbooks.com

Mythology Photography **Fiction** Fishing Christianity **Art** Cooking Essays Buddhism Freemasonry Medicine **Biology** Music **Ancient Egypt** Evolution Carpentry Physics Dance Geology **Mathematics** Fitness Shakespeare **Folklore** Yoga Marketing **Confidence** Immortality Biographies Poetry **Psychology** Witchcraft Electronics Chemistry History **Law** Accounting **Philosophy** Anthropology Alchemy Drama Quantum Mechanics Atheism Sexual Health **Ancient History Entrepreneurship** Languages Sport Paleontology Needlework Islam **Metaphysics** Investment Archaeology Parenting Statistics Criminology **Motivational**

AUSTRIA: HER PEOPLE AND THEIR HOMELANDS

*WORKS BY THE SAME AUTHOR
RELATING TO AUSTRIA*

PICTURES FROM BOHEMIA

LITERARY AND BIOGRAPHICAL STUDIES

A FORGOTTEN GREAT ENGLISHMAN

THE CARDINAL'S PAGE

THE GLEAMING DAWN

MARK TILLOTSON

JOHN WESTACOTT

REPORT ON TECHNICAL AND COMMERCIAL EDUCATION IN CENTRAL EUROPE

&c. &c.

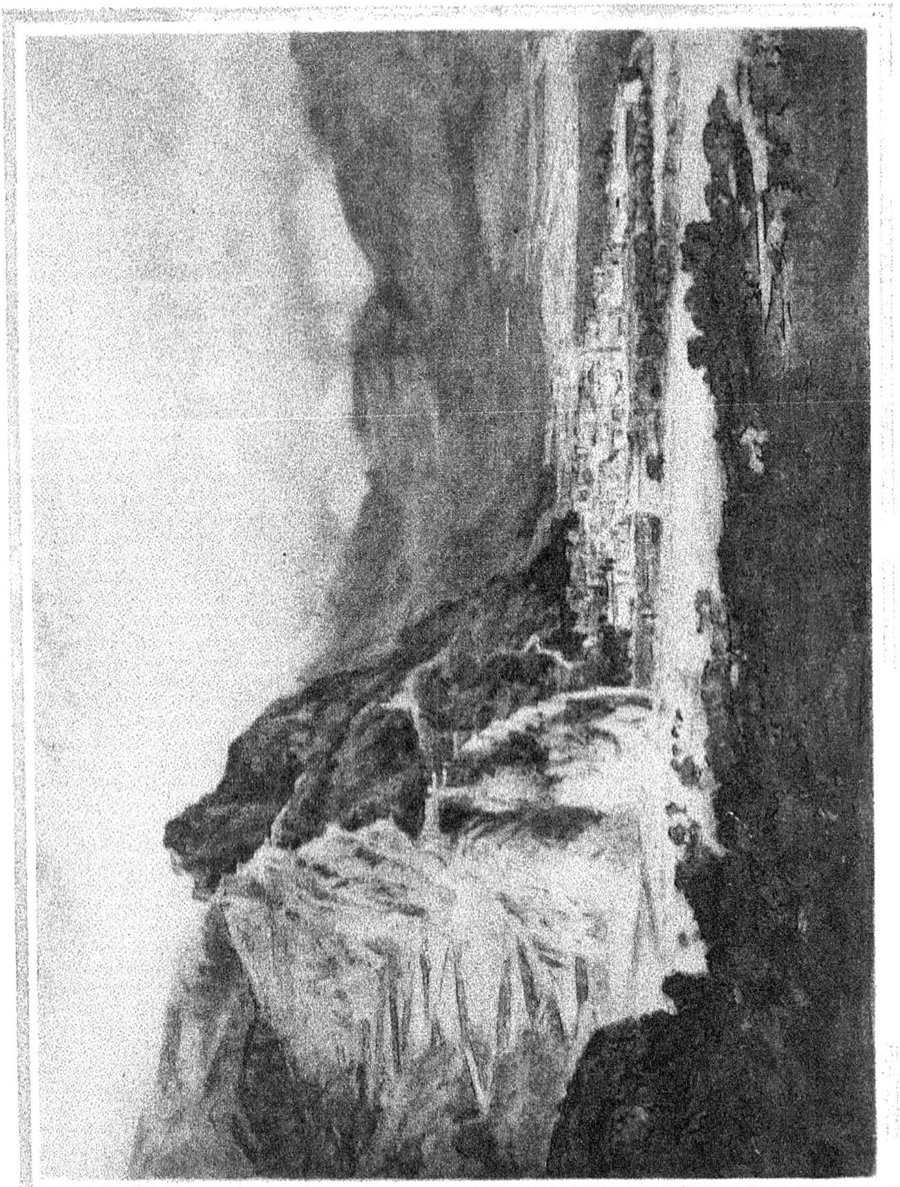

BY JAMES BAKER, F.R.G.S. F.R.Hist.Soc., KNIGHT OF THE IMPERIAL ORDER FRANCIS JOSEPH I., CORRESPONDING MEMBER OF THE ROYAL ACADEMY OF ARTS MADRID. WITH FORTY-EIGHT ILLUSTRATIONS BY DONALD MAXWELL

LONDON JOHN LANE THE BODLEY HEAD
NEW YORK JOHN LANE COMPANY
TORONTO BELL & COCKBURN MCMXIII

DB 26
.B 3

Gift
Publisher
JUL 7 1913

Turnbull & Spears, Printers, Edinburgh

TO
MY WIFE

NOTE

For the names of places no exact rule has been followed. Locally now in Austria the traveller will find the names of towns given in two, and even three, tongues; and it is necessary to know the name in the language preponderant in the district, and used in Maps and Guide-books. Frequently the dual name is given, such as the Slav and the Teuton, although the Slav accents have perforce been omitted.

CONTENTS

CHAP.		PAGE
I.	INTRODUCTORY	3
II.	INTO AUSTRIA VIA THE ELBE. NORTHERN AND EASTERN BOHEMIA	8
III.	THE CAPITAL OF BOHEMIA, PRAGUE	21
IV.	SOUTHERN AND WESTERN BOHEMIA	30
V.	THROUGH SILESIA TO MORAVIA	43
VI.	THE CHARM OF MORAVIA	55
VII.	GALICIA AND ITS PEOPLE	63
VIII.	IN THE HIGH TATRA MOUNTAINS	69
IX.	THROUGH LEMBERG TO THE BUKOWINA	77
X.	IN THE BUKOWINA	83
XI.	IN IMPERIAL VIENNA	91
XII.	LOWER AUSTRIA—THE SEMMERING	108
XIII.	STYRIA (THE STEIERMARK) AND GRAZ	114
XIV.	CARNIOLA (KRAIN)—LJUBLJANA (LAIBACH)	125
XV.	CARNIOLA, WOCHEIN FEISTRITZ, VELDES, AND ADELSBERG	132
XVI.	TRIEST AND ISTRIA	142
XVII.	DOWN THE ISTRIAN COAST TO DALMATIA, TO SEBENICO	149

Austria

CHAP.		PAGE
XVIII.	Down the Dalmatian Coast from Sebenico to Cattaro	157
XIX.	Through Küstenland, Gorizia (Görz), and Carinthia (Kärnten)	180
XX.	The Tauern Railway to Bad Gastein	193
XXI.	The Tauern Railway to Salzburg	199
XXII.	Salzburg and the Salzkammergut	206
XXIII.	The Salzkammergut	212
XXIV.	The Danube—from the Bavarian Frontier to Linz	227
XXV.	The Danube from Linz to Vienna	241
XXVI.	The Danube through the Wachau to Krems	259
XXVII.	The Danube from Krems to the Austrian Frontier	271
XXVIII.	Through the Tyrol from Lake Garda to Trent (Trient or Trento)	277
XXIX.	The Tyrol from Trent to Meran and Cortina	285
XXX.	Innsbruck and the Arlberg	294
	Index	303

ILLUSTRATIONS

Cattaro	*Frontispiece*
	FACING PAGE
Tetschen	10
Prague. The Palace, from Prince Furstenburg's Gardens	24
Charles Bridge, Prague	28
Karlstein	30
Tabor	32
Krumau	34
Budweis	36
Prachatic	38
Brünn	52
Krakau	64
Zakopane	70
Cernowitz	84
Aspernbrücke, Vienna	96
The Tower of St Stephen's, Vienna	106
Graz	120
Laibach	126
Veldes	136
Trieste—Twilight	142
The Grand Canal, Trieste	144
Rovigno, Istria	150
The Velibite Mountains	152
Pola	154
Lesina	164

Austria

	FACING PAGE
RAGUSA	168
THE WALLS OF RAGUSA	170
IN THE IZONZO VALLEY	182
MALLNITZ	198
SALZBURG	208
ZELL AM SEE	210
MONDSEE	214
LINZ	236
IN THE STODER VALLEY	240
MOLK	254
AGGSTEIN	260
DÜRRENSTEIN	262
STEIN	264
A VILLAGE IN GALICIA	278
THE SCENE WHICH INSPIRED DANTE'S INFERNO—THE LARINI DI MARCO NEAR TRIESTE	280
A BACK STREET IN TRENTO	282
ROSENGARTEN, FROM THE TSCHAMINTHAL	284
TRAFOI	286
SIGMUNDSKRON	288
BRUNECK, IN THE PUSTERTHAL	290
CRODA DA LAGO	292
INNSBRUCK	294
IN THE ARLBERG PASS	296
HALL IN TIROL	298

AUSTRIA: HER PEOPLE AND THEIR HOMELANDS

AUSTRIA

CHAPTER I

INTRODUCTORY

AUSTRIA as an Empire contains every type of Nature glory that Europe has to offer, and such varied races of humanity dwell within her borders that the student of history and ethnology is overwhelmed with dramatic incident and varied intensity of contrast.

And yet how little known is Austria to English readers. Of all that vast Empire, teeming with delightful beauty and exciting glories, certain points are known to the British traveller and diplomatist: the capitals such as Vienna, Prague, and Cracow, are known at least by name, although in sending a wire lately to Prague at a big English post office, I was given the German rate, and on doubting the price, was asked if it was not in Germany!

The glorious rivers of Austria, the Danube, Moldau or Vltava, to give its Bohemian name, and Elbe, are also known by name, but how few English are there who have wandered up the wild and intensely romantic ravines or klamms or grunds of the Elbe and Moldau, or halted on the famous historic spots on the Danube,

Austria

amidst the romantic hills overshadowing the beauteous wide sweeps of that mighty flood.

The Danube! That is sung of in the Niebelungen Lied, in Undine, and many legends and stories; that has witnessed such heroic scenes in both mediæval and modern times.

Austria's lesser rivers issue from mountain gorges that climb up to rugged, serrated mountain peaks far above the snow line, and from glacier heights they leap down to mirrored lakes that exceed in varied romantic beauty of both form and colour the better-known lakes of Italy or Switzerland.

The clusters of emerald and turquoise gems that lie amidst the mountains at Ischl and at St Wolfgang, at Veldes and Wochein-Feistritz, and in the Tyrol, have a wondrous, varied charm that is ever enticing and beauteous. The railways that penetrate these mountain fastnesses are marvels of engineering skill that excite the expert in such details.

There is also the sea-coast of Austria, down the Adriatic, combining the colour of Italy with the soft, grey elusiveness of the Grecian isles. The towns upon its shores are full of wondrous monuments of past glories, under Roman and Venetian rule; whilst the peoples of mingled Eastern and Western types, now living amidst these monuments, still retain much of their picturesque costume, and old habits of life and speech. The towns of Austria vary from the almost perfect mediæval walled town, with its watchman patrolling around its gates and walls and towers, to the most modern city, built entirely upon new ideas, a city without a slum; and the capitals of the various kingdoms and provinces, that make up this varied

Introductory

Empire, have in their splendid modern development preserved much of their historic glory.

The peasantry are yet full of mediæval custom, and their costume in many spots is brilliant in colour and quaint in style; but these same peasants are keenly alive to the scientific learning of the day, their knowledge gained under the very interesting and remarkable system of education adopted in Austria. The student of history, archæology, or ethnology will find hints in this volume of as yet untrodden fields of research. Vast libraries, or the archives of small towns, contain light upon our own history, when it has been linked, as it so often has been, with that of Austria; and the lover of romance can lave in a perfect sea of strange, weird legend, or historic fact yet stranger, and more weird and horrible, linked with the castles, abbeys, and monasteries that cluster so thickly on the hills and river banks, and yield so much to the lover of architecture, history, or folklore.

Not only in the ruins, or in the castles, that perchance for a thousand years have been inhabited, are preserved historic mementoes of the past, but in the palatial or tiny museums that are lovingly tended in city and townlet all over Austria. Art treasures, pictures, missals, books, armour, glass, domestic objects, needlework, all the past life is illustrated and jealously guarded.

In the matter of climate the traveller has enormous variety, from the mountain range of the Riesengebirge in the north, where the " snow men " even in May clothe the hills in white, to the soft, luxurious, southern air at Ragusa on the Adriatic, where summer ever smiles, and palms and roses flourish.

Austria

And the student in botany or geology has a vast variety of Nature's handiwork before him, sometimes embracing most unusual if not unique examples.

To the sportsman, the fisherman, and huntsman, Austria and her rivers, lakes, and forests offer big opportunities, for not only is Nature prolific with fish and game, but Austria in this, as in so many other things, takes care that the latest science assists Nature. In winter, sport of ski-ing and skating, and tobogganing or luging, as the French call it, can be revelled in on the mountain heights in glorious sunshine.

There are two things by which Austria has conquered the world, her music, and her industrial methods.

Her music in the days of Mozart and Haydn lit the intellectual world with its beauty, and to-day her composers, Dvořák, Strauss, Smetana, and her musicians, be they German or Slav, command the reverence and respect of all lovers of music.

One great work has been done in Austria, in all her dominions, by her remarkable educational system that decentralises, and yet in the end centralises, the highest types of scientific and technical education, enabling genius wherever found to advance and assist the nation; and thus it is that Austrian products, her artistic creations, and domestic furniture are seen in every home in the western world, and her land is tilled with scientific knowledge, so that an Irish journalist who had travelled with the author through Bohemia, wrote: "There is only one thing they cannot grow, and that is weeds."

With such a vast outlook over such an Empire, so full of varied and intense interests, where the people

Introductory

of many races, speaking varied tongues, are all pressing forward in national and industrial life, how in one volume give such an impression of the whole as to induce the reader to go to Austria, and there study and enjoy the glories and beauty of her Empire? But such is the aim of both artist and writer in this volume, and may that object be successfully attained.

CHAPTER II

INTO AUSTRIA VIA THE ELBE. NORTHERN AND EASTERN BOHEMIA

FOR the traveller from England there are two especial gates of entry into Austria, through France and over that most picturesque of railways, the Arlberg, to the pleasant town of Innsbruck, lying amidst the snowy Alps, or via the Hook of Holland to Dresden, and up through the rocky palisades of the Elbe to cross the frontier, afoot or riding, amidst the forests of Saxon Switzerland, or at the frontier railway town of Bodenbach on the Elbe.

It is by this latter route we commence our tour and study of Austria. There are of course other routes to Dresden, via Flushing, Ostend, or Calais, and Austria can also be entered by railways at such a point as Eger, for those going direct to Marienbad or Carlsbad, but this district we shall quickly reach also by the Dresden route.

Perhaps the most pleasantly picturesque way to enter Austria is to travel up from Dresden, by the comfortable and well-found Elbe saloon steamers, to disembark at Schandau, the last important German halting-place, send on the luggage to Herrenskretchen, and walk (or ride : ponies may be hired) a most delightful four and a half hours walk through the forest-clad mountains to this first Bohemian town.

Northern and Eastern Bohemia

The frontier is crossed between the height of the Grosse Winterberg and the strange, massive, natural arch of the Prebischthor, which is in Austria.

Standing on this strange and giddy outlook point, the traveller will begin to glean some faint idea of the picturesque, varied beauty of the kingdom of Bohemia, one of the richest jewels in the Austrian Imperial Crown.

A vast territory lies around of mountain peak and dark forest upland, and in the valleys lie the picturesque, prosperous villages, surrounded by meadow and fruit orchards, and cornland watered by innumerable streams that give fertility to the soil, and are often used as motive power for industrial work. In descending from this aerial outlook, one of the most romantic ravines in all Austria can be traversed, the Edmunds Klamm; these klamms, or defiles, or gorges, to give them an English title, are characteristic of the mountain passes in many parts of Austria; and in this Northern Bohemia lie also the fantastic and even grotesque mighty rock formations that have been dubbed " Rock towns." The two greatest of these strange Titanic groups of weird rocks lie in the extreme north of Bohemia on the borders of Prussian Silesia; Adersbach, and Weckelsdorf. These formations were supposed to be enchanted towns turned into stone, so like are the vast rock piles to man's fortifications. But beyond the great line of masses of rock, isolated piers start up and are formed into grotesque shapes of varied forms, men and women, animals, etc., and at their base are caverns and narrow passages that are awe-inspiring and weirdly strange.

The first time we saw Edmunds Klamm was in

early spring, and we dropped down into the narrow defile after a walk from the little town of Herrenskretchen to the village of Johnsdorf. Often since then have I pierced into these silent mountain recesses, beautiful at all seasons, but even in autumn never more lovely than on this day of spring, when the sombre pines that sprang from every rock ledge contrasted with the delicate, fresh, young green leaves of the birch; the winter's torrents were still frozen, and hung in crystal light-blue and white cascades over the grey, towering rocks; and these rocks were lit up with great splashes of sulphur-hued lichen, whilst overhead, above the mighty precipitous palisades, was the soft, clear blue sky in brilliant sunshine. Down through the gorge, rushes and hurtles, and foams onward the little river Kamnitz, rushing down rapids and over falls, but all at once it reaches a deeply worn bed, and all is still: and one can take a boat, and in absolute silence float on down the stream until another waterfall is reached, and the boat must be abandoned. A pleasant walk leads on through a gorge that reminds one of the Lyn Valley in Devon, or the Wye and its upper reaches, and yet here there is a vastness, and touches of colour not present in Welsh or Devon scenery. Then again a boat can be taken, and save in dry seasons the rapids of the little Kamnitz can be shot, down to the romantic village of Herrenskretchen on the broad Elbe.

This is as it were but a thumb-nail sketch of a marvellously beautiful scene, about which one could paint many pictures; but our vast subject and limited space enforce condensation, and this picture of Edmunds Klamm pleads to the reader to imagine

TETSCHEN

Northern and Eastern Bohemia

hundreds of such scenes as this in Bohemia, and in other parts of Austria, where her mountain streams carve out a beauty of varied charm in their course to Danube, or Elbe, or Moldau, or to her mountain lakes.

The Elbe from Herrenskretchen to Leitmeritz or Litomerice is full of beauty and interest. At Tetschen a diversion can be made from the river, and the railway utilised for excursions into a part of Bohemia that is crowded with strange scenery, and castles perched in romantic positions amidst mysterious rocky fastnesses.

The railway climbs slowly the hills until Tannenberg is reached, one of the highest points; and then one can drop down by various routes either to the plateaus surrounded by the Iser Mountains or still farther onward, either by motor or carriage or rail, to Reichenberg and Turnov (Turnau) and Trautenau, from whence a view of the Giant Mountains is gained.

In this district, wherein lie these towns, there are wonders of Nature and beauties of scenery, and historic castles and quaint towns that would pleasantly occupy months of travel. And herein lie also busy industries such as glass, ceramics, weaving, jewellery; and educational establishments for the development of these industries that will detain the enthusiast in artistic development many a day. At Reichenberg is the oldest weaving school in Europe, splendidly equipped, and an excellent industrial museum. At Turnov a jewellery school of extremely high order, and deeply interesting; at Trautenau an agricultural school, and in this district also are the remarkable castles of Burgstein or Sloup, a great castle scooped

Austria

out of an isolated standstone rock; the historic, picturesque fortress of Bezdez or Bösig, the castles of the Wallenstein family, and the Roll ruin from whence such a vast view can be had of this romantic district, and a score of other castles, many still inhabited, others picturesque ruins.

Not a volume but a pile of volumes might be written upon the legend and history and architecture of the castles of Bohemia. The whole of Bohemia is dotted with these strongholds, and some of the most characteristic are in this northern section of the country, although all Bohemia teems with them.

The castle of Friedland, the erstwhile home of Wallenstein, is exceptionally well placed; built around a basaltic mountain cone, now with extensive, handsome halls full of art and history treasures. The first building was a strong tower at the summit of the cone, and to-day the dungeons of the castle are at the summit, but embedded in the solid basalt. The date on this tower is 1014, and its fitful, fierce history can be traced until to-day.

Perhaps the weirdest of all these castles is that of Burgstein or Sloup near Haida. This was an isolated mass of sandstone left in a plainland and rising some 200 feet above the level. On its summit now flourish pine trees and other vegetation. But enter at its base, and by a narrow and V-shaped staircase, just wide enough for one person at a time to ascend, all the rooms, and armoury, and chapel, and stables of a castle can be entered; all scooped out of the solid rock. Around this impregnable fortress was a lake, and the only approach was defended by a drawbridge; and from this stronghold sallied forth

Northern and Eastern Bohemia

the robber baron who held it, and ravaged the country around. In its Hunger tower when opened were found relics of humanity, and inscriptions carved on the walls, and drawings of loaves of bread, the chalice, the Husite's sign; roses, death's-heads and crosses, a woman with a child, and a line of strokes, perhaps the tally of days of some poor, starving wretch, maimed but not killed when thrown down. These Hunger towers are always a part of all the mediæval castles in Central Europe.

Another castle, not so weird, but of more imposing dimensions, is that of Bösig or Bezdez. Here is a great Hunger tower, never yet opened; the walls are 15 feet in thickness. Another tall tower above, on the summit of the rocky ridge the castle walls enclose, commands a magnificent expanse of view, and the chapel is a charming example of fourteenth-century work. At one of the trefoil-headed windows were two niches that had both been walled up; on opening them a skeleton was found walled into the one, the other was empty; the awful problem of these two niches is full of strange, dramatic possibilities, and such problems are everywhere to be met with in these fascinating ruins, or still inhabited castles of Bohemia. In the volume " Pictures from Bohemia " I have sketched many of them, and developed some of them in my novels. In this district there is also the peculiarly strange type of scenery known as the Rock towns—wild labyrinths of gigantic rocks towering in the strangest of forms to the varied heights of hundreds of feet, even up to 600 feet. Some of the principal of these are near Jicin and Turnov, and from the latter place the

Austria

castles of Waldstein and Gros and Klein Skal can be visited.

The range of the Giant Mountains affords a series of pleasant excursions, the highest point, the Schneekoppe, often cannot be ascended in the spring because of the snow. I remember once in the second week in May intending to ascend it, but on our awaking in the little town at the foot of the mountain all was white around us, and the porter at the inn told us it had " Kolossal geschneit heute früh."

It had snowed colossally early in the morning, and tramping through half-melting snow is not possible. But at other times of the year the ascent is quite simple. The height is just upon 5300 feet, and the view from the summit is an immense and glorious one. It is on the frontier of Germany and Austria, and the view comprises vast stretches of both Empires. The network of railway that links up all parts of Bohemia will quickly run us down from Hohenelbe from whence the Giant Mountain excursions can be made, or from Trautenau to the central plainlands of Bohemia; but the roads are good, and I have run easily at fifty miles an hour over them in an automobile, and driven hundreds of miles in pair-horsed carriages, that can be hired at low rates in most of the towns. One of the great pleasures, keenly enjoyed by all in these towns is music. At Jicin we heard a remarkable orchestra, and a mixed-voice choir, all amateurs of every grade of society in the town: their rendering of choice music was excellent.

At Jicin we are within easy driving or motoring distance of a district that has been dubbed the Bohemian Paradise; and truly it is full of great

Northern and Eastern Bohemia

natural beauty, of strange hill form; vast, grotesque rock formations, lovely valleys and river gorges and meadows, and fruit lands that are richly cultivated. It embraces the mysterious ruins of the old castle of the Wallensteins, known as Waldstein, and the still more strange castle of Gros Skal with its horrible rock dungeons and subterranean passages; and near here is the town of Turnov (Turnau) that has much besides its jewellery school to induce a halt. The district is famous also for its precious stones, especially the rich-hued Bohemian garnet. Two places especially interesting are Rotstein, with its wonderful masses of gigantic rocks, and the little town of Rovensko, where they boast of having an arrangement for the bells unique in Europe. The bells, in a tower, are hung mouth upwards, and are let go and rung by men's feet on treadles; but there is a somewhat similar arrangement at East Bergholt near Dedham in England, only here the bells are on the ground in the churchyard, and not in a tower. We heard some good music at this small town, and the school children sing well.

·The strangest of all the castles in this district, so packed full of natural beauty and historic interest, is that of the defiant Trosky—two castles perched on two lofty peaks, once opponents, then linked with a great wall, and to-day a most imposing ruin that dominates the whole country for a hundred miles over the plainland. A good ending to a tour in this district can be made at Jung Bunzlau, or Mladá Boleslav, as the Cechs call it.

Not only is the district we have been sketching full of natural beauty and industrial interest, but histori-

Austria

cally it is important—both in mediæval times, when the lords of its numerous castles, the Waldsteins and Rosenbergs and others, played important parts in European history; and in the Prussian campaign of 1866, Jicin and Trautenau, Sadowa, and the Rock town of Prokov, were the scenes of bloody conflicts and decisive battles.

Before running into Prague, the capital of Bohemia, there are some points of interest in Eastern Bohemia that cannot be omitted from any book on Austria.

The town of Kutna Hora, or Kuttenberg, to give the German name, is full of mediæval monuments, recalling the important rôle that this town played as second city, and money-chest of the kingdom of Bohemia in the fourteenth and fifteenth centuries.

In many parts of Austria there is much material for the lover of folklore and legend, and for the historical romancist; and in Bohemia especially are the legends connected with the castles, and the history highly dramatic, and here in Kutna Hora are buildings that recall a terrible past, when religious wars were carried on with savage intensity, and yet a period when architecture and other arts flourished.

The great Church of St Barbara, a superb example of fourteenth- and early fifteenth-century architecture, contains some most remarkable monuments, and the other churches and civic buildings in and around the town, some dating back to the twelfth century, all tell of a great past history; and not far from the town, overshadowing the little village of Kank, is a hill, the Kahlenberg, that recalls vividly the terrors of the Hussite period.

Here was the silver mine of St Martin's, and in

Northern and Eastern Bohemia

Palacky's History is given a vivid description of the man-hunts which were adopted for catching the heretics, who were burnt or beheaded, until the executioner became so wearied and the prisoners so numerous, that they were leashed together in groups, driven to the pit's mouth, and the first one or two driven over, and these pulled all the others over, and thus they were hurled to the bottom of the mine, which was about 300 feet deep. History states that no less than 5496 men and women were hurled down this one shaft. The reliquary or bone house chapel at Sedlec, not far off, gives awful evidence of the murderous work of this Wiclif period.

There are many points of interest and historic towns in this eastern part of Bohemia, and in the life of "A forgotten Great Englishman," and in the novels, "The Gleaming Dawn" and the "Cardinals' Page," I have given the history and somewhat of the romance of this period, when Bohemia and England were intimately linked together: when Anne of Bohemia, the wife of Richard the Second of England, lived at Bristol Castle and received the dues of Bristol and Southampton as part of her dowry, and many Bohemians were resident in England.

Not far by train from Kutna Hora is a town most prettily situated on the Elbe, the historic Podiebrad. The castle still stands, though much altered, where the great King George of Podiebrad was born. Prince Hohenlohe now resides there, and it was from here that the famous Hohenlohe memoirs went forth to the world. This town, so famous in past ages, has lately renewed its life by the discovery of valuable medicinal waters, and Prince Hohenlohe has estab-

Austria

lished a Spa, since acquired by the town, that is attracting many to the old and interesting town.

'In all these towns there is a social and family life that is very homely, but full of pleasant culture. In the upper professional and official circles and the well-to-do intellectual tradesmen who mingle together, there is always a love of literature or history, and, above all, of music. Let me sketch two homes, one of a well-known doctor, the other of a learned imperial councillor. In the first, I met at dinner the principal chemist of the town and the Protestant pastor, both learned men: the chemist, a good historian and learned antiquary; the pastor, a clever linguist and a great patriot. The doctor's house was full of artistic treasures, books, pictures and sculpture; his wife and daughters were notable housekeepers, priding themselves on their table, loaded with their own delicious productions. The ladies, as is the custom in most Slav houses, and many Teuton, wait on their guests; but after dinner, whilst looking over some missals and historic treasures, we heard delightful music in another room, and quitting our books, we went in to see Madam at the piano, joining her son, who is a master of the violin, in a duet. So do the Bohemian ladies combine, and enjoy, the dual life of the careful housekeeper and the artist.

In the imperial councillor's home the wife was proud of her confections for the table, and loved to see her guests enjoy the products of her culinary skill, and after handing round delicious coffee, she sat down to the piano and played a song of her husband's translation from the English, set to music by herself, and

Northern and Eastern Bohemia

then rambled away into masterly rendered excerpts from their own Cech masters, Dvorak, Smetana, and, on being asked, some of Wagner.

\Another example of the outcome of Bohemian education in homelife was vividly presented at Domazlice (Taus), where during a luncheon the guests were waited upon by a bevy of very handsome girls, all delightfully dressed in white and cream-coloured dresses, enriched with elaborate needlework. We were told afterwards the whole luncheon had been prepared and cooked by these ladies, who were daughters of the best families of the district, and that their dresses were entirely their own handiwork: here also we had most excellent music.

\Of the beauty of the Bohemian women we will quote a German author, writing in 1841, of a popular Slav fête on the Island in the Moldau. He devotes great space to the beauty present: " One lovely face followed each other in quick succession," and after arguing on the probable reason for this beauty, adds, " Be this, however, as it may, Prague is decidedly a very garden of beauty. For the young ladies of 1841, I am ready to give my testimony most unreservedly "; and continues, " Titian, who studied the faces of lovely women for ninety-six years, and who, while at the Court of Charles V., spent five years in Germany, tells us, it was among the ladies of Prague that he found his ideal of a beautiful female head. If we go back beyond the times of Titian, we have the declaration of Charles IV. that Prague was a *hortus deliciarum.*"

\ I was fortunate once to be at a famous Slav fête with Walter Crane on this same island. All the elite of Bohemian Society were there, dressed in the

Austria

picturesque Slav costumes, and my artist friend and I agreed with Titian's dictum.

The outcome of the athletic drill of the Bohemians was evidenced not long since in London, by the presence there of a Cech team of athletes from Bohemia, who carried off the International Challenge Shield for Physical Drill, and their performance elicited high praise from the sporting and athletic journals in England, it being stated that drill to these Bohemians was not exercise but a religion; the whole team seemed animated by one soul. This drill can be seen in many towns, but at its best in Prague, the capital, that we are about to enter.

CHAPTER III

THE CAPITAL OF BOHEMIA, PRAGUE

THE one thing that at once arrests the attention in travelling in Bohemia, and, in fact, throughout Austria, is the intense cultivation of every scrap of land, be it mountain or plain, and the quick industry of the inhabitants. In running into Prague from either point of the compass this is very noteworthy, and upon arriving in Prague one at once sees the city is very much alive. This famous old city, with a tremendous history, Zlata Praha, Golden Prague, as the Slavs so love to call it, is being, or rather has been, transformed during the last twenty years. The crooked, nauseous, dirty streets through which one twisted and wandered thirty years ago have nearly all disappeared, much to the benefit and health of the inhabitants, but all the principal historic buildings have been preserved.

One still enters the inner town by that magnificent monument of mediæval times, the historic Powder Tower, and a narrow street, with historic buildings on either hand and a picturesque market place just away to the left, leads one into the Ring, the very heart of the city; with the Týn Church on the eastern side, and the Town Hall with its great balcony and little Gothic chapel, and famous clock tower on the western side, and rising in the centre the great

Austria

monument to their national hero, John Hus, that is to be unveiled in 1915, the five hundredth anniversary of his being burnt at Constance. What change works the whirligig of time. In Prague a Roman Catholic priest quietly stated to the author that he should not be surprised if Hus were canonised as a Saint, like Joan of Arc. Standing in this Ring or Grand Place of Prague, those who know the fascinating history of the city will be able to recall many a passionate, turbulent, intensely patriotic scene enacted here, when perhaps the streets around were blocked by the chains now hanging in the adjoining Town Hall.

Prague really consists of four ancient towns, known as the Old Town, the New Town, and the Little Town, and the Vyschrad, with the two outlying portions of the Hradschin and the Josephstown. To these have been added the modern independent towns of Karlin, Smichov, Vinohrady, and Zizkov.

The oldest part of the city, is the Vyschrad, the ancient acropolis of Prague, but the Hradschin, on the other bank of the Vltava, or Moldau, is said to have been founded about 752 A.D. by the Princess Libussa, who married Premysl, the ancestor of all the Bohemian rulers until the fourteenth century; from that date until the battle of the White Mountain in 1620 the history of the city is full of dramatic incident, the two most exciting periods being when Prague was intimately linked with England by the giving and receiving a queen—by the giving of Queen Anne to Richard the Second, and by receiving as Queen, Elizabeth, the princess who became the mother of Prince Rupert, the famous

The Capital of Bohemia, Prague

General, Admiral, Scientist, of our Commonwealth period.

As we stand before the Council Chamber and Town Hall, dating back to 1338, we can see by the fine new streets that radiate from this centre, how energetic and advanced are the Prague rulers of to-day. A broad street leads us into the Josephtown or ancient Ghetto, where is left the synagogue, built about 1212, and the old Jewish Town Hall, and the strange old Jewish burying ground, with numerous crowded tombs going far back into the centuries. In this quarter now are the handsome Rudolphinum or Picture Gallery, and the Museum of Industrial Art, wherein is housed perhaps the most remarkable collection of glass in the world, almost complete as regards the marvellously beautiful examples of Bohemian glass, but it also contains a wondrously remarkable and beautiful series of the glass of other lands.

Not far off is the Clementinum, with the University Library, wherein are the MSS. of Wyclif and Luther, and this takes us round to the front of the famous tower so noted for its architecture, leading us on to the renowned bridge, the Karluv Most, *i.e.* Charles Bridge.

On this bridge, with its lines of statues, has been enacted some of the most stirring and terrible scenes in Prague history, and to-day it is the spot that the student and traveller haunts. Here one can look up and down the Vltava's broad flood, up to the Cathedral of St Vitus and the Royal Palace of the Hradcany and back to the towers and domes of the New and Old Towns, and away down to the dark steep rock overhanging the river, on which is the Vyschrad, or castle, with its old churches near by, the kernel, or rather stem, whence all this beauty and strange romantic patriotic life has sprung.

We cross the bridge and note the various interesting groups of statues on either hand, and enter the Little Town or Malá Strana, where we are in the midst of the palaces of the great nobles of Bohemia, and where steep, picturesque streets lead up to the Royal Castle and the cathedral.

One of the best views of this noble group of buildings is from the Furstenberg Gardens, looking up to the long lines of the great palace, wherein is the great hall of 1484, and from a window of this Royal Palace the Imperial Councillors were thrown in 1618, bringing about the disastrous thirty years' war, and leading on to the almost complete extinction of the Slav power in Bohemia for more than two centuries. There is a great deal to hold the traveller in this part of Prague. Close by is the palace of the Wallensteins, and also the Parliament House of the kingdom of Bohemia, and many another palace of the Bohemian nobles.

Throughout Austria the traveller will quickly note the keen rivalry of the varied races that united form the great Austrian Empire. This rivalry, which at first sight seems to constitute a weakness, is really an immense power, for the keen emulation and the struggle for supremacy has enforced advancement on all lines, and throughout Austria many of the most famous institutions, museums, art galleries, schools, technical institutions, chambers of commerce, and savings banks are due largely to this race rivalry. The sons, aye, and daughters of one race will not per-

PRAGUE. THE PALACE, FROM PRINCE FURSTENBURG'S GARDENS

The Capital of Bohemia, Prague

mit a move onward of another race without striving, not only to come abreast of that movement, but to advance further in the science, art, culture, and movement of the time.

Nowhere is this valuable rivalry more keenly exercised than in Bohemia, and the remarkable educational institutions, the art galleries, and the Ethnographical, Art Trade, National and Naprstek's Museums, and the delicately and artistically decorated Cech Theatre, all give evidence of the intense vitality and culture of the Slavs in Bohemia; and the fact that the entries of names in the schools for the October session of 1911, the Cech children numbered 20,518, whilst the Germans only numbered 1632, suggests that it is with the Cechs that the future of Prague lies.

The brilliant costumes of the Cechs and their customs and folklore can well be studied in the Naprstek's Museum. M. Vojta Naprstek and Mrs Naprstek were remarkable people, and having made a modest sum in America returned to Prague with two objects: to advance the cause of Bohemia and collect all relics of her life and history, and to make England and English writers better known to Bohemians. In his life-time M. Naprstek made an extraordinary collection, and now this has developed into one of the most remarkable folks' museum in Europe.

In 1841 a German author, who travelled far over Central Europe and Russia, wrote five volumes upon his travels, and these were in a condensed form, published in one volume in English; this was one of the two books that appeared upon Austria in England between the years 1835 and 1889, being dated, London

Austria

1843. The author, a Herr J. G. Kohl, a pleasant writer and shrewd observer, gleaned much information from all the peoples of the Austrian Empire, and great was his delight at the scenery and art treasures in Bohemia, and the energy of the Bohemian excites his wonder, for he writes—

" Not only over the administration of their own country, but over the whole Empire, the Bohemians exercise great influence, owing to the important posts to which they have raised themselves by their ability and official aptitude." And of the pictures and treasures, he says, " To give an account of the picture galleries, libraries, and museums collected at the various castles of the Bohemian nobles, would, no doubt, be a highly interesting occupation, but would, at the same time, be found an herculean labour."

What would he say to-day of the public museums and galleries. The curator of an English museum, studying museums in Europe, stated that the great National Museum at Prague was far more advanced and worthy of note than museums in Dresden, Berlin, Leipzig or Hamburg.

In other parts of Austria it will be seen that other races, the Teuton and the Pole, are equally alive and keen for a cultured advancement and development of their kingdom or province, and thus the whole Empire has made tremendous strides ahead during the last quarter of a century.

I remember Prague when it was apparently a wholly German city; to-day the traveller will quickly see that it is a Slav city, but the Germans, although only about 6 per cent. of the population, have their theatre and schools, and the historic university, founded in

The Capital of Bohemia, Prague

1384, has nearly 2000 German students against about 4500 Cech students. The great technical school is also thus divided, having nearly a thousand German students to about 3000 Cechs.

From the height whereon stands the cathedral and Royal Palace some delightful walks can be had, and, above all, the Strahov monastery should be visited with its valuable library housed in a beautiful home.

Then not far off, through a lovely park which follows for a time the famous Hunger Wall, the Petrin height can be reached, whence is a most wonderful view of the whole of the city; all her domes and towers, and cupolas and the quaint " tent " towers, so characteristic of Prague, are far beneath, and the broad stream of the Ultava with its historic Charles Bridge and the newer bridges. Then the walk can be continued still through a well laid out park, until at the foot of the hill the gardens are reached, wherein is situated the excellently planned Ethnographical Museum. Wherein, as it were in life, by well dressed models in the various rich costumes, the home life of the people of the various districts at various epochs may be studied.

Prague is of course famous for its music: the home of Smetana and Dvorak, Kubelik, and Sevcik his famous master, and on the Sophia Island in the summer and at various halls, and at the theatres in the winter, there is ample opportunity of hearing excellent orchestras and some of the renowned bands of the Austrian army.

. The little steamers that run to the various villages up the river, give pleasant opportunity for excursions near Prague. Great works are being carried out for developing the navigation of the Ultava, and soon, by a great lock and dam improvement, boats will be able to come direct from Hamburg to Prague via the Elbe.

One of the pleasantest excursions on these small boats is up to St John's, and this river trip gives a good view of the dark grey rock on which stands the Vyschrad, the high castle whereon was built the first ruler's residence of Prague, that ruler known to legend as the father of Libussa. The later castle that played so fierce a part in the Husite wars is gone. The oldest buildings now left on this rocky height are two churches, one the romanesque chapel of St Martin, the other the church of St Peter and Paul, wherein is an interesting picture of the Vyschrad, as it was in earlier days, with walls and domes and buildings, all now disappeared. Perhaps still more interesting in this district is the Karlov church, built in 1350 by Charles IV.; its octagonal dome is said to be the largest Gothic dome, and it is of graceful proportions.

Prague and its adjoining towns give excellent examples of that problem of modern life, town planning. In the parent city slums have been swept away and beautiful streets have arisen on their sites; but Vinohrady, at the east of Prague, is an example of an entirely modern town, housing some 80,000 inhabitants without a slum. Town Hall, cathedral, theatres, schools, two delightfully laid out parks, all have been built during the last few years upon the site of the Royal vineyards, hence the name, Vinohrady. The streets are broad and lined with accacia trees, and the poor live in the upper or

CHARLES BRIDGE, PRAGUE

The Capital of Bohemia, Prague

lower parts of the houses, and thus get the same outlook as their richer brethren, and the inhabitants point with pride to the fact that all the work on their public buildings, including the fine wood carving and brass work in the cathedral, has been done by the workmen of the town. When asked why they did not use other trees than accacia, the retort was, " You forget our bee industry."

Thus does Prague interest the student of the problems of to-day by her advanced work in education, in music, in commercial vigour, and by her remarkable museums; and the student of the past, by her preservation of her famous monuments and her fierce dramatic history, but to give such a sketch of Prague and its history in a few pages, that will hint to the reader of all that will fascinate, is almost an impossibility; yet such a task in this volume will continually occur, for so many of the towns in the Austrian Empire hold one by their present-day beauty, and their historic past history.

CHAPTER IV

SOUTHERN AND WESTERN BOHEMIA

IN running south of Prague by motor, or train, one is quickly amidst the hills and in picturesque scenery. Throughout Bohemia, in the hill and mountain districts, there are always romantic castles perched on craggy summits, or hid cunningly in rocky clefts; these are perhaps more numerous in North Bohemia, but about twenty miles south of Prague is the most remarkable castle in all Bohemia, the royal treasure castle of Karlstein. I first saw this castle before it was restored, when the noble ruin and fine frescoes were covered with dust and debris, and great stone shot some two feet in diameter, lay about in the ruins, recalling the dramatic sieges of the fifteenth century. To-day this castle with its palace and three remarkable chapels, its halls and historical frescoes, has been carefully restored, so that one wanders in a vast range of buildings, much as they were when Charles IV. built them in the middle of the fifteenth century. Once on riding up to this castle we were met with the piercing cry, " Keep far from the castle, keep away from the castle, that you avoid danger of death." This, in Bohemian, was continually repeated through a speaking horn; it was the cry of the Middle Ages re-echoing in the twentieth century. We were being made to feel the dramatic fierceness of by-

KARLSTEIN

Southern and Western Bohemia

gone days. Aye, and one can go further back than into mediæval times, back into the pre-Christian era, still preserved in popular customs. A picturesque and curious sight is to be seen on Walpurgis night, the last day of April, when witches' fires must be burnt and a great noise made; for the witches are defeated on this night, and cattle and homestead are safe for the year from their attacks. No weirder sight is possible than to see on the Bohemian hills, as I once saw on the hills around this castle, these witch-fires gleaming on every height, burning besoms dipped in pitch being hurled flaming through the air, and the whole night filled with loud cries and shouts, and loud noises of all descriptions, to frighten the witches; for the next village may endow you with their witches, unless you make more noise. So may we live again in prehistoric times in this Central Europe.

If castles are more numerous in the north, brilliant costume is more prevalent in the south of Bohemia, and the towns are as interesting.

The town of Tabor, founded by Zizka, perched on its rocky height above the Jordan Lake with its walls and old watch towers and gateways, is a spot to linger in, and as everywhere in Austria one can live at one moment in mediæval times, and at the next be in the centre of the latest scientific developments. Here, in Tabor, is a great agricultural school, teaching the very latest discoveries in field, forest and garden work.

If we run farther south, at Budweis, we are approaching the Bohemian forest mountains, and are in a perfect network of picturesque scenery, great castles and towns, that for those who linger near

Austria

them give forth secrets of history and race feuds, and on Sundays and feast days especially, show a population eager in their patriotism and religion.

The railroad from Budweis to Linz has been called the grandmother of all the railways of Europe; at first it was a horse railroad, and it was stated that the levels were so difficult steam would never be used upon it.

An excellent example of the minute care and assiduity to neglect no detail and no source of knowledge, by the State, the Commune, and in some cases by the nobles, is to be seen near Budweis. Not far off is the great pile of modern building, the castle of Frauenberg, built somewhat after Windsor. But near this is the old castle or Jagdschloss, and this has been turned into a most perfect forestry exhibition.

In the courtyard were sections of giant pines 295 and 450 years old, and as we entered the house, most varied were the exhibits—every bird, animal, fish, reptile and insect, and every tree, plant, egg, to be found in the Schwarzenberg territory. Stags, eagles, boars, waterfowl, divers, storks, locusts, beetles, butterflies, all classed and arranged from the egg to full growth, or from baby animal to grandest example of full strength. All the furniture was of built-up forestry. Candelabra of horns and tusks, chairs and lounges, and tables of skins and claws. Examples of all the woods, including those used for resonant instruments, violins, guitars, etc. Strange examples of abnormal animals, every species of what an English hunter styles vermin. Enormous and most exact geological books of the century.

TABOR

Southern and Western Bohemia

Collections of the minerals and early implements of the stone and bronze ages, and some fine examples of early pottery; one great urn of black ware, eighteen inches across. In fact, so much was there to delight in and study here, that we regretted we had not given a whole day to the Jagdschloss. The castellan showed us with pride the last bear shot in the Bohmerwald on November 14, 1857. But the educational value of such a collection is beyond calculation, so scientifically yet so charmingly and artistically and amusingly arranged, for the comic element was not omitted.

The greatest of the castles of Prince Schwarzenberg, the descendant of the fighting powerful Rosenbergs of the Middle Ages, is at Krumau, or Krumlov, to give the Cech spelling, a vast pile of buildings on a rocky peak over the seething Vltava.

When Herr Kohl visited this castle in 1841 and said he wished to see as much as possible of the place, the officer to whom he spoke asked how many weeks he intended to devote to the inspection; and weeks it would take to understand the vast castle of Krumau, and especially to learn its history and legends. Prince Schwarzenberg has still his own army in the historic blue and white uniform, and the legends clinging to the castle, such as that of the White Lady, are numerous. The forerunners of the Schwarzenbergs, the Rosenbergs, were a defiant dominant race, and a certain Henry of Rosenberg made three magistrates, who came to advance a claim against him, eat the documents they brought, seals and all, and then set them free, whereupon he set the dogs after them.

Austria

I once, in calling alone at the castle, had an experience of these great boar hounds leaping around me, in their rough play, until they were called off by the daughter of the Seneschal of the castle. I have utilised this castle in "The Cardinal's Page." Herr Kohl says, "A moderately fertile writer might find material here for twenty romances."

Near Krumau, to the south, is the historic monastery of Hohenfurth, and the castle of Rosenberg, with its treasures of glass and pictures; and, if one drives north from Krumau by pleasant good roads, the mediæval town of Prachatic is reached.

' Here the double gateway with its tower and frescoed front, and the old walls and churches, carry one back in the ages; and when the Ring or central square of the town is entered, the frescoed and Sgraffitoed walls of many of the houses assist the illusion; at night especially one can re-people the town with the fierce combatants who fought for Pope or freedom, and captured and recaptured the town in mediæval days. From this old town it is a pleasant walk by the little river Blanie, out to the deep, green sloped valley, wherein lies the small town of Husinec, the birthplace of John Hus. On his house are the words, in Cech, "Mistr Jan Hus nar 8 Cervna 1369," and throughout this district, as indeed throughout Bohemia, the reverence for this hero of the fourteenth century is very pronounced. The curious fact being that it is the Roman Catholic population, which is Slav, that holds Hus in honour, the Protestant or Teutonic people being apathetic in regard to John Hus, although their own hero, Luther, was so deeply indebted to him.

KRUMAU

Southern and Western Bohemia

In such a little town in England it would be difficult to get good music, but here in Husinec (by the way not even mentioned in Baedeker's Austria), on going into the village inn on one visit, I saw a violin and flute on the table, and at a funeral the singing was excellent and a good band was there. On another occasion we heard an excellent orchestra and a string quartette of English girls, the Misses Lucas, who were pupils of Sevcik; a remarkable concert of classical music played in a superbly masterly fashion; would that in all our English small towns and villages we could get such music.

From Husinec the mountain district of the Bohemian Forest is easily gained by road or rail, and some delightful excursions can be made in this district of the Sumava. Up through the dark forests with the glorious scent of the pines, to famous points of view, or to such picturesque spots as the Black Lake, that can be reached from Eisenstein or from Spitzberg, a lake lying in a great circular wall of rocky heights, surrounded with dark fir-clad slopes, very like the volcanic lakes in the Eiffel Mountains.

From the heights around one can look across to the Bavarian Mountains, and the whole district is full of unsullied natural beauty. Somewhat to the north, at the foot of the mountains, in a vast fertile plain, lies the town of Domazlice or Taus. The great, tall watch-tower proclaims it a frontier town, and around it lived, and still live, a fine race of folk known as the Chods, the frontier watchers and guard, who had special privileges and in mediæval days were answerable to the king alone.

Austria

To-day, it is a wondrously picturesque sight to see these people in their blaze of colour, both men and women in picturesque dress. A few years since at a peasant's dance, some English writers thought an operatic scene had been arranged for their amusement, but it was only a fair day, and to the pipes a crowd of peasants were dancing. On Sundays all go to the church, the women-folk in their brilliant colours, carrying in one hand their prayer book, and in the other a clean handkerchief.

The districts from whence the peasants come can be told by the colours worn, and from the deep reds, and rich low-toned colours of this district, we pass on to the brilliant colours worn around Plzen or Pilsen, the famous brewery town.

But Pilsen is far more than a brewery town, here are also many important works, including the large Skoda establishment, where locomotives, and other machines, and the great guns are turned out for the Austrian navy.

The Sokol Athletic Society here is very active, having a good club house, and the Pilsen male voice choir is one of the most perfect in Europe; their part-singing, into which they throw all the Slav fire and yet render the pianissimo passages with delicate and exquisite tone, is a delightful treat to the musician, and at the theatre at Pilsen I once saw *King Lear* rendered, both scenically and dramatically, with wonderful power and beauty.

A visit to the town brewery is decidedly interesting, and the great hall, utilised for hospitality to famous groups of visitors, is worthy a visit for its decorations; while from a scientific point of

BUDWEIS

Southern and Western Bohemia

view the brewery is a revelation even to the general visitor.

The effect of this excellent light beer and good wine upon a lover of whisky was well exemplified by the exclamation of a Scotch journalist, who had been making a tour through Bohemia, and whose invariable habit it was to carry his native drink with him. When asked how he liked the beer and the wine, " Eh, mon," he exclaimed, " the whisky's had nae chance."

Rapidly we have to sketch in the various characteristics of the parts of this complex Empire of Austria. But we must not quit Bohemia without a word upon its great health resorts, so well known throughout the world, and Marienbad is easily reached by rail from Pilsen, passing through the quaint little town of Mies, near which, in a picturesque hill-country, lies the ruin of the Castle of Gutenstein, where Burian of Gutenstein held Peter Payne, the " Forgotten great Englishman," prisoner, whilst he wrote to the Pope and to King Henry VI. of England, striving to get a high price for his important prisoner, but neither Pope nor King would pay the price Johann Burian afterwards obtained from the Bohemian Wyclifites, viz.: two hundred schock of Groschen (a schock was sixty), five schock being the ordinary ransom for a man.

Here at Gutenstein we are amidst the hills that increase in height as we near Marienbad, where the mountains rise to about 2,000 to 3,000 feet, and the walks and excursions in the deep pine forests that clothe the hills are full of solemn beauty.

Marienbad is a juvenile bathing and health resort

Austria

compared to its more famous neighbour Carlsbad, only making its name early in the nineteenth century; but, thanks especially to the visits of King Edward VII., it has developed immensely, and is a charmingly built and well-organised health resort. The crisp mountain air and scent of the pines, especially in the early spring, being delightful. The pretty park with promenades and lakes, and the Ferdinand and Kreuz Wells are crowded with fashionable patients in the season. I once entered Marienbad in April, when every place was shut, and intense cold and snow prevailed, but now a winter-season for sports is established. Marienbad lies in a corner, as it were, between the Erzgebirge and the Bohmerwald, so that from here sorties may be made into both the mountain ranges, and the roads are good for motoring.

Carlsbad goes much further back in history than Marienbad, and the story that the springs were discovered, and the town founded by Carl IV. in the fourteenth century is not just to its antiquity, for it was known two centuries earlier, but its famous waters have secured to it an increasing fame, and to-day the town on the banks of the tumultuous rushing Tepl with its fifteen wells is the resort of patients and pleasure seekers from every part of the world, and the student of peculiar character can be well occupied in a stroll up the tree-sheltered and shop-bordered promenades of the New and Old Meadows (Neue and Alte Wiese). The special diseases cured here are gout, diabetes, and liver complaints, and the waters are generally good for stomach complaints.

Another health resort in this western portion of

PRACHATIC

Southern and Western Bohemia

Bohemia is Franzensbad, that lies not far from the historic town of Eger. Eger is a town well worth a visit, if only to stand in the death room of Wallenstein, and see the museum attached to it, and the ruins of the Kaiserburg with its double church.

One of the oldest of the health resorts of Bohemia is Teplitz, but owing probably to the great development of the coal industry in and near the town, as a health resort it is not now so much visited, although its waters retain their fame for curative powers.

But Teplitz has brought us nearly back to the Elbe by which we entered Austria and where we must quit Bohemia.

Not far from Teplitz is the busy port of Aussig on the Elbe, and just above the town rises up the giant stronghold of mediæval times, the Castle of Schreckenstein: once the key to the Elbe and the scene of many a desperate struggle.

The foundation of this castle dates from the year 820, when the Germans made raids into Bohemia, and counsel was sought how to stop this. A certain Strzek, whose name is decidedly Slav, suggested that a strong fortress should be established on the Elbe, wherein a strong fighter should live, so that the Germans should not go up or down the river. This was agreed to, and Strzek was told to chose the spot, and to build the fortress and occupy it himself: this he did upon the advantageous rocky height, and held the place in such a fashion that the Germans dared no more ascend the river.

There are other quaint legends of the foundation of this stronghold, but from this early date, down to the year 1310 when positive facts begin to be chronicled, legend fills up the void of history, and the history becomes more fierce and romantic than legend. Especially in 1426 the castle saw some terrible work in the Wyclifite wars. On the 16th June in this year, a mighty victory over the Crusaders was gained by the Wyclifites, and the slaughter was so great that 7000 Germans fell, with 500 knights and counts, and the booty included 37 schock of war waggons, richly laden; 3 schock of cannon and heavy guns; 66 schock of camp tents, and a mass of other weapons. As a schock means 60 the value of this capture was great, and on the following day the town of Aussig was stormed and the town set in flames.

Many a story and legend hangs around the old ruined walls of this castle. One of the wildest and most dramatic of these is called "Mathilde of Schreckenstein," and relates the strange deeds of Kuba of Strachov (*i.e.* Schreckenstein), who loved feuds and the chase; when there were no men to hunt, he would hunt bears and wolves. His revenge upon his enemies, his capture of Mathilde and her lover; the escape of the lover through the help of the Gnomes who lived in the mountains and Mathilde, and the ultimate revenge of the lover for the murder of his bride by Kuba, who hurled her from the battlements, make up one of those stories of love and combat of mediæval times that give such an insight into the fierce savagery and ardent devotion of the period. The wanderer amidst these Bohemian castles will glean from local volumes legend upon legend, and fact stranger than legend. Between the

Southern and Western Bohemia

years 1621 and 1648 this castle was five times besieged, so one gets fighting enough in its history.

Bohemia is the land of legend, and of song, and music, and if in old days it was the land of loyal knights and fierce robber barons, and passionate devoted religious and patriotic enthusiasts, to-day it retains much of this fervour, and the fisherman and sportsman, who can secure excellent sport in the forests and mountains, will hear many an old-time legend.

In one year something like a million head of game are killed in Bohemia, including wild boar, red deer, hares, pheasant, partridges, black cock, wild duck, quails, etc., and the Austrian government is everywhere careful to preserve and increase the fish in the streams. I have seen mountain streams in Bohemia black with trout.

And if Bohemia is interesting to historian, botanist and geologist and sportsman, it is also of great interest as an educational and industrial centre.

In old days it was the purse of the Empire because of its silver mines, to-day it is one of the richest divisions of Austria through its natural advantages, made much of by its energetic industrial leaders, and its splendid development of technical and artistic education.

It is not the purpose of this volume to give a series of figures, but rather descriptions of the people and their homelands that shall lead to a more intimate knowledge of Austria and her people. To emphasise these descriptions it may be stated that in the " Oesterreichisches Statistisches Handbook," Bohemia stands forth, in many ways, as a most important

Austria

kingdom of the Empire of Austria, in commerce, population, education, and municipal institutions. In the chapters upon the capital of the Empire, Vienna, some figures are given illustrating these facts.

CHAPTER V

THROUGH SILESIA TO MORAVIA

IN journeying from Bohemia to the capital of Moravia a most romantic stretch of country is traversed, that opens up possibilities of pleasant excursions in a country totally unknown to the ordinary tourist.

But if before leaving Bohemia, nearly on its eastern frontier at Wildenschwert, we bear north and running through the northern corner of Morvia enter Silesia, we are soon in the heart of the mountain district of the Sudeten, the highest peak of the district the Altvater, being on the frontier of Moravia and Silesia.

All around this peak are pleasant little towns that offer many quiet delights to the lover of nature, of sport, and of pedestrian tours. Perhaps one of the most pleasant of these halting spots is the new health resort of Karlsbrunn, a little town that reminds one of the earlier days of Marienbad, lying as it does deep in the hills, and surrounded with fir forests, with a reminiscence of the Bad Gastein, from the rushing stream of the Oppa that hurtles its way valleywards through the little town.

The buildings are, of course, not of the imposing style of either of these older health resorts, neither are the prices so imposing, as a room may be had here for two krone, say 1s. 9d., upwards, although on the Tariff

Austria

it is noted that in the season this price may be raised even three per cent.

The ascent of Altvater that rises 1490 metre, say 4600 feet, can be made direct from Karlsbrunn in two and a half hours, but perhaps the pleasantest route is to walk by the Oppa falls to the Schaferei in two hours, and then take the easy ascent to the summit.

The strange heavy building of the Habsburg Tower rises on the summit, and from its platform a glorious view is had of hill on hill, and dark forest interspersed with green fields and little villages, but no great towns to pollute the pure mountain air with smoke.

The members of the Tourist Union here are alive to the possibilities of this district for winter sport, and have marked out Ski runs with poles; for the snow is often very deep in this northern health resort, and famous sport is to be had on the hill-slopes around Karlsbrunn.

' The genuine nature lover will revel in tramps over the hills here, amidst the pines and pure unadulterated nature, through the little block house villages, where inns will be found with accommodation at very low rates, a krone a night, or even less, for a bed, and good wholesome living at equivalent rates. A rucksac or a knapsac is the proper baggage for such a tour, but the traveller who loves more *impedimenta* will find good accommodation at the larger towns.

One of these large towns is Jägerndorf, that lies to the east of Altvater at the Junction of the Black and Gold Oppa; the streams called Oppa here are very numerous; there are also the White and the Middle Oppa.

Through Silesia to Moravia

This frontier town, which lies on the borders of Silesia, has rapidly developed of late, and has now nearly 20,000 inhabitants, forming a pleasant place for a halt after roughing it on the hills.

ιThe student of social life in a small mountain town can here well study all that goes to make up the daily life under Austrian rule. The schools are excellent, and there is an important weaving school, as that industry is of great importance in the district, there being between thirty and forty cloth factories here, with an output of nearly a million pounds' worth of goods yearly.

From Jägerndorf, an important railway junction, it is only 18 miles to Troppau the capital of this Austrian Silesia. We run along the picturesque Oppa that separates Austria from Germany, leaving behind many a delightful hill excursion and robber's nest ruin, and enter the busy historical capital of Silesia.

ιAt the peace of Breslau, in 1742, Austria retained Troppau and a part of Jägerndorf, and in 1820 on account of a rising in Naples and Piedmont a congress was held here, but shifted to Laibach, the interesting town we shall visit in Carniola. But Troppau dates back to the twelfth century, and very early in the fourteenth century it was raised to a dukedom. One of the striking events in its history was the entry of the sardonic Wallenstein in the year 1627. To-day it is a bright well-organised town with very varied industries, a fine commercial school and museums. Especially should be visited the handsome Art and Trade Museum, an example of these establishments that in Austria, in all trade centres, do so much to

Austria

encourage research and development in every industry.

Around Troppau are many delightful spots, but above all the fine old castle of Gratz should be seen, for not only as a place of ancient birth, being mentioned in the eleventh century, and as the residence of Queen Kunigunde in the thirteenth century, but it is also famous for its siege by the Husites in the fifteenth century, when it was taken and burnt; and all music lovers should make a pilgrimage here, for from 1806 to 1811 Beethoven lived here, and in 1886 Liszt visited here.

But Troppau must not hold us, we must run on, quitting Silesia, taking a peep at Olmütz, and so journey on into the capital of Moravia, Brunn.

Moravia

In Silesia the preponderance of the inhabitants are Germans of the Teutonic stock, very many of the towns being wholly German, and others with a small sprinkling of Slavs. But in Moravia, the Slav proportion is much greater, and hence the type of life is different, and the costume of the peasants is more brilliant.

The student of ethnology has everywhere in Austria interesting facts brought before him, contrasts of temperament, contrasts of aspirations, ambitions and aims, and these contrasts are illustrated in the dress and in the habits and amusements of the manifold races that build up the Empire of Austria.

In Olmütz there are about 70 per cent. German and

Through Silesia to Moravia

30 per cent. Slavs or Cechs, and the educational establishments are divided, some for the Germans, some for the Cechs, and as usual the utilitarian side of education is well looked after, there being a Commercial school and two Trades' continuation schools in the town, besides the usual important gymnasiums, Real schools, teachers' training schools, or girls' household schools.

It is always of interest to study these educational establishments in Austria, and in connection with them the historical, trade and other museums that are generally, in even small towns, so well and originally organised. The two Rings (Ring is the usual designation all over Austria for the Central Square or *Grande Place*), the Upper and Lower Ring, are the centres of life in Olmutz. Time has played havoc with much in the town, but there are fragments of its earlier days in the Cathedral, and in the Town Hall, with its interesting museum, the history student will willingly linger; but perhaps, the most interesting monument of old times in Olmütz is the Church of St Moritz, said to be the biggest Gothic church in all Moravia.

Olmütz is rich in historical associations. In 1758, Frederick the Great besieged it, but had to raise the siege and return into Silesia, and in 1850, a Conference was held here, that resulted in, amongst other things, Schleswig-Holstein being handed over to the Danes.

But the capital of Moravia is calling us and although as we approach it a dark cloud heralds its presence, as do the smoke clouds of our North country English towns, yet, the country all around is very beautiful. The dwellers in Brünn, important centre as it is of the

Austria

cloth and leather trades of Austria, can quickly be in pastoral scenery, where picturesque rivers, much like the Wye and the Tyne in England, run through delightful scenery.

Brunn is a town full of interest from its historical buildings, or, as we enter from the railway station into the wide boulevard or Bahnring, the modern spirit of advancement of its inhabitants is soon very evident.

Good hotels, wide streets, the lamps hung with flowers in the most modern style, show the aim of its present inhabitants is to make their town beautiful in spite of the many factories that are in and around it, that have given it the title of the Austrian Manchester.

Broad flights of steps lead up from the Ring to the centre of the old town, and one is soon in the busy streets, some wide, that have replaced the old narrow streets, and others still narrow with picturesque buildings.

In the centre of the old town is the Rathhaus with its high towers and old arches, beneath one of which hangs the traditional Lindwurm, probably a crocodile. Within the courtyard is a delightful little gallery or loggia. The tympanum of the great doorway is richly decorated with sculpture, under well-carved canopies, the central figure being Justice with sword and balance. This building was rebuilt in 1311, after a fire, the town hall added about 1489, and the portal and loggia in 1511.

Some most quaint streets or rows lead from the Rathhaus to the Kraut or Vegetable Market, wherein rises up the Parnassus or Trinity Fountain, around

Through Silesia to Moravia

which are grouped the sellers of fruit and vegetables, and from the high slope above this fine, open square, a good view of the town is had, with its numerous spires, domes, towers, and fine old houses.

Near here is the Franzens Museum with a charming old courtyard, a rococo fountain in the centre, surrounded by pleasant trees; within is a collection worthy of some time being spent upon it, of prehistoric and ethnologic collections.

'In Brünn, as everywhere in Austria, commerce is made a science, and a fine commercial school and an excellent trades' museum teaches that science, the outcome being that Brünn goods are exported largely, and rumour has it that the fine cloth labelled in the tailor's shop as " Echt Englisch " (genuine English), is really Brünn cloth exported to England, and re-exported to Austria.

In prehistoric days ere Brünn's written history begins, the two heights which to-day so add to the picturesque in her centre, were probably the Kernel of her life.

To-day, lovely avenues lead up to the Franzensberg; near the summit is an obelisk " against Napoleon " erected in 1818, and dedicated by Franz I. to Austria's army and in thankfulness to faithful Moravia and Silesia.

'Pretty peeps are to be had between the trees of the cathedral and of the wide spread, smoky city. And we descend from the Franzensberg down to one of the Protestant churches, and through fine, wide, new streets, up past the great trades' museum to the foot of the Spielberg, the great hill and historic fortress of Brünn.

Austria

In spite of the great stand that Brünn and Moravia made for Protestantism, to-day there are only about 3000 Protestants in the town, and all trace here of the Moravian brotherhood is gone. In the Husite wars Brunn held for a time with Sigmund, and in 1419, received him right royally. Here John Capistran, the Franciscan monk, preached, but later Brunn, especially under the Protestant King George of Podiebrad, held fast to the Husite cause, and was one of the last towns to give in to the Papal power.

One can think over the fierce passages of history in the life of the towns, as one climbs slowly up the steep height, of about 900 feet, of the Spielberg.

The old deep-toned bells of the church, boom out over the wide plain below as we climb up to the monument to Count Radwit de Souches, who defended Brünn against the Swedes, and rising above is the old grim fortress of the Spielberg, beneath which are the terrible dungeons wherein so many prisoners have been tortured and died. Here Silvio Pellico was imprisoned, and in one of the " Martyr Holes " the Emperor Joseph II. spent an hour, and on coming out said, " I am the last prisoner in these cells," and the torture was stopped for ever.

It was an English ambassador who brought about this result, for he had studied various types of imprisonment, and had written: " better be hung in England than be pardoned in Austria," and sent to the Spielberg; and Kaiser Joseph said he would prove if this were true. But to-day the Spielberg is a joy to the dwellers in Brünn and to all who climb its height, and as we went down its pleasant gardens and tree-

Through Silesia to Moravia

clad slopes, and noted some of the cannon-balls still in the walls, young recruits were singing gaily and the hot sun was lighting up the vast plain below.

Brünn numbers about 125,000 inhabitants, nearly two-thirds being Teutons, and a little over one-third Cechs, but I was told in 1911 that the Slavs were rapidly increasing as the poor, the work people, were largely Slavs; but this development of the Slav population is noticeable throughout Bohemia and Moravia, and in other parts of Austria. But all, irrespective of race, benefit by the excellent system of Austrian education, and here not only are the town trades looked after, but there are winter schools for agriculturists and small holders, whose holdings vary from six to eighteen hectare.

In the town, the wages run, for men, from 4s. 6d. to 6s. per day, and in the Textiles, for women, from 2s. to 3s. a day. But there is a good deal of home industry done by the small holders as in other parts of Austria, and this is badly paid, a whole family earning about a pound a week. But these small holders have geese and ducks and a cow, and so eke out their living.

In curious corners, and in the churches, there is still much of the old history of Brünn to be seen; and as an example of modern enterprise, the splendid building of the Chamber of Commerce well exemplifies the business energy of her merchants. Its portal of blue-grey marble is adorned with carved symbolic heads. The walls of the fine hall for meetings are of Silesian marble, the windows of good stained-glass, and the rooms are furnished in excellent taste with good local work.

Austria

These Chambers of Commerce are not as in England, supported by private subscriptions, but every one who pays a State duty of 8 kroners and upwards, pay 5 per cent. of that amount of duty to the Chamber, thus every merchant down to the smallest shopkeeper is interested in the work of the Chamber, and can vote for the election of Director. The work in these Chambers is very thorough, opening up new avenues of trade, stating types of trade, and stability of districts and customers; the reference library here, being new, has only 17,000 volumes.

Just a reference to one other modern institution in Brünn and we must quit this interesting town, but the Artist's House or academy is one of the latest additions to Brünn's public buildings. This is built in the crude Secession style, with ugly and glaring decorations and glass, but within was a very good exhibition of the work of Moravian artists, some of the post impressionists' order madly striving for effect, and others gaining effect and impressing the lover of art by excellent work, both in landscape and figures.

And yet amidst all this modern advancement the old heathen customs die hardly in Central Europe — one might rather say they live vigorously. Many of them have, of course, been modified, and transplanted into the Greek or Roman churches, and survive in the religious ceremonies of to-day. One of the quaintest of these old-world customs, is that kept up on Palm Sunday here in Moravia. The peasants cling to their old customs as they cling to their brilliant picturesque costumes. A fête day in a Moravian village is a brilliant spectacle.

BRÜNN

Through Silesia to Moravia

The women folk in their wide distended short petticoats of every hue, their brilliant bodices with lace or silk kerchiefs thrown over the shoulders, and their many coloured headdresses, all form operatic groups when a festival or church fête is being celebrated. The men wear white jackets, with brilliant coloured facings and rosettes or bobs to collar and lapels; white breeches with black work upon them and top boots and broad hats with coloured ribbons, or perchance long white overcoats laced with black or coloured work. And it is such a crowd as this that assembles on Palm Sunday to " Carry out death." Death is the goddess Morena, the dark death goddess of the Slavs.

The figure to represent the goddess is made up of straw or flax and rags, and dressed to represent Morena. Crowds assemble in the township or village, and bear her out to the nearest deep brook or pond, singing as they go, and the Moravians are very musical. The songs are sometimes sad and doleful, and then as in all Slav music, swiftly change to bright lightness with jocular words. At the brook a heavy blow is first dealt at Morena by one of the leaders of the crowd with an iron-bound stick, then all try and deal some blow at her, and everyone essays to tear off a bit of her clothing. This they guard carefully for the year, as it constitutes a charm against sickness and death; just as the catkins or palms are treasured up from those blessed in the churches on Palm Sunday. At last after a terrific assault on her, poor Morena is tossed into the water and safely drowned. Death is defeated; winter is over; and with palm branches or branches of spring-bursting trees, entwined with

Austria

coloured ribbons, and with coloured eggs in their hands the troop of peasants go jovially back to their homes. Nature is awake again, the death god is defeated, and music, and dances and merriment are heard instead of the doleful chants with which they bore out Morena from homestead and township.

CHAPTER VI

THE CHARM OF MORAVIA

FOR landscapes the Moravian artist has glorious opportunities. But a few miles from Brunn there is a delightful district full of beauty along the banks of the pretty river Zwitta. One of the favourite spots is called Adamsthal, and a little further north is Blansko. From either of these, the whole district can be explored and it is full of charm, reminding one of our Wye and Dart, but adding to their charm of precipitous rock scenery very remarkable stalactite caverns that rival even Adelsberg in beauty, if not in size. All these wild idyllic districts throughout Austria have many romantic legends connected with precipice and cavern and lake.

We have too much space to cover, and a crowd of matter presses for admission into this volume, but there is a legend linked with this district of the Machocha (stepmother) avalanche, that is so full of retributive Nemesis that we give it.

Some hundreds of years ago there lived in Willimowitz (it will be noticed that most of these names are Slav) a miner who had lost his wife, and to give a mother to his young son, he married a poor, but pretty maiden. To her also was born a son, but as the child was too much petted, it grew up sickly and weakly, and the stepmother was jealous and

Austria

envious of the strength of her stepson. So she consulted an old woman learned in charms, and by her was advised to seek out, and pluck a certain special herbweed.

Whilst seeking in the forest for this weed, she was met by a charcoal burner, who told her that the stronger and healthier grew the stepson, the weaker would become her own child. So long as they both breathed the same air her child could never recover strength. Then an awful determination seized upon the worried mother. She called the stepson to her in the forest, and taking him to an awful precipice, where the cliffs sank sheer into the valley, she begged him to pick a herb from the edge of the cliff, for that herb would make his little brother strong and well again. She would hold him so that he should not slip.

The boy stooped over the rocks to pick the herb, and his cruel stepmother, pretending to hold him, gave him a push that hurled him into the abyss, and without a look, she hurried away to her home to find her own son, dead.

The next morning some charcoal burners on going at dawn to their work heard the moaning and cries of a child, and they found the stepson caught in the branches of a tree. They rescued him, and whilst they were succouring him and listening to his tale of how his stepmother had pushed him from the summit above, they heard a fearful shriek from a woman's voice, and from the cliff sprang the maddened mother pressing her dead child still in her arms, but no tree rescued her from the death she had intended for her stepson. And to-day, through the howling, raging storms, and soughing and hissing of the wind through

The Charm of Moravia

rocks and pines, one can hear the cries of a child, the screams of a woman, and all flee from the spot; for misfortune awaits him, who lingers in the sound of these cries of the Machocha or stepmother.

Machocha the spot is called, where this great avalanche or mountain-slide worked its ravage, and left a wild wondrous beauty spot for the modern traveller to marvel over; where leaping rivulet, and little lakes, add to the charm of broken cliff and forest scenery.

To the north of Brünn, there is picturesque scenery and an interesting folk; in running south, there is very much of interest. The whole district is excellently cultivated, and the towns have characteristic and historic monuments that will repay frequent halts, and we are going over the ground where Napoleon emphasised Austerlitz and Wagram.

Rising hill-chains break up the scenery, and the cultivated plains are dotted with prosperous villages and busy little towns. The costume of the Slav peasants is often extremely picturesque. It was a group from Ungarisch-Hradisch, an old town on the river March, that Mr Walter Crane once sketched for me in all their quaint and brilliant-coloured dress; for the Moravian peasants make pleasant old-world groups in their long white coats with coloured fringes, and embroidered breeches, and the gay parti-coloured dress of the women, with brilliant head-dress; and as in Bohemia, romantic castles, many inhabited, others in ruins, are thickly dotted in most picturesque situations over river and on hill height.

One of the richest districts for scenery and historic interest is the Thaya valley. Foolishly, local books compare it to the Rhine because of its hills and numerous castles. In old days, when the Rhine was a purely pastoral river, this may not have libelled the river Thaya, but to-day, the beauty of the Thaya heights and river bends, far exceeds that of the factory and town-crowded Rhine.

The little town of Znaim makes a good halting place for this district, and the town itself is romantically situated and historically important.

'To an Englishman the educational establishments of these small Austrian towns are extremely noteworthy. Here in Znaim, a town of only 16,000 inhabitants, is a series of remarkable establishments to develop and raise the manufactures and agriculture of the district. In addition to all the usual folk, burger, real and gymnasium schools, there is a technical school for the pottery industry, a two-class agriculture and vine-yard school, trades and commercial continuation schools, and a state and province vine cultivation school, with practising ground.

\The corporate life of these small towns is also very alert, and societies for amusement, music, fishing, shooting, boating, skating, gymnastics, tennis, are formed, and prevent effectually the dullness of provincial small town life, so complained of in other countries.

The outcome of the schools is a busy commerce in the articles invented or improved by the teaching in this district; the various varieties of pottery from Majolica to the common brown ware, and in garden and field produce especially, in preserved fruits, or vegetables, and pickles.

But Znaim charms perchance the most for the

The Charm of Moravia

natural beauties around it. It was a brilliant day, early in May, that I first drove out of the town of Znaim, across the great busy market-place, noticing the dark shades of the head-dresses, and of the women's dress generally, for the majority of the inhabitants here are of the German stock; at the village of Hodnitz we took up an old man as a guide, who was to take us to one of the nature-wonders of the place, the ice-exuding holes, where ice is plentiful in the hottest summer, in fact the hotter the summer the more the ice.

We left our vehicle at the foot of a hill, and after a lovely walk between the pines, scrambled up over smoothly worn blocks of rock to the ice holes, but there was no ice: " kein Eis da " (no ice there), exclaims our guide, so on we went until we came up to a glorious view, the Thaya winding below between the dark pine forests with a vast expanse of hill country and rocky slopes.

Vast masses of rock were lying round, over these we climbed up to a plateau where stands a monument, and scrambling down below this we soon felt there was ice near, at fissures in the rocks deathly cold blasts or currents of air were felt, and soon we came to an aperture, a great doorway of rock with flat slabs half hanging overhead, and here were great streams of ice, and all round were holes in the mountain from whence issued the deathly chilly puffs of the icy air.

A wild, strange, weirdly romantic spot.

From this height we passed down over smooth slippery slabs of rock, some moss covered, and over our heads hung great ferns and rose tall pines, to more *Eis Gruben*, where we broke off icicles 4 inches long,

Austria

and then passed down where a mighty avalanche had cleared away all trees.

It was a wild, savage scene we were amidst. The bright sun was gone, and an inky sky spread overhead, and ere we reached the foot of the hill where our carriage was to await us, the crashing storm broke, and we crouched behind a pile of cut timbers for some shelter against rain, hail, intense flashes of lightning and deafening peals of thunder.

At length we were able to move ahead, and get into the village where a funeral was proceeding, all the women in black and all the onlookers in dark clothing; the men, with priest and acolyte clustered round the coffin as the prayers were said before the house, the women being grouped near the house, a curiously dramatic ending to the awful storm we had just passed through.

If the ice caverns were interesting, so also is the Castle of Frain, that as one passes along the valley comes out majestically on a bold, high, jagged brown rock, its high white upper buildings rising above the fir trees, and its brown, square, solitary towers looking mysteriously down on the piers of natural rock. The river winds beneath and a weir forms a pretty foreground.

There is a great deal of interest in this castle, which dates from 960 A.D., and is still inhabited, having had many a romantic and stirring passage in its history.

The major domo who showed us over the halls and towers, and its art treasures, said he could not remember ever to have had any English there before; and this statement I have frequently met with in

The Charm of Moravia

some of the most gloriously beautiful, and historically exciting spots in Austria.

If the neighbourhood of Znaim is full of beauty and Sehenswürdigkeiten (things worth seeing), so also is the town itself, with its historic buildings, besides the modern buildings for culture and amusement.

It was on a Sunday morning that we were awakened at 5 A.M. by an excellent band; and when we went up to the old palace, that is now partly a barrack, we found the soldiers busy cleaning their coats and accoutrements. The whole town breathes of history, and history in these towns has been full of intense passion and fierce drama. Ottocarius Rex is carved on the palace gateway, reminding one that Ottakar I. founded Znaim in 1226, and through all its history Znaim has had an eventful life, especially when it warmly sided with the Reformation in the fifteenth century, and again in the seventeenth century, when Wallenstein with his staff resided here.

A curious link with the past is the little Wenzel's chapel that stands not far from the interesting church of St Nicholas. This chapel, dedicated to Wencelaus, the patron saint of Bohemia, is a double church, one superimposed on the other as at Eger, and the strange fact is that in the upper church the Roman Catholic rites are celebrated, whilst in the lower church the worship is in the Protestant faith. It had been noised abroad in the town that we were English; and whilst we were studying this remarkable architectural monument, the upper church being in Romanesque style, and the lower in the earlier style with galleries in the heavy walls, we were asked if we were Evangelistic. We answered we were Protestants, and re-

Austria

ceived a warm greeting, and the pastor was sent for, who told us there were only a hundred Protestants in the town, but the little group, who soon crowded round us, showed their intense warmth of feeling in the faith of Hus. But the Roman Catholics of to-day in Bohemia and Moravia are decidedly broad-minded, and their churches are often plainer than our own ritualistic churches.

From near this little church we could see how the town is perched up upon the rock over the beautiful valley of the Thaya, and people and town, and all the charm and fascination of history and scenery, held us in their sway, and tempted us to pay a return visit to Moravia.

CHAPTER VII

GALICIA AND ITS PEOPLE

TO enter Galicia from Southern Moravia we pierce through the Beskiden Mountains that are linked with the most northern chains of the vast range generally known as the Carpathians. These mountains are not high, running only to about 4000 feet, but they are full of charming spots and romantic beauty, and a happy hunting ground for geologist, botanist, and sportsman. Upon entering Galicia we are soon in touch with the great river Vistula, that plays so important a part in the history and commerce of the province and the ancient kingdom of Poland. Travelling over the great well-watered plains of the province, Cracow is the first town of importance we arrive at upon this route, and Cracow is a fascinating town not only from its history and all the monuments of its great past that are preserved to it, but also by reason of its people and their picturesque costume and quaint customs.

Here under Austrian rule the Pole is free to speak his own tongue, and to sing his own songs. Arriving, as I have done on more than one occasion, from the Polish Provinces of Russia and Germany, the contrast of the life of the Pole in these three divisions of the old kingdom is very noteworthy.

To stand in the Ring or central square of Cracow is for the lover of history a moment of keen emotion.

Austria

Here have been enunciated, and fought out, some of the most passionate struggles of humanity in Europe, and Cracow has preserved enough of her historic buildings vividly to rebuild the past and its history.

The great church of St Mary with its two towers rises up above the great Cloth Hall, and the scene within, especially upon a fête day, impresses one with the fervour of the peasants for their religion, and, as the incense rises before the elaborately beautiful high altar, the work of Veit Stoss, the low bending worshippers form a mass of colour of every hue. The men to-day are not so vivid in colour as formerly, but the long white coat with red and black facings, with the varied coloured vests with contrasting fringes, are still everywhere to be seen, and the jackets of brilliant red and blue, when the long white coat is not hiding them, make church and market place a kaleidoscope of colour.

The groups of women in the market outside the church are full of rich beauty of colour and picturesque dress. Alas, the cheapness of modern clothes, compared with these carefully made, enduring, brilliant costumes, is steadily reducing the wearing of the old dress.

As one stands at the entrance to the old Cloth Hall and looks up at the two towers of St Mary's, one is shown hanging by a chain to the archway a great rough knife to which a gruesome legend is attached. It was with this knife that one of the brothers, the twin architects of the two towers, slew the other, because his tower was approaching completion too rapidly, and in advance of the work of the murderer.

As one looks around at the varied types of houses

KRAKAU

Galicia and its People

that form the square, one is struck by a peculiarity, some of the houses being very narrow with little frontage, others with broad, handsome façades.

But few would guess at the quaint reason, for this inequality of houses built apparently at the same period. It arises from a law that only the higher nobles be permitted to have houses with five windows on each floor, the lesser nobles were allowed three windows, and the plain burghers but two, and it strikes one quaintly to see a burgher's little house with but two windows squeezed between two patrician houses with five or three windows.

Austria is not afraid to allow the Poles in Galicia to speak and sing of their history, and with pride, tinged perhaps with a little sadness, the Poles of Cracow show you their monuments to their national heroes in the cathedral. The one to John Sobieski, the saviour of Vienna, has but a simple gold ring on the black marble tomb with the initials J. S. and the numeral III between them. On Kosciuszko's tomb is only the name, but when I last stood there a quantity of wreaths and flowers were laid upon their great hero's grave; he was not forgotten.

Not far off from the cathedral is the great palace or castle that rises so majestically and picturesquely over the broad flood of the Vistula.

As one of my hosts in Cracow remarked, the buildings here were all influenced by Italian workmen, and the castle is in the Italian style — three tiers of arcades with great archways and mighty towers and embattled and machiolated walls. The view of this vast pile of buildings from the river is especially interesting.

Austria

I once, at Midsummer, witnessed a very picturesque fête on the Vistula below this castle; an old Pagan custom, still heartily enacted. The maidens throw wreaths of flowers into the river and the floods carry them down, and the young men watch for them as they flow down the stream and seize them as they near the shore. These wreaths were on boards to which were attached lights, and soon thousands of lights were seen floating down the river, and later, processions with torches were formed and the castle illuminated. This quaint custom dates from pre-historic times and is called Swieto wiankóu, the festival of wreaths. It celebrates the advent of summer, but its exact significance is not known.

One must penetrate into some of the houses to see what a beauty of architecture and decoration was attained in the heyday of Cracow's history. There is preserved in the Café Sauer, in an upper room, the beautiful Italian roof and low relief of an old chapel, with figures of the Apostles and other religious emblems; and another interesting expressive memento of the past is the great bundle of heavy chains that are hung at the corner of Slawkovska Street, one of the main streets. These are the chains that used to shut off the Jews from the central town, and confine them to the Ghetto.

These quaint memorials give glimpses into the stirring history of the old city, already in the eleventh century a city of importance, and from the time it became the capital of Poland, about 1312, until under Sigismund III. that dignity was shifted to Warsaw, Cracow held a foremost place in the history of Europe.

As one enters the city from the railway station there

Galicia and its People

is an interesting relic of Cracow's former greatness in the round, low tower and gateway, known as the Florian gate, built in 1498: an old plan of this shows it sunk in the outer moat then filled with water, with the strong walls and towers of defence beyond it, and within the walls the towers of the churches and high-gabled houses. Perhaps the greatest glory of Cracow is the fact that John Sobieski was born here in 1629, the son of the Castellan of Cracow, and he it was who, on 15th August, 1683, set out from Cracow, joining his small forces with the army of Charles of Lorraine, and thus commanding only 70,000 men; on the 12th September, he crushingly overwhelmed the vast Turkish force of 300,000 encamped round Vienna, and saved Europe from the Mohammedan flood.

In the volume which my old friend, Professor Morfill, wrote on "Poland" there is the translation of a most interesting letter from Sobieski to his wife, dated: "The 13th September, at night." With the significant heading, "In the Tent of the Vizier." Small wonder that to-day the Austrian government gives freedom to the Poles in education, and the use of their national tongue, when this glorious deliverance must ever be remembered. Sobieski's tent, whence he dated this letter, may be seen in the museum in the Cloth Hall, and here also amidst many objects of intense, historical interest are the pictures of the great Polish painters, Matejko and Siemiradzki.

Cracow holds us by her history, by her people, and by the life of to-day. Just outside the town is that remarkable conical hill, the Kosciuszko Hill, the upper cone of which is composed of earth brought from all parts of the world wherever Poles live, and from this

Austria

height we can look out over the city and the country round, and see the life of the people, artisan and peasant; and leaving unsaid so much about that life and the interesting monuments of Cracow, here say adieu to her towers and spires.

The country all around Cracow and stretching away southward is flat, and agriculture is almost the sole occupation of the people. The peasantry in their white jackets and blue breeches and jack boots, the women with their large shawls and brilliant head-dress, form picturesque groups in the country market-places and in the fields that are well cultivated. Horses, and especially ponies, are very plentiful in the fields, dairy work flourishes, and poultry is well looked after.

But if the central portion of Galicia is flat, on her border lands are the various sections of the great Carpathian Mountains, and south of Cracow, about a hundred kilometres as the crow flies, is a paradise for sportsman, fisherman, or mountaineer, botanist, or geologist, in that section of the Carpathians known as the High Tatra Mountains.

CHAPTER VIII

IN THE HIGH TATRA MOUNTAINS

THE marvellous diversity of life and scenery in Austria lends a strange and delightful charm to travelling amongst her people.

Dramatic changes are continuously succeeding each other, and this is strikingly illustrated in journeying from Cracow to that romantically encircled plateau of the Carpathians, whereon lies the picturesque little town of Zakopane.

We happened on one occasion to leave Cracow for the mountains at 7 A.M., and as we steamed out of the ancient capital all her towers stood out in fine effect under the morning sun, and over the plainland rose up that conical hill of Polish earth, dominating the flat land around it.

But we soon ran into the hill country with fir forest and sloping meadowland, and picturesque villages and pleasant little towns.

Amidst the white and grey houses of the villages, we see tiny dots of children guarding the geese or cows; one tiny mite of about four years was in charge of a flock of geese; the women folk in blue skirts and red jackets, or in red skirts and soft, brown jackets, busy in garden and field.

The country is well tilled, and the roads are fairly good, and it is noteworthy to see the quantity of small stock in every village.

Austria

At Chabówka one begins to get to the uplands, and here starts the new railway, opened in 1901, that has done so much to develop the district. A rich, fruitful district with plenty of fruit trees and wide, open meadows, and away in the distance, like soft clouds in the horizon, rises up the gloom of the vast blocks of the mountain ranges.

But we climb on, rising slowly over the vast plain to Nowy Targ, and the elusive Carpathians still keep far away, but soon isolated peaks are near, and then to the south-east and east a grand serrated range is seen, and we are in the mountain uplands, with the rich grass and soft scent of the hay. The men in the fields have white vests, and white breeches decorated with black needlework, and the women love a rich old gold tone for their head-dress.

At Poronin we are in the peculiar mountain bay, or recess, in which Zakopane lies nestled at the base, and all around is a glorious view of the mighty range of heights. Vast towering blocks, ridge on ridge, like a tumbling sea, dark, mysterious. A rushing river dashes down from the hills and pierces through a vast amphitheatre of soft grass, here and there dotted with yellow corn, and amidst the landscape are figures of women-folk in deep red dresses capped by the old gold head-dress.

Zakopane is a pleasant, bright little town, unique in itself, and yet slightly reminiscent of some of the Swiss towns in far bygone days, before crowds of British and Americans had captured and overwhelmed the district.

Good small hotels, well-built houses, and numerous pensions are situated in pleasant avenues leading

ZAKOPANE.

In the High Tatra Mountains

away to the pine forests that shade the country roads, and, towering up over the town, the vast heights and strangely shaped peaks, and serrated ridges of the Tatra Mountains, the highest of all that vast mountain range that shuts off east from west known as the Carpathians, a range that circles round Eastern Europe for a distance of nearly 900 miles.

Our artist friend was arranging to get a characteristic bit of the Tatra heights from Zakopane, and at once the curious crooked peak that seems to rise sheer from the meadows by the rushing little river, the White Dunajec, called loudly for supremacy. This height of the Giewont dominates all views in the district, and delightful it is to wander up by the side of the brawling, tumbling, rushing stream, in the glorious pure air with the soft scent of the pines, mingled with the hay, amidst which are working men, women, and children, all in richly coloured and interesting costumes. The river reminds one of the Usk, and the scene around of Switzerland, with a more brilliantly dressed peasantry. We found a good view of the whole encircling range was had from the exercising ground of the Sokol, the presence of this gymnastic union proving that we were in a Slav district, if the brilliant colours worn by the peasants had not already asserted the fact.

·It was intensely hot in the valley on this afternoon, but in the night Zakopane was to show us its power of ₁uick atmospheric change; for, after dinner, when all the guests of the Dr Chramiece Institution, where we were staying, were amusing themselves with

Austria

music and cards, and a Tombola was being drawn, in spite of the lights the whole room was flooded with lightning, and the crashes of thunder were nerve-shattering, and the next morning, on looking out over the pine-tops, lo, the mountains were white with snow.

Zakopane is perhaps the best centre for expeditions into the heart of the Carpathians in Austrian territory; the Hungarian frontier is not far off, but in this volume we are only dealing with Austria, and, in the Carpathians, Austria has enough nature wonders, to hold entranced the lover of wild, titanic, dramatic scenery.

Guides and ponies and light vehicles can easily be provided for covering the distance to the foot of the peaks to be climbed, or for crossing some of the forest passes, and for the pedestrian who loves walking, without too adventurous climbing, there are some glorious walks near Zakopane, and the idea of danger and the necessity of carrying arms in the mountains is too stupid to refer to, had not some writers suggested such a folly.

One lovely walk is up to the now deserted ironworks of Kuźnice. Here is a very large school for teaching housewifery, and in my walks I fell in with a Pole from Posen whose daughter was being educated here. There were three ranks of girls, the first paying 1500 Kronen a year, the second 1000, and the third a small fee, but these helped with the work and agreed to stay five years. We had a long talk upon the contrast of Prussian and Austrian rule of the Poles as we walked on between the grand lines of

In the High Tatra Mountains

sombre pines, with rushing mountain torrents making pleasant music on either side of the forest road; and far above the pines were the great grey craggy peaks, high in the sunlight.

The water power is used for a paper mill; at about 3500 feet up is a good restaurant, spotlessly clean, and with beautiful flowers on the tables, and in the windows. We saw, as we returned, a pretty sketch suggestive of the Real Presence, namely, a timber church, so crowded that all round the door the peasants were clustered, but one man had gone from the crowded door, and was alone; standing in his picturesque costume, with his ear glued to a chink in the timber, that he might hear and join in the service of God.

One of the favourite excursions is to the strange, weird little lake called the Morskie Oko, or Meeresauge, the " Eye of the sea," about 4500 feet above sea level, a strange wild spot, with the grey bare rocks running down to the little lake that suggest weird fantasy and legend, with the mountains above it towering to the height of 8000 or 9000 feet.

Of the dangerous sport, rock-climbing, there is plenty to be had in these mountains, and in excursions to the marvellously romantic Koscieliska Valley we saw some famous spots for tests of nerve and endurance, known as rock-climbs by local enthusiasts. But the charm and wonder of this valley and the narrow defile that leads on into the heart of the mountains is indescribable. To reach it, we pass over a wide, open plateau, with good views of the precipitous mountains, and on the hill-slopes is a vast sanatorium.

Austria

There are many of these buildings here, and they do not accord with the scenery, like the picturesque block-houses often decorated with excellently carved frontals.

But we leave the plateau and descend into the valley, that narrows into a tremendous gorge like a gigantic Cheddar.

Little pure streams, the sources of rivers, start out from beneath the rocks, as the Ombla in Dalmatia, or the Aire at Malham in Yorkshire.

The towering cliffs take strange shapes, such as the "Sleeping knight" or animal forms. A vast amphitheatre opens out of sheer precipices of over 1000 feet, and our peasant lad tells of stalactite caverns. He has brought candles with him, and we scramble up a goat's path to a cave some 300 feet above the footpath to a small cavern as yet unexplored. Another of these grottos beneath a wall of rock, rising sheer up 600 feet, is called the Smocza Jama, and not far off is the Kraków Klam or defile, and at the end of this cleft, between the rocks, was a great bastion as Königstein on the Elbe, but 1000 feet high. One rock looked as a great eagle stooping for flight, and the whole surroundings were full of wild wonder and majestic beauty, the colouring superb, and the fresh cool mountain air full of invigorating life. At the entrance to the defile, is an excellent block-house restaurant, and our guide, in his picturesque Zakopane costume, formed a good study as he sat out on the grass, sipping his hot light Polish tea.

Another expedition that gives a wondrous view of the great range of the Tatra Mountains is to the Bukowiner Hohe, through the picturesque little

In the High Tatra Mountains

townlet of Poronin. The peasants peculiar dress is of white sheepskin jackets inlaid with coloured leathers with astrachan-like collars and fringes. Highly decorated breeches with coloured pockets and stripes worked down the sides, and red or other coloured bobs. A round black hat with coloured ribbons or cords is worn. The women love a dark red dress, but especially the soft old-gold head-dress.

When we arrived on the great elevated plateau the scene was strangely beautiful. Zakopane lies as it were in a quadrangle, and on three sides of it are these great chains and peaks that shut it off from Hungary, the fourth or plain side is the exit to Galicia, and though the wind was bitterly cold, we lingered long over the view, for all the peaks around were made charming by the cloud effects, and we felt that these Tatra Mountains held much of glory and beauty as yet unknown save to the very few.

And if Zakopane has so much of natural beauty, it is interesting as a health resort; it has also two educational institutions of importance, that all interested in art technical training should visit. Both the wood-carving and the lace-making schools of Zakopane are deservedly famous.

In the wood-working schools is taught and executed the famous Zakopane style of house-decorating and wood-carving generally, and, in fact, every fashion of manipulating and utilising wood, from the homely household utensils to the inspired wood sculpture of sacred and dramatic subjects, and in the lace schools are produced delicate and original designs from the

Austria

richly worked, luxuriously expensive bed coverlets, and ladies dresses, to the simply designed collarette. Here as everywhere in Austria, this scientific technical education is developed, by utility being beautified by the artistic.

CHAPTER IX

THROUGH LEMBERG TO THE BUKOWINA

GALICIA, the province so little known to the English traveller, is, as we have seen, very full of towns and villages and natural scenery of varied types. In population Galicia ranks as the highest of all the Austrian provinces even exceeding the population of the kingdom of Bohemia, by a million, and we are now *en route*, away from the mountains over the plain lands to Lemberg, the capital of Galicia, and the seat of the Galician Diet.

Lwów, to give the Polish name, or Lemberg, before 1861, when the Diet was formed, was a poor, almost ruined town, undrained, no schools; then in 1866 a Constitution was granted, and to-day, after less than fifty years, it is a beautiful city, full of great monuments, handsome buildings, and lovely parks. The Diet House, situated in a charming garden, is a handsome building richly decorated within.

With a population just upon 200,000 inhabitants, there is an air of alertness and vivacity in her streets and promenades, that are bordered with handsome modern buildings and good statues and monuments to her heroes and benefactors, especially a vigorous equestrian monument to Sobieski. Perhaps the best spot to get a good general view of the town is from the very pretty Kilinski Park, whence the swift

Austria

development of the town can be studied, and in this park is a vivid realistic panorama of the great victory of Kosciuszko at Raclawice, near Cracow, wherein all the vigorous details give an opportunity of comparing the houses and dress of the Galician Polish peasant then and to-day.

From the height in the park the square tower of the Rathaus and the dome of the cathedral and all the lines of the streets can be traced. Below is the deep valley of green pines and birches, and beyond the rising hills, and on the right the pyramid of Kopiec, and beneath in the pretty gardens of the park, is a fine monument to Kilinski, the brave shoemaker patriot, who fought bravely in 1796, and, after imprisonment in St Petersburg, returned to his shoemaking and wrote his valuable recollections.

Another fine point of view is from the High Castle Hill, with a view to the east of the vast plain where on August 25th, 1675, Sobieski defeated 40,000 Turks and Tartars, and freed the town of Lemberg.

Away to the east one sees where Russia and Austria meet.

On the north hill is a plateau where the castle once stood, and some of the walls are left, and here is a great mound piled up by patriotic Poles, and from its summit the view can well be studied, including the town with its towers and domes and swiftly increasing well-designed streets.

Although so modern in its development the town has many noble institutions of benevolence, and especially of education, and for trade developments its educational establishments are remarkable. I called especial attention to these in my report for

Through Lemberg to the Bukowina

the Board of Education on Technical and Commercial Education in Central Europe (C.D. 419), but since that visit the schools and institutions have been extended by such important buildings as the New Art Trade School, opened in 1910, a most spacious building, where the pupils are turning out some really remarkable work in wood, iron, and other materials, and of artistic work generally, and yet another development is the Technological Institution, where men who are at work can learn the highest technique of their trades. An institution that shows the energy and alertness of the people, of Lwów to give the Polish name, is the new Chamber of Commerce, with its handsome rooms superbly decorated with rich marbles and mosaics and furnished in soft grey blue tones. The hall is illuminated with good frescoes of industries, and furnished in excellent taste. All these modern buildings are of local work and illustrate the local technique. The Library consists of 60,000 volumes.

And if Lemberg is developing rapidly she also remembers her history, and in the Dzieduszycki Museum are some intensely interesting collections of prehistoric weapons and peasants' weapons, and household utensils and dresses. Two very remarkable finds made in 1907, about ten miles from the town, are an elephant, almost intact, skin and all, and a rhinoceros, found in boring for oil wells, and preserved so astoundingly, presumably by the oily soil. Another interesting historical museum of books and pictures is the Ossolinski Museum, collected by Prince Lubomirski. Here the history of Galicia can be studied in volume and illustration, and by some most interesting relics of bygone days. The churches are interesting, especially the Roman Catholic and the Ruthenian cathedrals. In the former, dating from the fourteenth century, a chapel has been illustrated and decorated by the professors of the Art School.

The theatre is always interesting at Lemberg. The great classics of all nations are played here and the work of their national dramatists. When last there I saw a remarkable drama entitled "Eros and Psyche," illustrating the antagonistic forces of soul and love over brute passion and strength throughout the ages—an absorbing series of scenes most intensely rendered.

How much we must leave out in so short a description of such a town, where the cultured prosperity of its learned residents makes a visit so pleasant.

The general idea of the city is one of fine open streets, with many gardens and promenades, good modern buildings and statues, fine churches and monasteries, and numerous schools, technical institutes, an old university, a modern polytechnic, fine banks and shops, and a free eager townspeople, interspersed with the peasants in their brilliant costume. A town with many of the amenities of life, and a strenuous populace eager in life's race.

One word must be said of the Jews, who in their long gaberdines, and with long hair and little corkscrew curls, form so noticeable a feature in the streets. Out of 200,000 inhabitants there are 60,000 Jews.

The provincial life of the peasant in Galicia may well be studied in some of the villages near Lemberg, and the artist or photographer can obtain most delightful pictures of village scenes and peasant homes. We drove out one day to the village of Sokolniki,

Through Lemberg to the Bukowina

where the houses were bordered on long commons, where ducks and geese in crowds revelled in the green herbage and the numerous ponds, and the cows and horses were grazing in quiet peace where willows gave pleasant shade.

At one clear pond half a dozen women in the most brilliant shades of red were busy, washing their many-coloured garments. The cottages were interesting, hung with holy pictures; in one living room, where was the usual big stove and bed, the room was decorated with little figures of Mary and Christ, and flowers were in the room, and no less than seventeen sacred pictures around the walls. There was a little holy water vase, over which the rosary of beads was hung up. This was a home where there were six children, and we went into the kitchen, also well kept. In another cottage, where a sturdy farmer met us, and showed an interest in our being English, we had a chat on the holdings and the common rights. He turned out to be the Woigt, or *Maire*, of the village. He was dressed in the usual long coarse shirt, that comes down to the jackboots, a blue vest and white breeches, and a long white coat. In winter they wear a grey or fur coat. There was the usual school in the village, and little church, and the children in reds and blues were a pretty sight as they trooped out over the common. At the wells they use the same arrangement as the Shaduf in Egypt, and the tillage is good, every part of the land being utilised.

On returning to the city we passed a great cattle market with a very large amount of stock, horses, ponies, and cattle; and also small stock, such as fowls, geese, etc. The Galician peasants are not

Austria

so alert and *vive* as the Bohemians, but they are decidedly industrious and solid.

'As we journeyed on down through Galicia we noted the activity of the peasants with their second and third crops of hay, their horses and cattle, maize, flax, and potatoes, hemp being sown between the potatoes, and at every village were the flocks of geese. In the fields with the cattle were the figures in the grey-white coats guarding them, and as we crossed the Dniester we had a wide view over the vast plains with, away to the west, the distant Carpathians looming up.

At Jezupol we noted the names of the stations were in Ruthenian, as well as in Polish and German. The Ruthenians have absolute freedom in Galicia.

We were nearing now that strange corner of Europe the Bukowina, set as it were in a bay of the Carpathians and hemmed in by Hungary on the west, Roumania on the south, Russia on the east. A veritable epitome, we were told, we should find here of Austria, with all its varied peoples.

CHAPTER X

IN THE BUKOWINA

How slightly many parts of Austria are known in England was illustrated by a conversation with the well-known historian, Professor Oman, who, on hearing I was about to travel in the Bukowina, said, "I only know one Englishman who has ever been in the Bukowina, and if you get there you will be the second." I sent him a post-card from Zadagora, to prove I had "got there." And yet the Bukowina is a peculiarly interesting corner of Europe.

Here are clustered together Poles, Ruthenians, Roumanians, Germans, Magyars, Jews, Armenians, Bulgarians, Cechs, Lipowaners (*i.e.* old faith Russians), Turks, Gypsies; and the variety of religions is a strange study. Greek Orthodox and Greek Catholic, Roman Catholic and Armenian Catholic, Armenian Orthodox, Old Believers (the Lipowaners), Protestants; even the Jews have two sects, orthodox and reform. The wealth of the Greek Oriental body is very great—it possesses in territory a third of the province, largely forest land. The dress of this population is as varied and interesting as their religions. And Czernowitz, the capital, is an epitome in strangely varied scenes of this independent Crown land of Austria, that has its own "Landtag" or local parliament.

Austria

The Bukowina has also its own weather, and *that* is excessively independent. During the remarkable drought in the summer of 1911, which affected other parts of Austria, here there were floods and torrents of rain for two months.

In September we visited it, and as we neared Czernowitz we saw the quaint figures of the peasants guarding their flocks under umbrellas, and everything was sodden. In the city, in the Austrian Platz, the principle square and market place, the women peasants in their white cloth oriental head-dress and long brown coats, beneath which hung the long white shirt over the bare legs, bore umbrellas; and the men, some in curious little round Garibaldi hats over their long wavy hair, wore the long brown skin coats, with many buttons, and grey-white breeches, decorated with needlework. But the peasants' dress varies according to race, and is of great variety.

The city has very many fine buildings; the race rivalry here, as everywhere in Austria, is a spur to perfection, and an interesting way to study the variety of the educated classes of the district is to visit the "Houses," *i.e.* clubs of the different nationalities.

In the Polish house is a fine hall for dances, and a theatre, the wood-work being all carved in the Zakopane style; the drop scene is a picture of the Tatra district, with a figure of a guide in that local dress. Here educational work, and the ever present "Sokol," is carried on as in all Slav districts.

Just opposite is the German national house, a remarkably fine building, the courtyard being like a bit of old Nuremberg. Here too is a fine theatre with

CERNOWITZ

In the Bukowina

rather heavy decorations, and an excellent restaurant in old German style.

In the Roumanian's house one gets the quaint Roumanian music, and there is a large garden; but to show there is friendliness between the races, as we entered, being with some well-known Poles, Polish airs were at once played by the excellent orchestra. In the Jewish house was a very big hall with gold and red decorations. It is in these houses, or national homes, the national character is sustained, and retained. The Ruthenians also have their special house.

Perhaps the churches, the religious establishments and benevolent institutions should claim the first word in Czernowitz, for they are innumerable and wonderfully varied; every creed seems to have its hospitals and homes.

The wealth of the Greek orthodox body is well illustrated by the vast palace of the archbishop, a building with its many domes and towers and gables, that serves too as a seminary and meeting-place of the Synod, and rarely could a more imposing and richly decorated hall be found than that of the great hall where the Synod meets. Its marble arches and arcades on black marble columns, supporting a deeply coffered, richly decorated ceiling. The walls are of alabaster. From the windows are lovely views of the palace gardens and the valley of the Pruth.

Churches of the various sects, and the rich new synagogue are all worthy of study for their architecture and for the folk and peasantry that frequent them, as all are very fervid in their religion. But if religious edifices are numerous so also are the civil

Austria

buildings. The home of the Landesregierung is a handsome simple building with gardens before it, the Palais de Justice is also a fine building.

One of the most striking modern buildings is the new Savings Bank, built in the latest Secession style, and elaborately fitted up with most modern sanitation, ladies and gentlemen's waiting and toilette rooms. The council room is upholstered in soft crushed strawberry hues, with inlaid woods and elaborate electric light fittings. Even the door locks are in gilt and in lovely designs. The handsome main stairway has stained-glass windows and elaborate lamps on the pillars in brass and coloured metal. The great hall for general meetings is beautifully decorated, and even the chairs are most artistic. The whole gives an idea of the thrift of the peasantry who get 4 per cent. for their cash, and are charged 6 per cent. for loans. It is considered an honour to be on the council of this bank.

The Chamber of Commerce is another splendid building; the meeting hall is in grey and red tones, with a rich ceiling and handsome electroliers; the chimneys are of red marble and glass mosaics, and brass with inlet enamels form part of the decorations. Well-executed frescoes of agriculture, industry, and Mercury illustrate the object of the Chamber, which has widespread correspondence, and works scientifically, developing local commerce and agriculture. It is certainly housed more luxuriously, and holds far more classified information than most English Chambers of Commerce.

We were fortunate in our introductions in Czernowitz, and our kindly host, in his artistically furnished

In the Bukowina

home, gave us a glimpse of the cultured professional home and business life of Czernowitz.

Music one finds everywhere in Austria, and here, as so often elsewhere, our hostess was a lover of art and music, and a connoiseur in housekeeping and cooking; one of her hobbies was the collecting of old brass-work of Jewish homes and ceremonial, and a remarkable collection she had acquired. Her daughter spoke English well, and we here had an illustration of character, for, at the end of a delightful lunch, our artist friend suddenly exclaimed to his fair neighbour : " Oh ! I've left my mackintosh in that village, on the ground. I was sitting on it." We had left him sketching near Sadagora, four miles off, so, instead of driving with us to Ludi Horecza, he had to get out to Sadagora, where he found his mackintosh hanging up on a tree that he might see it; and a tiny mite being near, he gave it some coppers. With these the child ran back to its parents, and then there was a talk and a struggle ; and at last the small mite came timidly back, took the artist's hand and kissed it. This is the type of life amidst which we are asked if it is safe to travel.

The little town of Sadogora is a remarkable one, reminding one still in its Eastern bazaar-like streets, rough mighty cobble stones and mud, of Turkish or Russian rule. We cross the Pruth to reach it, and pass numerous settlements of Bulgarians, who have captured the market-gardening of the district. It happened to be a fair day, and crowds of cattle, especially horses, were on the road, and many peasants picturesquely dressed. The women in the market-place were rich in colour, and nearly all had

Austria

slung over their shoulders their bags in many colours of needlework harmonising with the white embroidered shirts and many-coloured heavy aprons.

The great marvel of Sadagora is the synagogue and palace, where lives and works the Wonder Rabbi Friedmann, to whom come pious or benefit-seeking Jews from all parts of Europe.

We went over the synagogue, and were met by a cluster of old Jews in their long robes and curls, and they opened the Tara Rolls for our inspection, and showed us the rich satin hangings, and then as a great favour we were shown (for a consideration) the private room of the Wonder Rabbi, with a little peep-hole through which he may see, though himself unseen. He rarely shows himself, but accepts offerings, and gives his blessing and prayers. In this room was a rich hanging of about seventeenth-century Spanish needlework for the Rolls, to be used at Pentecost; we were told it cost 70,000 roubles and was given by a devotée, who won it in a lottery for 1800 roubles. The palace of the Rabbi is opposite the synagogue, and we were told strange stories of the gifts given him, and the objects of those who sought him out.

On returning to Czernowitz we drove through the Volksgarten with its lovely avenues, shooting galleries, and halls for dancing.

As usual the trades are looked after by education, and there are weaving and agricultural schools, and English games are played, as out on the vast exercising ground we saw football in full swing, several games going, but no hopeless, senseless crowd looking on.

The road out to this breezy downland is called Russian Street, and from it a great view is had away

In the Bukowina

to the spurs of the Carpathians, the valley of Pruth, and the dark forest slopes, whilst in the valleys were sugar factories, and breweries and saw-mills, and the queer little town of Sadagora in the plains in the distance.

In driving out to the strange little church of Horecza, we saw well the peasant homes, little cottages with pretty flower gardens, and in a lovely, quiet tree-shaded valley we saw the old church, once a mosque. Within it is supported by four pillars, and over the west door is a fresco of heaven and hell and judgment. Here, as in the bishop's splendid palace, was the sign of the Holy Ghost, a face in the centre of six wings; hung upon this was a handkerchief, as an offering, as I have seen shreds of cloth hung in the mosque of Omar, and pieces of ribbon on the figures of favourite saints in Italy and France.

There were five *tourelles* to the church, to represent the world's five Continents, and three big towers, denoting the dominion of the orthodox Church.

There are other towns in the Bukowina that are full of interest, for the people and their history, and for the scenery.

One of the favourite resorts is Dorna Watra, near the Roumanian and Hungarian frontiers, and not far from the Siebenburgen. It lies on the mountain spurs, about 2500 feet above sea-level, and is a growing health resort, with fine Curhaus and baths for gout and rheumatism, for which its waters and mud baths are most curative.

There are five sources and two bath establishments, and the pretty rivers and picturesque villages make it a pleasant resort.

Austria

If the Bukowina, this unknown land to Britons, is deeply interesting through its marvellously varied races, its history has also many points of fascinating study.

It was Finnish-Mongolian in its prehistoric days, then Scythian, then Dacian and Gothic, until the Huns burst over the land. Later on came the Wends; the Avars and Magyars dominated here until the thirteenth century, when we get the Mongolians in this mountain land bay. It is not until 1360 that real history begins, and in 1395 the Castle of Cecina on the hill, that is so prominent in the view near Czernowitz, was built. In later times Sobięski won a great victory over the Turks at Bojan, and the Swedes in the eighteenth century worked ravage here, and were defeated near Czernowitz. It was not until 1775 that Austria occupied it, and in 1861 it obtained autonomy, since when it dates its rapid development.

But with this flying glance at what is a strangely interesting corner of Europe, we must quit the Bukowina, leaving far more than half its history unrecorded.

CHAPTER XI

IN IMPERIAL VIENNA

OUR chapters and pictures of some of the home lands of the Empire of Austria have been as it were but "happy prologues to the swelling act of the imperial theme," and Vienna, the beautiful capital of this strangely interesting, diversified Empire, is, the chief gem of this mighty jewel set in central Europe, that glitters with coruscating flashes, and adds lustre to the whole theme.

The homelands of Austria, as we have seen, and shall see, have much self-government, but it is Vienna, the seat of the Imperial Parliament, the home of the Emperor, that holds these lands and their peoples, binding them into one great power. But Vienna is not Austria, as Paris is France. Vienna is moved and managed by the strong forces that surge around her, and she in turn controls and stems those forces, and her influence from Parliament and the imperial throne, checks and softens too fierce or rash developments, that might wreck imperial unity.

Vienna is placed in a worthy setting for this imperial task.

· It is nigh on forty years since I first landed from a Danube steamer on her quays, and marvellous have been the developments I have watched in frequent subsequent visits. To-day Vienna is a beautiful city, surpassing, I think, Paris and Berlin, and in her environs, in the lovely crownland of Lower Austria, she has all around her glories of scenery unmatched by the surroundings of any other capital.

There are two centres in Vienna, the one in the heart of the city, in front of that wonderful building with its high, tapering spire, St Stephen's cathedral, that for seven hundred years has been a holy shrine of the Viennese. The spire that tells of Vienna from afar, they owe to Hans of Prachatic, that strange, quaint town, where we halted, in Bohemia.

But the work of Hans, after much reparation, had to be rebuilt, in the early sixties of the nineteenth century. Upon the old tower, they maintained by a most ingenious method a system of fire alarm: to quote Herr Kohl, who gives an elaborate account of the old tower and the struggle to prevent its decay, " No less than seven hundred steps must be mounted to reach the tower, where the watchers have their dwelling and place of abode. The arrangements made for ascertaining the exact locality of a fire are very peculiar and interesting. On the parapets of the four windows, looking east, west, north and south are four telescopes. Each glass, or as they call the whole apparatus here, every " toposkop " commands a fourth of the whole circular sea of houses, stretching on every side of the church. Each quadrant is divided by circles and radii into sections, and by the aid of the glass, the section in which the burning house lies, is easily ascertained. The individual house is discovered with the same ease. By every " toposkop " there lies a thick book containing the

In Imperial Vienna

names of all the house owners in each section, and thus the house can not only be ascertained but named. When the name is found it is written on a slip of paper, which is enclosed in a brass ball. This ball is thrown down a pipe, and it passes rapidly, like a winged messenger of evil tidings, down to the dwelling of the sexton, where it is picked up by a watchman constantly in attendance there, and carried to the city authorities. Here it is opened and the name of the unfortunate house made known to those whom it may concern. In the description the operation appears somewhat long, but it is performed with tolerable rapidity and certainty, and the " toposkop " can be used as well by night as by day. In the more remote parts of the suburb, the point is, of course, more difficult to ascertain, as the angles of vision and position become smaller in the " toposkop."

At this period the wits of Vienna had a joke about St Stephen, who they said had been made a widower lately, and upon the innocent stranger asking how that could be, the reply was, " Because it has pleased the fates and the safety police to relieve him of his cross." We must return to St Stephen's ere quitting the capital. It is a centre that draws one to it again and again.

The other centre of Vienna is in the beautiful garden space on the Ring, where rises up yet another tall spire over the handsome Rathaus; and not far off is the classical building wherein sits the Reichstag. From these two centres Vienna and Austria are ruled; but from Schönbrunn, on the outskirts of Vienna, comes the mighty influencing power of the Imperial Crown, for some sixty years borne by Francis Joseph

Austria

I., who ever wields the highest controlling power, and moulds and bends the authorities for the welfare of the State.

Just a word upon this " Mark " of the East, this Oester-Reich and its history. The first mention of its being so-called was in 976 under the Babenbergers; and the present reigning family the Habsburgs, under Rudolf I., assumed power in 1278. But it was not until 1526, after all the turmoil and fighting of the distracted fifteenth century, with the fierce religious factions, and in the midst of the Turkish wars, that by conjunction with the kingdoms of Bohemia and Hungary, Austria became a monarchy. The history of the evolution and development of this monarchy into the powerful Empire it has become is full of fiercely dramatic, tragic, and romantic incidents, and Vienna has been the centre of this drama.

From this modern centre of the capital, where we halted before the Rathaus, to get a glimpse at her history, the picturesque tree and garden-planted Ring encircles the city, and by electric tram, or in a droshky, we can visit all the historic spots, the great ecclesiastical and lay monuments, that so richly embellish Vienna.

A statue of Pallas Athenae rises before the Greek portico of the Parliament House, a statue that has given opportunity to the wits of Vienna to say that they have placed all the learning outside the building, but the *coup d'œil* from this statue of all the great and handsome buildings around, with the lovely well-kept gardens surrounding them, is one difficult to surpass for beauty.

In Imperial Vienna

The Rathaus, the Hofburg Theatre, the University, the delicate gothic of the Votive Church, and stretching away to the right the long line of trees, and the vast handsome buildings of the Imperial Museum, with its superb collections of industrial art, and the famous picture gallery, that holds the collections once housed in the Belvedere, and very much more of inestimable value, all these handsome and interesting buildings are in view. Many and many a day can be spent on this Ring, amidst the art treasures, and in the museums housed in the Rathaus and elsewhere; in the Volksgarten, that is on the other side of the Ring, is music, such as the Viennese love; whilst not far off is the luxurious and artistic opera house. On the other side of the Ring, round about the Schiller-Platz, are many of the public official offices of the Empire. As throughout Austria, music is everywhere in Vienna; the Austrian military bands are certainly the finest in Europe for delicacy and expressiveness of execution, and the various orchestras, under enthusiastic directors, give excellent renderings of the best music; of course never forgetting the light joyous music the Viennese love. The museums, picture galleries, and educational establishments of Vienna are excessively numerous, and if Vienna has no such mighty High Technical school of such collossal proportions as Charlottenburg, Austria's system, as we have seen, of this type of education, and the Polytechnic and textile and technical schools here, and spread everywhere through the Empire, have perhaps done more for the artisan of Austria and the artistic trades of the Empire than has the system of Germany. Yet other valuable agencies for developing the trade and commerce of the Empire are the Chambers of Commerce, and in Vienna is established one of the most handsomely housed, and minutely appointed and well organised chambers it is possible to imagine. A handsome building with well-appointed rooms for council and general meetings; maps, and a very exhaustive library of reference, and docketed statistics, with information upon every part of the world where the Austrian manufacturer or merchant may hope to do business. The chamber, that is supported as are all the Austrian chambers, by a slight tax from all trades however small, has sent out important embassies over the world, to bring back samples, prices, and business regulations, for the information of Austrian business men.

Very numerous are the philanthropic institutions in Vienna, and the poor relief system is less calculated to make unemployables than our own system, and some of their charitable institutions are marvellously equipped, notably the N.O. Landes—Central Kinderheim, a foundling hospital, called a Home (Heim) to get rid of the term foundling, opened in 1910 and governed by the Province. There are about 17,000 children in all under the care of this Home, mostly, of course, boarded out. In the Home the mothers and the infants are marvellously cared for in spotlessly clean rooms, with every possible medical and surgical aid. The very latest scientific discoveries are available, and the power-driving fires are arranged with a new smokeless invention, so that the neighbourhood is not injured by the smoke of the chimneys.

If Vienna cares for the poor, and her sick, she by no means forgets enjoyment. The " Lustige Wiener,"

ASPERNBRÜCKE, VIENNA

In Imperial Vienna

the joyous Viennese, is no false appellation. If the climate is somewhat treacherous, and the extremes of heat and cold are very great in Vienna, and the changes very sudden, the open air life in Vienna is revelled in, and numerous are the parks and gardens where excellent or jovial music, and good entertainment is to be had. In the centre of the town there is the Volksgarten, and all the world goes to the Prater, the long beautiful drive, with gardens on either side, that runs for miles from the canal in the centre of the city down to the Danube.

Here is every type of amusement, and every class of restaurant, from the aristocratic Sacher down to the cheapest beer garden, but all with music. The whole park has over 4000 acres of space, and it is one of the prettiest sights in Europe to see there the children's first communion procession in carriages at Whitsuntide. The children are dressed all in white with white flower-decorated carriages; or one may see the more elaborately decorated vehicles for a Flower Corso, when the fair beauties of Vienna strive to outrival each other in their personal beauty, or the artistry of the decorations of their carriages or triumphal car, and also in their horses, for the Viennese pride themselves on their horseflesh.

All around Vienna are beautiful spots of public resort. One of the nearest being Schönbrunn, the usual residence of the Emperor; this with its well-kept Versailles-like gardens, always open to the public, and its famous Gloriette, from whence is a far entrancing view, is a favourite resort of the Viennese. Here lodged Napoleon, and here lived and died his son, the young Duke of Reichstadt, "L'Aiglon." Another

Austria

spot of interest is the Kahlenberg, reached either by steamboat or railway, and especially interesting from the fact that on the mountain slope is the garden or walk, where Beethoven loved to stroll. From the summit is a glorious view of the vast city on the plain below, the far winding Danube, and the lower spurs of the Carpathians, and the Styrian Alps.

Not far off is a newer resort, with a splendidly arranged people's restaurant and garden, the Krapfenwald, where thousands can hear good music, and get good refreshments and intellectual entertainment, at very low prices, and near by on another height is a more luxurious and expensive resort, the Cobenzl, with its luxuriously appointed castle hotel and restaurant; from the terrace is a splendid panorama of the country around.

An interesting proof of Vienna's advancement in all modern developments, is her series of handsomely fitted drawing-room tram cars; by which tourists in parties can visit the city and its environs. The tram cars have polished wood panellings, lounge chairs, smoking and writing tables; and they halt in sidings, while visits are paid to the various churches and show places, making day or half day tours. But as a set off against this the cabs (Droshkys) are very expensive and not good; the peculiar system of extras for the railway stations is irritating to travellers.

The reader who longs for statistics as proof and evidence of the strivings and prosperity of the country will find a mass of figures that are very full of interest not only to the statistician, but to the ethnologist and philanthropist, in the volume issued by the Royal and Imperial Statistical Central Commission,

In Imperial Vienna

entitled, " Oesterreichisches Statistisches Handbuch " and in the " Statistisches Jahrbuch der Autonomen Landesverwaltung," etc.

There is no space, or place, in this descriptive volume for many figures, but before leaving the capital of the Empire, just a glimpse may perhaps be allowed into the figures that prove how this composite Empire of seventeen homelands is made up.

In the question of population and race, the Slavs and Poles number over 10,000,000, the Germans over 9,000,000, and the Ruthenians, Serbs, Croats, Italians, etc., over 6,000,000. There are also the Jews and residents of other nationalities. The homelands with the greatest population are Galicia, with over 7,000,000, Bohemia with more than 6,000,000, Lower Austria, that contains Vienna, with over 3,000,000, and Moravia with about 2,000,000, and the Steirmark, Styria, with 1,500,000 inhabitants. No other land or province has over 1,000,000 inhabitants in its borders.

In the matter of tourists and visitors to watering places, Bohemia, as in matters of finance, comes out easily first, she having about 130,000 guests yearly; whilst Lower Austria, which comes next, has about 75,000 guests visiting her health resorts.

The figures referring to technical schools and agricultural and forestry schools, are full of significance, as also are those relating to the commercial schools, and the Chambers of Commerce; all go to show what a remarkable system has been built up by self-help and governmental organisation, and the eagerness of the people to take advantage of these well-organised institutions.

In the trade schools, the continuation and drawing

schools, and the agricultural and forestry schools, Bohemia is first in the number of pupils attending. Lower Austria comes next, and Moravia follows, but at a long distance.

In the matter of newspapers, Lower Austria with the capital leads, with an issue of about 1300 journals, Bohemia follows with over 1100, Moravia and Galicia being again third and fourth, and so above the other districts. The system of savings banks is well organised; as we have seen the buildings are generally handsome in construction, and the arrangements assist thrift and largely help the development of the country. In Bohemia there are 216 Gemeindes and town savings banks, 9 Verein or society's banks, and three district banks, in all 228. In Lower Austria, 53 Gemeinde and 29 Verein, in all 82; in Moravia, 82 Gemeinde and 4 Verein, in all 86 banks; and in every province there are a goodly number of these banks, and the amounts deposited are very considerable.

Even the most casual tourist will note the excellent tillage nearly everywhere in Austria, hardly a scrap of ground being uncultivated, and the statistics given of the mileage of roads planted with fruit trees prove how careful the peasant holders are of land space, and, as many of the roads are district property, how the communes combine for the general good.

The disposal of the produce of the land is largely helped by the river traffic, and one of the great interests on the river boats is to watch the varied peasantry dealing with their produce, passing with loads of their wares to and fro to the markets by this means of transit; and of course heavier traffic in corn, etc., is also so dealt with.

In Imperial Vienna

In the matter of factories, both large and small, as also in the case of house and home labour, the statistics prove that the order of precedence with the varied homelands is much the same, Bohemia having the largest number employed in industrial work; Galicia comes next, followed by Lower Austria, and then comes Moravia. In the matter of what are known as giant (Riesen) establishments, that is establishments mustering over 1000 hands, Bohemia has 33 such works, Moravia 20, Lower Austria 16, Silesia 14, and Galicia only 9, whilst in the smaller workshops Galicia comes second.

In spite of the fact that, as everywhere in Europe, prices have risen greatly during the last few years, living is very cheap in Austria, and the staple commodities, such as bread, potatoes, are very low in price, and often, in the restaurants, the cheapest dishes to have in Austria are exactly what would be dearest in England, such as venison, partridge, omelettes, etc.

These few figures will give some slight insight into the general life of the people, and prove which are the provinces that largely maintain the wealth of the Austrian Empire, although, as we shall see as we pass onward through the other lands, there is everywhere a wealth of natural beauty and an industrious folk; but the other lands than these four principal divisions are more occupied with agriculture and forestry, and have not so thick a population dealing in great industries.

Some reference must be made to the government of this Empire of Austria that with the kingdom of Hungary forms the great balancing power of Central Europe.

Austria

There are two books which have appeared during the twentieth century, in the last decade, that are very useful towards getting some grasp of the central and local government of Austria, one in French, "L'Autriche a l'aube de XX Siecle," by Max Marse, the other a voluminous work full of detail and statistics, " Austria-Hungary," by Geoffrey Drage ; for the latest figures, of course, we must go to the latest Government publications, and to the publications of the various provinces and cities ; in this volume it is only possible to give a slight sketch of the system of government adopted, the better to understand the life of the people in this complex Empire.

The central authority is the Reichsrath, and for local matters there are seventeen diets or provincial parliaments, and these deal with all local taxation, public works, sanitation, the control of all charitable institutions, etc. ; in many provinces we have seen the handsome buildings arranged for the local diets.

The Reichsrath, *i.e.* the House of Lords and House of Deputies, deals with the army and navy estimates and general budget; railways, education, public health, right of meeting, the press, general imperial matters ; and complaint is made that since the introduction of payment of members the professional delegate has greatly increased.

There are also councils for the communes and for the towns, and the progressive districts force on their local councils towards the advancement of each especial district, and in travelling through the various cities and communes the work of the council, whether progressive or dilatory, is soon in evidence, and the

In Imperial Vienna

progressive are in a far larger majority than the *laissez faire* bodies.

There is great freedom in Austria. In coming either from Russia or from Germany, especially from the Polish provinces, this freedom is at once evident. In Austria everyone has a right to speak in his own tongue, and to sing his own songs; there is great freedom of the Press, and freedom of meeting, and in 1907 Universal Suffrage was introduced for all men over twenty-four. I was present at the first Universal Suffrage election, and there was absolute freedom of voting.

The economic situation of Austria has greatly improved; there is a notable increase of the people's savings deposited in the banks, amounting almost to the savings of the French people, and the credit of the National Bank is such that the rate of discount is on a par with the other great powers.

This has been brought about by the vigorous action of the Government. One of the notable examples of prompt and valuable action was in 1901, when at a probable period of depression, that did have a great effect in other countries, great works were undertaken by the State, especially the development of important productive railways to be carried out from 1901 to 1905. Six great lines were projected and eighteen lesser lines, and some most important canals and river development work, and, says Max Marse, the industrial life of Austria received an immense impulse from this work. As we pass over some of these new lines, the additional local impulse and development will be very evident. To quote Geoffrey Drage, "Not only has the State acquired vast assets in constructive works, but, as may be seen by the steadiness of the Government bonds, it has placed its credit on a sound footing."

Mention has already been made of the excellent mode in which local industries are fostered and advanced and expounded by education. Mr Drage makes very numerous references to my Report on Technical and Commercial Education (C.D. 419) in Austria and especially Bohemia, issued by the Board of Education in 1900, and as we travel on we shall see more of the outcome of this valuable educational system. The State aids largely also museums and libraries, which so advantageously help scientific and professional education, and fosters this education by scholarships. But this work is also greatly aided by the " pious donor " and benefactor, and by self-help and local patriotism.

Since 1873, the date of my first visit to Austria, there has come a great change over the industrial life in town and country. Hours have been lessened, wages increased, and the sanitation in the works marvellously improved, until to-day many are far in advance of our English workshops; especially is this noticeable in the glass works, and also in the machine works, as we saw at Pilsen; but still the rate of wage is low, but the manner of living is economic.

The army of the Dual Empire commands 2,250,000 men, for in this Hungary must be included (although this volume is not referring in any way to the kingdom of Hungary). The navy is also rapidly developing, and will shortly bring Austria into the rank of one of the great naval powers. That most delightful historian and far-seeing man, Palacky, the author

In Imperial Vienna

of the great history of Bohemia, in 1848, said, in a work entitled "Oesterreichs Staatsidee," that the upholding of the Austrian Empire was a political necessity; and that if it were not, it must be created; and all in Austria and Hungary know this.

All the various races are earnestly struggling for development; for race advancement; and in England we get most exaggerated reports of the strife between these races; but speak to Cech, or Pole, or Hungarian, all of whom are ardent patriots, devotees of their own race, and the suggestion that the Austrian Empire should break up is at once scouted as impossible—" should there come a common danger all would unite at once" were the words of one of the most eminent of these patriots.

We have referred to the balance of population in Austria, but the better to understand the race difficulties and aspirations we give the division of the population in Austria and Hungary. This amounts to $48\frac{1}{2}$ millions, and is divided into 24 million Slavs, 11 million Germans, $8\frac{3}{4}$ million Magyars, 3 million Roumanians, and $\frac{3}{4}$ of a million Italians, and there are Jews, etc.

This slight review of the political and industrial situation in Austria may, as we travel onward through their glorious inheritance, help to illuminate the life of the Austrian people whilst we are still halting in the midst of her capital, which in her artistic and beneficent development has proved that her civic rulers recognise the magnitude of their city, and the dignity due to the capital of the Empire.

One can see in Vienna, especially on holy days, large groups of the rural population visiting some especial shrine in the vast cathedral of St Stephen. They enter, a picturesque, parti-coloured group in their local distinctive costume, that at once tells the district from whence they come. Some white-headed old man leads them, perhaps bearing a small banner or cross. The clatter of their feet is subdued as they slowly reach the centre of the nave, and then they halt, and for a few moments all look around in wonder at the upsoaring sombre columns, intensified with the glory of the coloured windows: and then, slowly, the women in their brilliant head-dresses bow their heads, and the men, bareheaded, bend also in reverence, and the whole mass of varied colour sinks slowly to the earth, and the silent prayers go up in this glorious building, grey and sombre with antiquity, for those left at home in the distant villages.

The evening service is always a favourite one at St Stephen's, for then all are permitted to go up to the high altar, and one can sit in the richly carved stalls, and before the service begins, become absorbed in the beauty of form and colour, and all the fascinations of history that are around us. The building goes back to just before the power of the Habsburgs took rule over Austria, and from that date till late in the fifteenth century it was continually being enriched with additional work.

There is one other church we must refer to for its historic interest, as it is the modern burial-place of the Imperial family, and the tragic deaths of so many of the Habsburgs make this one of the saddest spots to visit it is possible to conceive. As the long-robed monk shows tomb after tomb, all the fierce tragic history of this family comes visibly to the mind. Here

THE TOWER OF ST STEPHEN'S, VIENNA

In Imperial Vienna

is also the tomb of " L'Aiglon," the young Duke of Reichstadt, Napoleon's son; but one is glad to ascend again to the upper air, and pass onward into the brisk life of the city, and we are quickly in the Hof Garten, amidst the flowers and trees, and pass thence into the Volksgarten, where the music rings forth, and the gay throng recalls us to all the bright joyous life that the Viennese love: although their life is by no means a life *pour rire*, or *pour s'amuser*, as we have seen from the hints at the energetic, strenuous advancement in science, art, and commerce that her palatial buildings, the homes of these arts, prove she loves and reveres.

Vienna is a city to linger in, and to visit and re-visit; then gradually all the wealth of her institutions, her museums, libraries, art galleries, and public buildings slowly prove their immensity, and the enormous interest and value of the collections. The history of Austria can then be better understood, and one sallies forth by the gate of the glorious river, the Danube, into one of the most picturesque and historic districts the world has to show.

CHAPTER XII

LOWER AUSTRIA—THE SEMMERING

THE two crown lands of Lower and Upper Austria are small in extent, but they are of great importance geographically and historically.

Lower Austria as the seat of the capital, and as containing a stretch of the Danube that is commercially of great value, and historically of the deepest interest; it also contains some remarkable mountain scenery, the popular region of the Semmering.

At the Prater Quay is the large building wherein the vast business of the Danube Steamship Company is transacted, and by one of their handsome saloon boats we can most comfortably visit all the scenes on the Danube. Before quitting Vienna we must say a word upon the work of this company, that is of great importance commercially and from the tourist point of view. They run 45 passenger boats, 89 freight steamers, and have a fleet of 838 merchandise boats, the latter with nearly half a million tonnage.

Their saloon steamers are handsome vessels, extremely well found, and with good restaurants on board, and with some special cabins for sleeping, ranging from two to six in number, on each boat, but with made-up beds in the saloon, which are quite comfortable, ranging from a dozen up to forty.

Lower Austria—The Semmering

One can live delightfully and very cheaply on these boats, the charge for meals being very reasonable, and the cost of a bed per night is two kroner, *i.e.* 1s. 8d. It is of interest to note that " By Imperial Patent First Danube Steam-Navigation Company " was granted to John Andrews and Joseph Prichards on April 17, 1828, and their first boat ran on September 17, 1830, an earlier attempt to start steamboats on the Danube having failed.

The boundary of Lower Austria stretches to Enns, nearly to Linz, the capital of Upper Austria, and through this province the Danube would bear us to within sight of Passau in Bavaria, but we must leave our excursion upon the Danube until our return from the Adriatic, and link this lower stretch of the river with the chapter upon Upper Austria; for the course of the Danube through Austria is through these two crown lands, quitting Bavaria just after leaving Passau, running through Upper Austria to Linz, and on through Lower Austria to Vienna, and entering Hungary just before reaching Posony (Pressburg).

If Lower Austria thus includes some most deeply interesting and romantically beautiful river scenery, it also embraces a succession of towns and villages situated upon upland slopes and lofty mountain ranges, with scenery of the most varied and idyllic beauty.

The Viennese are thus most fortunate, placed in the heart of Europe, with these delightful pleasure and health resorts at their doors.

The mountains claim us first, and we run south from Vienna by the Southern Railway, through a part

Austria

of Lower Austria that has become the playground of Vienna.

It is curious to call on an official in Vienna, and to hear he is at Baden, and then to be told that he comes in every morning; but this Baden, only seventeen miles from Vienna, is a pleasant town on the varied hill slopes, rising above the little river Schwechat that has become a favourite watering-place, the Richmond of Vienna, with good hotels, Curhaus, and, of course, good music, and plenty of amusements and baths. The hills around run up to 1000 and 1500 feet, giving health and picturesque promenades.

But far more glorious scenery awaits us as we go farther south, running through the vine district of Voslau, that produces the excellent red and white wine known by that name.

The whole district is picturesque and full of scenes that make walking excursions in the district a delight. Castles and ruins and pretty villages, and scattered towns that are pleasant halting-places, and as at Wiener Neustadt the historian and antiquary will find much to detain him.

In not so far bygone days the railway broke off, and we had to go by diligence over the Semmering Pass, but since 1854 this mountain chain has been conquered by the iron road, and one can quickly be at the summit, 3000 to 4000 feet above sea-level.

Austria is famous for its remarkably beautiful mountain railways, as the Arlberg and the new Tauern railways; but if these are grandiose, we shall cross them both shortly, yet this Semmering railway is hardly surpassed by them in strange beauty and sudden surprises.

Lower Austria—The Semmering

The mountain pass, that now by steam links Vienna with the Adriatic, has ever been a route from Central Europe to the east; and in 1184 Markgraf Ottokar V. built a refuge or hospice here, as a halting-place for the pilgrims to the Holy Land. The little town of Spittal, on the southern slope of the range, by its name, commemorates this fact, and the pass was used for heavy goods, and became an important route in the fourteenth, fifteenth, and sixteenth centuries. But it appears that, not until 1728, was a really good road made over this pass, and then it was necessary to utilise a couple of hundred horses daily to assist the hauling of goods over the pass. The new road, superseded by the railway, but still used for local traffic and pedestrians, was made in 1841.

It was a certain Karl Ghega, an Austrian, born in Vienna, and a Doctor of Mathematics of Padua, who, at the age of eighteen, becoming an Austrian official in the Works Department, became enamoured with the development of railways in England, and visited that country, and Germany, Belgium, and France, to study railway work, in 1836 and 1837, and again he made a second visit to England in 1842, when he also went to America, and after a tremendous struggle against opponents of every type, including his brother engineers and the Press, the work was carried through, and after trial trips the line was opened for passenger traffic on the 17th July 1854, the Emperor Francis Joseph, a young man of twenty-four, being the first passenger.

And truly it has opened a wealth of beauty and a wonder of continuous sudden changes and surprises to the traveller.

Austria

At Gloggnitz, one is still in the lowlands, with rich fields, through which the river winds, and cultured uplands. Then quickly we begin to ascend, and the marvel of this early engineering feat begins to excite one.

We twist round hill sides, through tunnels, and getting different views of scenes, now on a level, then far below, catching glimpses of snow on the heights far above. We are rising up from the level of vineyards to the pine level; the views embrace vast stretches of landscape or deep, rocky ravines, with, as at Klamm, a grand old castle ruin perched on its rocky height. Then we crawl round on a dizzy viaduct that gives a grand glimpse down through the pines to the rich valleys, and so skirt the vast, rocky wall of the Weinzettelwand, perhaps one of the finest, if not most dramatic, scenes on the route. A double tiered viaduct, 150 feet high, takes us over the deep Kalte Rinne, that is a ravine wide enough to give us time for a good long look at the very beautiful view. Another viaduct, not of so dizzy a height, leads us on to more tunnels, and we pull up at the Semmering Station.

Just a couple of hours from the plainland and crowded city streets of Vienna, and here we are amidst the scent of the pines, with peasant girls offering one Edelweiss blossoms. A trudge up through the winding forest road quickly brings one to the villas and hotels of the Semmering.

We tramped up this road once on September 16th, a hot fatiguing walk in the heat, but misty clouds swept round us, and on the morning of the 17th, when we awoke, snow lay all around, and from the terrace

Lower Austria—The Semmering

of the hotel (built by the Southern Railway) there was a vast view of rocky, bare mountain ranges and pine-clad peaks, all glittering in the first, pure snow of autumn. One can be quickly in the deep silent forest of the resinous pines, and in winter, skiing and toboganning is to be had on splendid runs.

On another occasion when, in May, I was again on the Semmering, at a luncheon on the great balcony where one can sit and revel in such a glorious view, it was my lot to propose prosperity to Austria. With such a vast view of this corner of the beauty of that Empire, the words of Goethe came to my mind—

"Oh wunderschön ist Gottes Erde
Und schön aur Ihr, ein Mensch zu sein."

The pure exhilarating air, the vast scene, the strange, delightful beauty made one feel—

"God's in His Heaven, all's right with the world."

We could look out northward over the beautiful province of Lower Austria, that has other charms in its river scenery to call us back again; for on the Semmering we are on its frontier, and in descending the heights on the southern side we shall enter Styria, the ancient Steirmark of Austria.

CHAPTER XIII

STYRIA (THE STEIERMARK) AND GRAZ

THE province or dukedom of Styria is but very little known to the English-speaking traveller, and to say you are English, especially if one confesses to a desire to study more nearly than *en passant* the life in the towns and in the villages of this fair province, is at once to receive from every section of the people a hearty welcome, and every assistance to gain a knowledge of their historic monuments and their ofttimes quaint folklore.

The entry into this province, via the Semmering, is so very beautiful, one has a presentiment there must come a reaction from the elation of mind at the remarkable scenery that one looks out upon, as we emerge from the tunnel, some 3000 feet up on the mountain height. We know we are slowly dropping down to the sea-level of the Adriatic. But as we drop to the plain level and from snowy mountain heights, wander amidst low-lying towns, surprises are in store that intensely stir the mind, and allow no dull moment of apathy to clog the brain with weariness or *ennui*.

The Steiermark is a large province, and we shall skirt its western frontier when running through the Tauern Mountains; but in descending to Triest we run through its entire length, from north to south, and

Styria (The Steiermark) and Graz

so get a fair idea of its fertile land and pleasant towns.

There are about a million and a half inhabitants in the province, nearly a million being Germans, the rest of Slav or Slovak origin, with a sprinkling of Italians, Poles, and Croats. Agriculture is the principal industry; in fact, a local writer in piteous tones pleads that the capital, Graz, is not a " world town " with many chimneys and great industries. But even as we descend from the mountain heights, we quickly see that forestry and agriculture are scientifically developed.

We have already descended about 800 feet when we arrive at Mürzzuschlag, where the river Murz, that afterwards becomes the greater Mur, winds through a lovely valley embowered in low, forest-clad hills, the higher crags towering above. Here is a good halting-place for the botanist or geologist, for these hills have a rich flora and varied geological formations.

The valleys, as we creep downwards, are smilingly prosperous, and here and there, as at Wartberg, a fine old ruin gives work for the historian, and interest to the archæologist. Often, in early spring and in autumn, this valley is flooded, and the rush of water is tremendous. That there is a certain amount of artisan life in the district is evidenced at Bruck, where many busy factories pour forth their workers in the evening. Here the lines branch off for Villach and the Karawanken Alps, and for the lakes in the Salzkammergut, and it is but a short run for Ischl. All these places we shall visit later on, continuing now, down on the southern route, for another thirty-four miles to the capital town of Styria, Graz.

Austria

Graz

Graz, formerly spelt Gratz and pronounced "Grates," rhyming to "gerate" (it has succeeded), as a quaint poem by Gottfried Leitner expresses it, in relating the legend of the founding of the town by wanderers from the bank of the Isar in Bavaria. But Graz goes back to Celtic and Roman times, and the museums in this and neighbouring towns are very rich from finds in the district.

Throughout this volume we are utilising notes made on the spot, and the pamphlets and volumes issued locally upon the history of the district. In nearly every town in Austria there is always a learned knot of enthusiasts who love their homeland, and are proud of its history; and someone, schoolmaster, curator, priest, or historian, as a labour of love, produces a book that is generally very interesting; and there are also the unions or societies for promoting tourist travel in every centre, who also issue useful booklets, often very well written.

Here in Graz, in addition to local guides, there is a most carefully written history of the Steiermark by Dr F. Mayer, the Director of the "Landes-Oberrealschule" (Higher modern school). The title page of this gives a quaint view of the town in 1634, with the castle and fortress on the precipitous, rocky plateau above the river Mur, and the numerous domes, spires and towers on either side of the river. The picturesque castle height, with its strong, red tower, at once arrests the eye, as one runs into the town. This Schlossberg is the acropolis of the Steiermark, and one instinctively makes for it on

Styria (The Steiermark) and Graz

arriving in the town, which is the capital of the Mark, and returns to it again and again, either wandering up through the lovely parks and gardens below, or quickly reaching the summit, 1650 feet above sea-level, by a lift.

From the plateau is a vast view of the great plain and the dark-red roofed town, the grey Mur rushing through the midst of the city; the last time I looked upon it, it was in flood, a fierce, turbulent river.

Away to the south is a low range of hills, and beyond is the vast loom of the mountains; and at the west side of the hill one looks down on a lovely valley, through which pierces the Mur, whilst beyond to the north are all the piled Alps, the dark forest slopes, and nearer the picturesque hills and dotted villas.

At the spot where this view comes in, is a monument, a lion defending a flag, erected " To the heroic defenders of this Schlossberg against French dominance, 1809," erected in 1909.

Below to the south-east lies the vast town, filling much space, with many trees shaded between the houses. At sunset, the bells ring out from the many church towers, and seem to tell of the life of the city.

Upon this height, as we look out over so much of Steiermark, we can listen to a few words about the life of the people of this important homeland of Austria; for the story of the settling of this Markgrave gives an idea of the race struggles through the ages in all Austria, where sometimes one race, sometimes another, has remained dominant, or in the majority.

In the fifth or sixth century before Christ, the Celtic

Austria

folk overran this district, driving out the earlier people of whom little is known, save that they lived by hunting and fishing, and by the land. Probably about the same period the Etruscans, those artistic settlers in North Italy, came over the Alps for their commerce, and brought their products here, their weapons, their household implements, vases, and household and personal ornaments; and as the Etruscans faded from history, the Roman merchants took up the story, and from the Roman port of Aquileia (towards which we are travelling) came also to the plains and the valleys of the Mur, and brought their industrial products in exchange for the agricultural products of the district.

The Noric branch of the Celts were not merely agriculturists; they understood mining and many trades, and lived in towns and did much business, especially with salt. They understood mining for copper, iron, and gold, obtaining the latter also from the rivers, and they wove woollen articles, making ten varieties of material from sheep's wool, and by a mixture of copper and tin produced a fine, gold-like bronze that they used for weapons and implements, and the excellence of Noric iron weapons was renowned. They also coined money, imprinted with Roman letters.

Many of these articles have been found in the Tumuli and urn burying-places, and some beautiful examples are in the Graz Landes Museum. In Maria Rast a great find was made of over a hundred urns with bracelets, brooches, rings, etc.; these also are in the Joanneum Museum in Graz.

In the year 113 B.C. the Romans had assisted these

Styria (The Steiermark) and Graz

Celtic tribes against the Teutons, and later on the Steiermark became part of the Roman province of Norricum, and the Celtic roads were developed, and Roman roads, especially the great military road from Aquileia on the Adriatic, to the famous Danube road, ran through the land, with, of course, the usual stations and military forts or castles. Valuable remains of this Roman period are in the museum, as well as relics of the various religions of the Celts, and all the various gods the Romans brought in their train, Egyptian, Syrian, and especially Mithras, the Sun god of the Persians, to whom many altars were erected. Christianity was early adopted; the precise date is not known, but in the persecution of Diocletian in 303 a Bishop Victorin suffered martyrdom, and in the fifth century the Church here was well organised. After the fall of the Western Roman Empire the Avars, and with them the Slavs, overran the district and settled here. They are described as a peace-loving folk, having the organisation, somewhat as it is to-day in Russia, of the family, and groups of families, ruled by a Starosta; these again grouped into a community under a Zupan; and these communities had watch-towers and fortresses and earthworks into which the people fled for refuge in war time. They had their own gods of which Morena, the god of winter and death, was one of the chief, and they believed in eternal life.

The neighbours of this Slavic folk were the Bajuvaren or Bavarians, also heathen until 696. Strife ensuing between the Avars and the Slavonians the latter called in the Bavarian Duke Tassilo to their aid, and later on, he going against the Franks, was

Austria

crushed by Charlemagne, and then it came about that the Germans occupied the land; and as all unoccupied land belonged to the Crown, and the Slavs only thinly populated the territory, it was divided amongst nobles and churches, and monasteries, and the Slavs were utilised as workers on the land. Many Celtic, and still more Slavic names are left in the district, and the tenacity of the Slavs for their ancient customs and their picturesque costumes will be seen in many parts of Austria. This slight sketch of the peopling of the Steiermark is fairly illustrative, with slight variations, of the peopling of the whole of Austria.

But Graz is more German, therefore one sees but little costume in the city.

The central point in this city of nearly 200,000 inhabitants is the Hauptplatz, with its busy market, town hall, monument and fountains representing the four great rivers of the Steirmark—the Mur, Drave, Save, and Enns. But the most interesting point for the traveller is the old courtyard of the Landhaus, which is in the Italian renaissance style, with a triple story of arcades, arches, and stairways. On the west side is the famous well, a masterpiece of open metal work, dating about 1590. The diet hall and the wine cellar are worth visiting, but the strangest and unique building that should draw every lover of history to Graz is a massive building on the south side of this courtyard. A ring at the bell will bring the custodian, who is a lover of the marvellous collection entrusted to his care. Here in this Zeughaus or Arsenal is the most remarkable collection, or rather **armoury, of mediæval** weapons the world has to show.

GRAZ

Styria (The Steiermark) and Graz

This is not a show lot of beautiful pieces of armour and weapons as at Dresden, Madrid, Berlin and elsewhere, but a real armoury of four wide floors all stocked with mediæval armour, waiting, waiting, for a phantom army to come and be harnessed and armed. Here are 28,000 weapons; 14,000 men could be armed. Here are 2500 suits of plate-armour besides those in chain. Every possible type of offensive and defensive weapon is here, and many ingenious devices for crippling and maiming the enemy. It is notable that there are no suits of armour for men 6 feet in height, nor for big men; but as the custodian lovingly handled weapons and armour, he proved they must have been very muscular men to wield these weapons and bear this armour. To wander through these solid, dim floors, with all this preparation for a bygone war, that comes not again, is to experience a most strange sensation; and many of the pieces are very beautiful works of art, and others are devilish for their cruel ingenuity.[1]

Another most remarkable collection is that in the Kunstgewerbe (art trade) Museum.

This is housed in a fine, spacious building finished in 1895, near the old Joannuem Museum that holds the antique, geological, and botanical collections.

One often hears statements upon Austria founded upon trivial knowledge, or upon visits paid years ago. The development of every town and district in Austria has been tremendous during the last two decades, and this museum is an example of this great work. Here

---

[1] See article in the *Morning Post*, "The Armoury at Graz," August 24th, 1910, by J. B.

Austria

are indeed historical and folk museums, filled with artistic relics of past ages, arranged with every care and foresight, dwelling-rooms of the district at various periods, tools, personal ornaments, glass, musical instruments, dresses, iron work, porcelain; and the exhibits are so hung that they can easily be taken into the technical schools for study, reproduction, or to incite invention or design. There is a whole suite of rooms, illustrating the life of the Steiermark with figures in costume.

The technical school is a magnificent building with four faculties, and most elaborate and important arrangements and apparatus for chemistry, engineering, building. The university is also a very handsome building with an anatomical and physiological annex, and a physical institute adjoining, linked with a pretty garden and an observatory, and an excellent library and botanical garden; there are about 2000 students studying here. As far back as 1841 the technical school of the Johanneum was said to be one of the three schools in Austria, and Graz also had her agriculture school and model farm and polytechnic association.

A very pleasant ending to a visit to Graz is to cross the rushing Mur from the west part of the town by the old bridge, to wind up through the narrow and busy streets, passing the cathedral, that in spite of restoration is worth a halt, and then to work up through the lovely Stadtpark, with its beautiful flowers, shady trees, and often excellent music (a Bosnian regiment was playing once when we lingered here), then to climb the steep Schlossberg, and visit the old clock tower and the Turkish Wells, and once

Styria (The Steiermark) and Graz

more we can look out over the wonderful view, down over the picturesque town, and try to recall all the historic reminiscences Graz has brought to mind.

On quitting Graz we turned southward, through the Steiermark, and sometimes when the river is in flood the valley is widely flooded. There are many small spots of interest, but Marburg on the Drave makes a useful halting-place, if only to study the excellent and painstaking methods of fruit culture, and the school established for teaching this.

All through Southern, and, in fact, all over Austria great care has to be taken to note which race peoples the district in order not to offend susceptibilities; in Graz, as we have seen, it was German that was predominant, and therefore one would be careful not to use the Slav salutations; but as we run southwards we come into a Slav district, and at Cilli we are amidst a Wendish population, one of these towns whose name dates back to the Celtic Roman period. This makes a pleasant halting spot, a bright town; the old square towers in the Schlossberg form a picturesque bit in the landscape, and the church bells have a glorious tone. To those studying Roman life the museum is well worth an hour amongst its local finds.

The little river Sann adds to the beauty of the scenery, that is very diversified with high hills and rocky defiles, ruins of castles, pretty villages, and small towns. At Römerbad the station is remarkably pretty, and, as the name implies, here are curative baths known to the Romans, and the country around, both in forest, pastoral, and rock scenery, is full of pleasant

Austria

charm. But we are approaching the frontier of Styria, that is bounded by the Save which flows into the Sann, and must quit this interesting mark that has played no mean part in the history of Austria.

CHAPTER XIV

CARNIOLA (KRAIN)—LJUBLJANA (LAIBACH)

THE scenery as we enter Carniola, or Krain, along the banks of the Save, is full of beauty, and just a mile or two before crossing the frontier at Trifail we have great cliffs that are really open coal quarries; and at Sagor, the frontier town, are grand hills and cliffs rising sheer 400 to 800 feet in height. We are not far from Hungary, and by following the Save eastwards Agram is quickly reached; but we journey on, along its banks to the westward, emerging from the ravines, and soon get a fine view of the Julian Alps that promise plenty of work for the rock and mountain climber, and glorious scenery for the lover of nature.

The capital of the province, Ljubljana, or Laibach, forms an excellent centre for exploring the district, and is a most interesting and pleasant place to sojourn in. Railways branch off to that most fascinating district of Alpine heights and idyllic lakes, Veldes and Wochein Feistritz, and into Gorizia; southward into Istria and on to Triest and the Adriatic; and eastwards to Hungary. Both history and modern development tend to hold the traveller for some days in the capital of Carniola, or Krain as the Germans call this Duchy; and in the near neighbourhood we can study the peasant life in this homeland of Austria.

If in the Steiermark Germans predominate, here in

Austria

Carniola the Slav is in the ascendant, there being over 500,000 Slowenisch to about 28,000 Germans, and patriotism and race devotion is shown in the eagerness of the people to be abreast with all developments. With the military garrison there are about 50,000 inhabitants in the capital, and the diet-house for the local Parliament is a handsome building, with club and reading rooms for the members, who are elected by four classes of voters: the rich domain holders, the towns, the peasants, and the general voter. The Justice Palace, or Law Courts, is also a fine building, and around it are pleasant gardens and lakes and avenues of chestnut trees.

The Government House is another handsome building, the residence of the Stadthalter; and in passing from this through the poorer part of the town, that is well kept and clean, one sees a part of the old Roman walls. The view from the south embraces the pleasant shady avenues and gardens, the river from which the town is named, and above all rises the great mass of the castle, upon its dominating tree-covered hill, whilst beyond are the green picturesque hills.

The town has been greatly developed of late; one passes through the old Ghetto, but no Jews are there now. The old town hall is a picturesque building with balconies and arches, but the building that will hold the visitor, wherein he can study the history of this district and the folklore of the people, is the Rudolphinum, where the museum of the province is installed.

Here the life of the district can be gleaned from the well-arranged exhibits, and it was interesting on one occasion when there to see a school of lads, some

LAIBACH

Carniola(Krain)—Ljubljana(Laibach)

without shoes, but decidedly clean, others well dressed, all studying the life and history of their homeland.

The finds go back to the earliest lake-dwellers and Neolithic times, including some remarkable pottery with encrusted ornamentation, etc.; thence to the Bronze epoch, and a very rich collection of the Iron period, that a local writer gives here as 900-400 B.C. Belonging to the later Iron or Celtic epoch are richly decorated swords, and a beautiful helmet collar, with cheek pieces, upon which birds are chiselled. The collection of the Roman period is also very rich, especially in glass, and what is perhaps yet more interesting, are the finds of the folk migration period and the first Slavic settlers.

The history is carried on to later days, when the struggle with the Moslem was desperate, and a flag of 1593 recalls this epoch in their history.

Here, as elsewhere in Austria, the life of the folk of to-day and yesterday is illustrated by models and actual furniture, and household utensils of their homes, and figures in the bright costumes. We went out on the balcony of the museum, and looked out over the town. As we had entered the city on this occasion, on the eve of Corpus Christi, many peasants were flocking in for the procession, and we noted the tone of colour of many was a quiet grey, with a whitish head-dress, but on the morrow we were to see all the more brilliant-coloured dress of Upper Carniola, and these dresses and the whole home-life of the folk is illustrated in the museum.

Before climbing up to the castle we made an excursion with the learned curator of the museum out to the village of Roznik, and in chatting with the

Austria

peasants learnt that the small-holders worked about 5 acres of ground, and that the pay for workers in harvest time was 4 Kronen a day, in winter 2 to 3 Kronen, but most of the hands engaged in this work were women.

In the factories the girls earned 1.50 to 3 Kroner, the men 3 to 5, really less than on the fields, because they were also insured against sickness. From this village we went on to St Veit, where we found them busy sweeping the roads and decorating with young trees and flags for Corpus Christi.

We had a chat in the house of a young carpenter, who was also a small-holder of about $1\frac{1}{2}$ acres. A smart, bright young fellow, full of life and keenness in his work with wood, and in his fowls and pigs, and in his garden. We went into his workshops; the technical schools had made him love and know his work. In his kitchen all was clean. A white towel was hung up for drying hands. The cooking utensils were of bright metal, well polished; there was a cake-mould amongst them. In the sleeping-room for the children all was clean and airy, and a big room, with two beds in it, served as sitting-room, the beds having tidy, pretty coverlets over them. Here were flowers on a table, and flowers were wreathed over a pier-glass and a crucifix. Everything was absolutely sweet and pure.

We next visited a well-to-do farmer's house, who farmed 60 to 70 acres. He cultivated hops and corn, and kept cows. We went into his sitting-room and kitchen and three bedrooms, all clean and orderly. He was just putting up a new hop-oven with expensive screen methods, and an excellent and unusual arrange-

Carniola(Krain)—Ljubljana(Laibach)

ment was his smoke chamber above the kitchen, that utilised all the smoke for drying meats, etc. From the farmer we got the prices of food for the towns, and found that it averaged: bread, 1½d. per lb; potatoes, ½d. per lb.; meat, 6d. to 1s. per lb. At first he was very reticent and reserved, but at last became very friendly, and his wife came and offered us a slice of their excellent brown bread, which, with a Slav, is a mark of friendship.

We were fortunate to have introductions to a Landrath, a Mr Lindtner, who was full of information, and most kindly courteous in his assistance, and with him we were enabled to see the Corpus Christi procession from the balcony of the Parliament buildings.

The troops were paraded, all wearing oak leaves in their hats, a tribute to spring; and as the procession passed beneath us it was a pretty and impressive spectacle. All the artistic and patriotic societies took part. The national white head-dress of the women was prominent, and as the first blessing was pronounced the cannon roared out from the great castle that was above us, and the bells clanged forth, and the people lit candles in their windows to greet the procession as it passed. Women in the National costume, bands of music, the Philharmonic Society, Mariastift Society; little children all in white, bearing candles and flowers; officials of the town, monks, and, last of all, the bishop under a gold canopy in his rich vestments, and priests in gold and white. When the bishop halted to bless the troops, with the people in their brilliant colours all grouped around, the scene was full of beauty, and recalled

Austria

the fierce history through which the people have passed.

'The study of life here in the great market-place, and in the churches gives many tokens of the life of the people; and a climb up the tree-clad height to the great fortress above, affords in either a morning or evening light a wide and beautiful prospect of the town and all the country around. The castle buildings, now used as barracks, are still very imposing, with great round towers and overhanging bartizans, and the views from the platform are superb. To the north-west are the big range of hills, and the Alps with the famous Triglav. To the west is the rich plain land intersected by rivers. In descending from the height we saw the pretty house of General Radetzky, the General of the Italian wars, and the walk down through the shady avenues with the birds singing in the bushes gave a delightful finish to the visit to this pleasant town that suffered so terribly in the awful earthquake of 1895. It was here that the Congress was held in 1821. That the people of Laibach are very alive to modern developments was evidenced in the handsome, well-arranged "Slavonitz" newspaper office, where everything was up to date, with a good library, each editor having his own room.

Carniola, like Styria, has a history that carries one far back into the dim, misty ages of the beginning of the human race. The rich plain we looked down upon from the great castle height was once a great lake, and as we have seen in the museum, rich finds have been made of these beginnings of history. Legend says Jason and the Argonauts passed here on

Carniola(Krain)—Ljubljana(Laibach)

the way from Colchis in distant Circassia; and of the occupation of the Celts there is ample and valuable evidence in the museum. After the Celts came the Romans, laying their high roads, and with more perfect organisation, and the rich finds of gold and silver objects prove, that this was a rich province under Roman rule.

In the fifth and sixth centuries the West Goths under Alaric, the East Goths under Theodore, and the Longobards under Alboin, destroyed much of this Roman civilisation, and the Huns led by Attila continued the work.

In the sixth century the Slavs appeared, and with them the Avars, and the history of this district developed as we have described the history of the Styrians, until in 1335 the Habsburgers came into power. Being near the Turkish border the district suffered heavily in the fifteenth and sixteenth centuries from Moslem invasion, and Laibach was attacked but never taken.

CHAPTER XV

CARNIOLA, WOCHEIN FEISTRITZ, VELDES, AND ADELSBERG

BEFORE proceeding on the southern route through Carniola to the vast caverns of Adelsburg we must make a north-western excursion to the district that Sir Humphry Davy so loved, and often visited in the eighteenth century.

This district can also be reached by the Tauern route to or from Triest, but it may be included in the chapter on Carniola, as here may be studied amidst scenes of remarkable beauty the Fauna and Flora of Carniola, and the sportsman, and fisherman, and Alpinist will have in this province wide scope for their pet pleasures.

It was in rather a dramatic fashion that I first learned that this rich corner of Europe was well known to a famous Englishman in the eighteenth century. I had arranged a journey for a party of British writers and journalists through Bosnia, and on our return when we arrived in Carniola, a well-printed and well-illustrated newspaper was handed to us in English and German, with a hearty welcome to the English guests; and to our astonishment more than one good portrait of Sir Humphry Davy.

In the welcome it was stated that the English were the " pathfinders," the pioneers, of the foreigners who

Carniola, Wochein Feistritz

since have visited this country, and continued: "One of the most important English naturalists, Sir Humphry Davy, made our country known to the world, as J. Gilbert, who followed the traces of the famous Briton in 1861-62 and 1863, writes in his highly interesting book of travels. He (Humphry Davy), the greatest ornament of the most fashionable London Society, the representative of European fame, had to come to the distant country of Carniola in order to find a place "where a man can rejoice in his life." And then followed a lengthy and learned article upon the early English travellers who had studied Carniola, and especially upon those sent by the Royal Society as far back as 1648 and 1672, when Dr Edward Brown made a long stay here. It was in 1818 that Humphry Davy first visited the district; and then again in 1827, staying at Laibach and in the district for a month, returning again in August; and then, being very ill in England in March 1828, with young Dr Tobin started on a tour and arrived in Laibach on May 4th, putting up at the Inn Detela, which stood where now stands the Union Hotel, where we had halted in Laibach. Davy remained in the district until October, then went on to Triest for a few days, and returned again; hunting, fishing and geologising as before, and exploring until the 30th October.

One of his notes on the district runs thus: "I have again and again visited Laibach, and again and again learned much that is new and beautiful, and wonderful, in the district. The valley of the Save and its waterfalls and lakes enticed me the most; I know nothing in Europe more gloriously beautiful."

Austria

It was strange that this document dealing with Sir Humphry Davy's rapture at the scenes we were visiting, should fall into my hands, for, but just before leaving England, I had been working to have a plaque placed on the house where Davy began his scientific work in Clifton, at the home of Dr Beddoes, and Signor Marconi had unveiled that plaque, a fact that deeply interested our Carniola hosts when I told them of the incident. The journal gave a most interesting account of succeeding English savants, explorers, etc., especially of Gilbert and Churchill of the Geological Society, and also a detailed account of the district, from which we must cull items upon the various points of interest.

Davy's raptures over the Wochein Lake and waterfall one can quickly understand when walking along the shores of that idyllic scene. Where the river runs into the lake it is of that strange, lovely turquoise hue so rare, and yet so often seen in this district, whilst the lake is of a dark green tone. A steep scramble and climb leads us up over the lake to the Savica Falls. A little wooden bench is here, just as there was when Sir Humphry Davy came, day after day, to revel in the scene.

And truly a wondrous and wild scene it is. The mighty fall leaping 250 feet, from between the bare grey rocks that climb some 1800 feet above, down into a turquoise pool; and then a little fall spending itself in cascades, these forming into a rushing torrent. A rainbow hovered over the pool, coming and vanishing as the light played upon it from behind the fleecy clouds.

The eternal roar, and thunder, and hiss of the

Carniola, Wochein Feistritz

waters made titanic music for the ear, and on looking back through the deep forest, a glimpse of a lovely lake was had, with the light falling upon it. Then again we looked up at the fleecy-white foaming turquoise-hued fall, and thought that this was the Save, that great river that flowed into the Danube. We are here, as it were, at the foot of the famous mountain, the giant of the district, the triple peaked Triglav, rising above the seven Triglav lakes to the height of 9400 feet.

The local Alpinists are a jovial and musical company with a pleasant wit, and I was astonished to receive at a dinner at Veldes an important document with many seals, endorsed in English, " In the service of its Majesty, ' The Triglav.' " The document was signed " Rex Triglavenses I.," and conferred upon me the " insignia of an honorary citizen and Knight of the Triglav Kingdom." The insignia was a handsome badge, enamelled in the local colours of red, yellow, green, and blue, with an edelweiss in white in the centre, and the legend " Reg Terg-lovense " around it. I found " his Majesty " was really Professor Belar who had climbed the mountain twenty-five times.

We had some glorious music on this evening, from a choir of peasants in pretty and brilliant costume, who came from the Rotwein Klamm, and sang their Slav part songs with vivid fervour and expressive intonation; and also from the " Glasbene Matice " a men's choir from Laibach, who also sang Slav part songs superbly. The Slav greeting in this district is " Zivio " pronounced Jee, vio; it is equivalent to the Bohemian Na Zdar, but, of course, this should not be used in a German locality, as also it is best not to use in a Slav district, " Hoch," or " Leb wohl," or " Auf Wiedersehen."

'The road from Feistritz to Veldes is full of enchanting charm, and from it the lake is looked down upon, lying like a jewel set in pearls of snow peaks. Here some of the rushing streams are of delicate emerald green, and the grey peaks rise up into the blue heavens, until they are snow and cloud wreathed.

At Veldes we drove to the Louisenbad, and on the balcony sat and wrote, and revelled in the soft beauteous scene of castle and lake and little island of St Maria im See.[1]

In spring the slopes of these mountains we have looked out upon are a field of superb colour of myriads of flowers, and on the lake side are baths of hot and cold springs, or for the summer there are lake swimming baths, and rowing and shooting and fishing can be enjoyed; and for the lover of early folklore, stories of heathen Celtic gods, and of mediæval legends; and peasant customs that recall both stories and legends and primitive faiths.

We shall visit this district again in passing up from Triest to Carinthia, the adjoining homeland; but we may give the sportsman and botanist a short hint of the pleasure to be had in this nature-favoured spot that Humphry Davy loved so well.

In Carniola, so famous for its Alpine beauty, the botanist will indeed find a paradise. In Austria itself, just as one may find every type of landscape scenery, so also the flora is of infinite variety; and the fauna

---

[1] The Weissenfels lakes that are on the frontier of Carniola-Carinthia are referred to in the latter section in an excursion from Villach.

VELDES

Carniola, Wochein Feistritz

is of especial interest; neither the naturalist, the sportsman, the geologist, nor the fisherman need depart empty-handed.

The flora is particularly varied, for here we shall find both Alpine flowers and those too that gladden the shores of the Mediterranean. Its inhabitants claim that in this respect Carniola is the most interesting country in Europe.

Amongst the rarer plants, we might mention *Festuca aurea* (only found on the Vremscica), as also *Festuca carniolica* (upon Nanos and in the valley Rasatal), *Fritillaria tenella* (at Gaberk), *Fritillaria meleagris* (at Laibach, etc.), and the scarce *Pœonia corallina* (upon Nanos and Baba), *Delphinium hybridum* (at Vrem), *Aconitum albicans* (Wocheiner Alps), *Ranunculus Thora* (at Kumberg), *Arabis scopoliana* (on the Schneeberg and also at Nanos), *Potentilla carniolica*, *Potentilla nitida* (in various localities), two rare varieties of *Trifolium-noricum* and *panonicum*, the attractive *Geraneum argenteum* (on the Crna prst and Lisec), *Euphorbia lucida* and *Euphorbia nicœensis* (Zirknitzer See and at Vrem respectively); and the following varieties of Viola may be found — *uliginosa, Zoisii, pinnata, cornuta*. Among the Gentians, *Gentiana Fröhlichii* is not uncommon, as also *Gentiana triglavensis*; and amongst others we might mention are *Valeriana supina, Scabiosa graminifolia*, as also *silenifolia*; *Chrysanthemum macrophyllum*; *Centaurea heleniifolia, Echinops ritro* and *Crepis grandiflora*.

The animal world of Carniola is very varied, as varied as the variety of the levels of the country. The great Alpine ranges of the Julian, Karawanken, and other mountain heights, the lower pine forest hills, and the level grassy plains, give a vast variety to the fauna of the district.

On the Julian Alps are the chamois and roebuck; on the Karawanken the ibex, or horned goat; eagles float over the lower mountain heights, and in the forests are blackcock, heathcock, ptarmigan and grouse; and in the deep forests wolves and bears are yet to be met with. Hares are plentiful, and wild cats not scarce, and wild geese and ducks are in the lower moors and woods.

The fisherman can have good sport in lake and stream with the various types of excellent trout, carp, pike, and a fish known as wells, the sheath fish; and as we shall see at Adelsberg, for the curious and specialist, the underworld of Carniola has its own peculiar fauna, and even flora, that accommodate themselves to the utter darkness of the numerous caverns.

To reach Adelsberg from Veldes we must travel back again to Laibach through Radmannsdorf and Krainburg, both pretty spots for a halt, the latter town being an excellent centre for mountain excursions. We follow along the Save, that valley that a hundred years ago Humphry Davy described as the most beautiful in Europe, and yet to-day, how very few English-speaking travellers know its beauty. We shall be again in the near neighbourhood of all this nature glory, when travelling up from the brilliant sunshine of Dalmatia, and halt to explore Gorizia, and all the exquisite beauty of Carinthia, two territories that border on Carniola.

In leaving Laibach to journey due south, we are

Veldes and Adelsberg

at once in a district full of strange problems for the naturalist. We cross the vast moor or "Moss" that has yielded so much of the life of the lake dwellers, and run along the river which later on plays such tricks of appearing and disappearing, like the rivers in the Tatra and in Yorkshire, and the Ombla that we shall see in Dalmatia. We halt at the pleasant little town of Adelsberg, where, although it is only a place of a couple of thousand inhabitants, yet the express trains stop, for the marvellous stalactite caverns bring about 50,000 people here annually, and the number would be quintupled did the world know what is to be seen in the netherworld of this region.

Before visiting the vast caverns, it is as well to visit one of the inns in the town for refreshment; for the tramp through the underworld lasts two to three or more hours, and is tiring because of the exciting interest aroused.

The little church in the town is worth a visit, especially if one sees as I once saw, a crowd of Slav children who had come to visit the caverns, all in their bright colours, here kneeling at their prayers before starting homeward.

The entrance to the caverns is a little way from the town, up a fine avenue of chestnuts, with lovely meadows below, through which runs the little river Poik that we met at Laibach under the name of the Upper Laibach. Then one passes up between grey rocks, and pines, soon coming to the arched gate of the cavern entrance. No torches are needed now, as all is lit up by electricity, and even a little railway is laid for the long stretches in the caverns for the weakly traveller. These things detract somewhat from the mysterious weird grimness, and the vast gloom of the caverns, but the light shews us marvels of beauty the torches could never reveal.

There are 20 kilometres of caverns (12 miles). Vast halls, long mighty corridors, intricate mazes, and beauteous niches on either hand as one enters and passes up the long tunnel, and then soon, far beneath, we can hear Poik rushing onward in its black depths. One longs to halt, but we are told this is nothing, and so it proves when the vast spacious Gothic halls are entered. The pure, lovely, colossal stalactites and stalagmites assume all types of form. The vast ballroom has great pendants of stalactites, and here, on Whit Monday and August the 15th, a peasants' dance is held, and 10,000 people throng the caverns. But it is best, at least at first, to be nearly alone; the awe and wonder is intense. At one place is the tower of Pisa, at another an organ, and fantastic pillars like palms. In the mausoleum are great sarcophagi. The entry into the Francis Joseph's Hall is very striking, and from here to the Calvary is a succession of wonders. Terrific! imposing! are the exclamations that come to the lips. In one place the masses glitter as with rain-drops. Some of the pillars and domes are as set with brilliants. The colours vary from purest white to soft deep sepia. On the Belvedere one looks down on the three lakes of Tarturus, and as one enters the Loible pass a giant lion guards the path.

Once when we were in these vast, sombre, dark yet glittering halls, a weird, strange, soft cry came through the night beyond us, echoing, and, as it were, wailing, pleading amidst the pillars and arches. It

Veldes and Adelsberg

was some children singing in a far-distant part of this netherworld. On this occasion I was furnished with much information by Mr Perko, the Secretary of the Government Commission that rules the caverns, and he showed me the strange string-like weed, that grows in this world of night, and the blind eel-like fish that live here. Some of the halls are 130 feet in height and nearly 200 feet in length; and great stretches containing new wonders not yet shown to the public, are being pierced through. It is a thousand Cheddars in one, and it is more wonderful than the great caverns of Han in Belgium. In one place was a fallen pillar, very like the famous pillar at the temple of Karnac. The age of an old twin column was given as 190,000 years. Perhaps the most beautiful and wondrous point is to stand on the top of the Hill of Calvary with its crucifix, and hundreds of pillars and pinnacles, and intricate mazes all around one. Other wonders are in dark caverns, where light suddenly reveals the most delicate beauty of form and colour. But we must leave this netherworld and journey southward, and soon cross the frontier of lovely Carniola, and enter the Küstenland, or coast land, and the province of Istria.

CHAPTER XVI

TRIEST AND ISTRIA

AUSTRIA is pre-eminently the land of dramatic surprises, and, after all the beauties of Carniola and the mysteries of Adelsberg, we cross, in descending to the Adriatic coast, that most barren yet ruggedly beautiful district of the Karst mountains.

It is an enlarged Dartmoor, with a wholly different scheme of colour. Here the rock is of light grey, with rich deep purple heather, and the rushing streams are of that wonderful turquoise blue I know of in no other district. It is said that all this barren rocky waste was richly afforested in Roman days, and that the Romans destroyed the forests to build their galleys. But Austria's schemes for education and agriculture and forestry are again making this wild lime stone region of bare rock, fresh and green with foliage, and the spines of larch and pine. One passes miles of young trees making good headway, and soon this district that for 2000 years has been a desolate waste, will be a profit-yielding forest-land.

We soon come to Opcina, which has quite lately been made a health-resort suburb of Triest. A mountain resort with the pure air of the altitude of 13 to 1500 feet, including sea bathing! An impossibility it sounds, but a lift connects Opcina with the sea level of Triest, so that one can live up here amidst pines, and

TRIESTE — TWILIGHT

Triest and Istria

rocks, and heather, and descend for a morning's sea plunge to the level of palms and roses. The look-out over the Adriatic, lying soft and blue in the sunlight along the indented shore, will charm the traveller, who gets thus his first glimpse of Adria's sea; and landward the view is very varied, with the grey scarps of the Karst leading up to the nearly bare uplands; but the villages on the lower slopes are in rich vegetation of vines, and chestnuts, and pasturage. There are good hotels, and pensions, and bathing establishments on this height, some linked with the sea-baths at the foot of the mountains. The ordinary rail takes a long time to get down to Triest, as it dives into tunnels, and winds and twists down the mountain side, giving glimpses of the sea, and the town of Triest and its harbour spread far below.

The city of Triest has a very modern appearance, and at first sight there seems to be little to detain the traveller, but the monuments that are left are of great interest, and excursions may be made by water to points of great beauty. I first entered Triest by water on returning from Greece in 1886, by the Florio Rubatino line of steamers, and as we entered the harbour the low sloping, green lands and ridges of the hills in the distance, and dotted houses, told of more cultivation than on the Grecian hills. The town itself was all varied with green from the open tree-shaded spaces, and, as it was in the spring, the chestnuts and Judas trees were in flower.

To-day the fine buildings at the quay of the Austrian Lloyd's palatial offices, and opposite the palace of Prince Hohenlohe, the Stadtholder of the province of Triest, with the town hall, enclose a handsome square, the harbour and busy shipping forming the front. The peculiarity of the clocks always striking the hour twice, had worried me, because one could get no satisfactory explanation of these redundant strikings, but Prince Hohenlohe, upon my putting the question to him, said it was because so often people did not hear the first striking; but another reason given was that the clock of St Mark's strikes twice, and Triest likes to copy Venetian customs.

There are scenes in Triest, on the canal, that vividly recall Venice, with her narrow waters, her rich-toned sails, and public buildings. But Venice has not the hills to climb that Triest can give you, neither has it the terrific Bora that sweeps down off the Karst mountains, that seem to shelter the city, and tears great ships from their moorings, and will even lift people bodily and hurl them into the harbour. The city has nearly doubled its population during these last twenty years, and now numbers considerably over 200,000 inhabitants, largely an Italian-speaking people.

Triest and its district has a population of Italians, and Slovaks, with a small proportion of Germans, and a sprinkling of Servian or Croats and Slavs, but Italian is the language mostly used, although German is understood in all the public offices and large business premises.

There are winding routes for carriages through streets and piazzas named after famous writers, such as Silvia Pellico, Goldoni, that lead up to the upper old town and the castle and cathedral, but for the pedestrian the most interesting way is to climb by

THE GRAND CANAL, TRIESTE

Triest and Istria

"The Steps of the Giants," that give occasion for frequent halts to look down on the city below and study the people who clamber up and down these steps, but it is a hot climb on a warm day.

Arrived at the summit, from the embattled platform near the cathedral, a great view repays the climber. Far over the brown-roofed houses of the whole city, with the dark smoke rising from the shipbuilding yards, out to the Mole and lighthouse, and far out to the open Mediterranean beyond. The bay is sheltered from the east and north by the dark hills and jutting headlands. Then when one has drunk in the view one can turn aside and enter the cathedral, some parts of which have stood since the days of Rome's dominance. In the tower, at the entrance, may be seen a pillar of the Roman Temple that stood upon this site; and in the Lapidarium, a tree-shaded space with a museum near by, some most beautiful relics of Roman sculpture and architecture, and also a fine monument to Winckelmann, who was killed here in 1768. The interior of the cathedral is at first a great puzzle to the archæologist. It is really two early churches of the fifth and sixth centuries, linked by a fourteenth-century nave. The inlaid marbles and mosaics are of exceptional value. The cathedral is dedicated to St Giusto, our St Just, and the frescoes illustrating his life are remarkable. The church is unfortunately very dark, and it requires good eyesight to be able to examine the really interesting details of this strange and impressive building.

To obtain even a wider view of the landscape around, if permission is obtained, the castle height can be climbed, and the grey ridges of the Karst mountains can be seen, as well as the distant Alps. It is hoped in Triest that even the dreaded Bora will be tamed, as the afforestation of the Karst goes on; and certainly the fresh vigour of the young trees we saw in some of the rocky districts promised thorough success to this bold movement, that should be a tremendous lesson to some British, or especially Irish, grumblers at home difficulties of cultivation, because of indifferent soil.

Triest, like Pilsen, is noted for its beer, for here is located the great brewery of Dreher, producing yearly something like a million and a half hectolitres of the well-known light beer.

It is a most interesting study to stroll along the harbour and quays of Triest, and watch the arrival of the Ocean liners, or still more, the small local steamers from the near ports and islands of the Adriatic; and numerous are the excursions one can arrange. In the town there are pleasant walks in the Giardino Publico, where the band plays, and the people are in light-hearted crowds, all orderly, but jovial. One sees but little quaint costume; now and then a grey-coloured head-dress, but most of the girls are bareheaded. Another popular place is the Boschetto, a lovely wooded hill with oaks, ash, and many trees, with shady little paths and water-courses, and peeps down to the city below and the hills beyond. Here, in the groves in spring, one can hear the music and laughter of the crowds, and in the retired paths the song of the nightingales.

Of the numerous excursions near Triest the one that all take is to Miramar that lies just across the bay. The pleasant way to reach this is by boat; one can get there by rail or tramway, but the approach to this stately château and its beautiful gardens by water is by far the most impressive. On landing at the marble steps we ascend into the beautiful gardens, with their bowers and seats in shady avenues looking out on to glorious flowers. Perhaps between tall dark cypress trees, on the blue waters of the bay there floats a tiny boat with deep orange sails, under the paler blue of the sky. All is beauty, colour, and soft, contented peace; and then one looks away to the white marble palace, and remembers that it was the home of Maximilian and his wife—he, executed in Mexico, and she lingering on in Laachen as a demented widow. The rooms within the castle are very lovely and hold many art treasures; but their greatest beauty is the superb views from the windows upon the beauteous bay, and the charm of landscape around it. A day that gives very much to remember is one spent in a trip to Capo d'Istria. A call at the offices of the Austrian Lloyd's will secure much useful information upon the possibilities of short or long tours on the Adriatic, and also interesting local booklets that give valuable notes.

Capo d'Istria can be reached in various ways; its name implies it is a headland of Istria, formerly an island, and as one sails around the great point the whole bay opens out, and soon a great building, that we were told was the Carceria, is seen.

The little town is very quiet now, but on entering the Piazza one halts almost with a shock of surprise. Here is a miniature Venice. The Campanile, the Lion of St Mark, and farther on the great cathedral, and the Palazzo communale, with its Venetian windows,

Austria

and estrade for public announcements. A veritable bit of Venice.

Once when visiting here, Il Brolo, the three old churches and a monastery, with the rich old cloisters had been utilised for an Istrian exhibition, and some remarkable historic pictures and relics of the province had been collected. Among their special art treasures were Carpaccio's Virgin and Child, and a rich collection of Pyxs and Chalices. In one of the churches a Gewerbeschule (Trade-school) has been established.

The whole little town is full of rich corners and quaint bits, and many of the houses of the former patrician families still speak of their former state. But Istria must not too long detain us, although in our tour down the Dalmatian coast we shall halt at a couple of points at the extreme south of the Istrian promontory.

CHAPTER XVII

DOWN THE ISTRIAN COAST TO DALMATIA, TO SEBENICO

THE fleet of Austrian Lloyd steamers that make the tour of the Dalmatian coast are varied; some fine vessels of big tonnage with every possible comfort, others smaller, suitable for calling in at the smaller ports, with not such luxurious accommodation, but with all reasonable comforts, and it is on these steamers that one sees more of the real life of the people, and there is a marvellous deal of pleasurable, exciting, and deeply interesting life, antiquity, and beauty to be seen on this journey.

'Leaving Triest, we recede from the city and glide out over the wondrous-hued sea; as we look back a deep cloud hangs over the town, proving how much of work there is in the capital of Istria, the great seaport of Austria; but we soon lose sight of the smoke, and see only the white and richly coloured sailed boats, and the Medusae in the clear blue waters, and the beautiful outline of the distant hills. We are sailing into one of the most romantic lands left to modern life, over a sea that is full of beauty, but that can show its passion, especially in the northern part, known as the Quarnero and Quarnerolo, the two sections forming the beautiful gulf that we shall traverse on our return route for Abbazia.

Austria

At first, after leaving the Gulf of Triest, we sail down the Gulf of Venice, noting the strange deep red hue of the earth on this coast, getting a view of Mount Maggiore, near Abbazia, and a glimpse of Venice. But we soon bear eastward and begin to see the islands and towns on the Istrian coast that are so full of antique lore and remains, and whose people offer so many traits in speech and in customs to interest the linguist and the ethnologist. Rovigno is one of these towns that well repays a halt. Here, again, is Venetian influence dominant in the architecture of the cathedral, the campanile of which rises high above the city dwellings. Sailing onwards we soon reach the small isle of Brioni, a lovely little spot with most charming walks—groves of arbutus and laurels that are filled with nightingales, or of palms and magnolias, scenting the air with their flowers. The sweet scent of the flowers and the hay makes one feel we are back in idyllic days, alone amidst nature, and then we light upon excavations, with rich Roman remains, villas, and temples, and we hear that Pliny wrote of this island, and that in later mediæval times it was well known. Then suddenly, after a lovely, silent walk amidst pastoral scenes, we come back to the harbour to see a fine hotel with a Kursaal, and all the amenities of life of to-day. On one evening we spent here we looked out over a roseate silver sea, with the little boats with their rich-hued, ruddy orange sails, standing out against the setting sun, whilst eastward were the silver ripplets from the moon that was arising over the silent wooded islet; all seemed to speak

ROVIGNO, ISTRIA

Down the Istrian Coast

of absolute peace and beauty; but farther away rose up on the sea the dark black mass of an ironclad, and lights sprang up in the distance of a town; it was Pola, the great naval seaport of Austria.

The first visit to Pola gives one almost a shock as we steam in between the silent and wooded islets. Suddenly we meet three or four torpedo boats, then an ironclad. White-sailed yachts are dotted here and there; The surprise of an Austrian who had never seen an ironclad, was intense at this sight. "Dass ist kein Kriegsschiff" (that is no warship), he muttered repeatedly, *sotto voce.* "What do you think it is?" I asked. "I don't know, but it is no ship." He could not believe such a dingy, dark-coloured wall of iron could be a ship, and as one of them lay against the rocky islets it did look like part rock, or too solid to float. But it is not the Austrian navy that draws the traveller to Pola, although the Marine Museum, with historic relics of Lepanto, and other episodes in Austrian history, is worthy of a visit. But the one thing that all go to linger over is the great arena standing on the rocky hillside, in lonely grandeur, where once 20,000 spectators looked on at the games in Roman days. The interior of the arena is a good deal filled in by debris of past ages, but the outer walls are in good condition, and some excavation has been done. Pola reminds one frequently of the Isle of Wight by its modern life; and then in its churches one is pleasantly thrown back into mediæval days; and then again by such monuments as the Temple of Augustus with its relics and the handsome Sergius triumphal arch, we are back once more in the midst of Rome's imperial days.

There are excellent hotels in Pola, and delightful music. Travellers, especially those with good introductions, can spend a most enjoyable time here; in the near vicinity are crowds of places where the historian and antiquary can revel in the past life of the district, and modern sport is not neglected. As all the boats call in at Pola, and it is also linked with the rail, it makes an excellent halting-spot for exploring the promontory of Istria.

But we are now on the borders of Dalmatia, that country into which Titus went. A learned canon once travelled thither to find out why Titus took this journey; he came back deeply impressed with the country and its beauties, but never solved the Titus problem.

As we sail on southward we pass the two islands of Lussino, the sea in the evening being tinted with opal and gold, and in the far distance the grey islands and white towns stand up against the varied outlines of the Velebit mountains. Here the Austrian hills begin to assume that strange, soft grey elusiveness in certain lights that is so characteristic of Greek scenery, whereas at other times cloud-covered, they are stern, rugged, and hard in outline. After having passed the open gulf of Quarnero there is rarely any sea to affect unpleasantly the weakest passenger.

The myriad islands and islets break all force to influence a good-sized ship, and the beauty and interest is continuous. The only thing is, one wants to remain on deck all night, the afterglow and mysterious

THE VELIBITE MOUNTAINS

Down the Istrian Coast

weirdness of the gloaming is so enticing, and then very frequently one feels compelled to be up before sunrise to see some famous spot.

I once entered Zara at 3 a.m. and went ashore in the darkness, just as the first faint gleams of dawn gave glimpses of towers and buildings. It was one of the most impressive walks I have ever taken. All was so silent. I met no one, but I passed through narrow streets and under archways, and suddenly came into the square before the cathedral. The grey gloaming was increasing. I could trace the Romanesque arches, and the tall towers, and all seemed to breathe of the dead past in the darkness and silence, the life of the centuries seemed present. Far, far back, even to a thousand years B.C., legend says Zara was an important town, and the Romans have left many a monument here, and on through the troublous ages Zara has always been of importance. The curiously varied races that have fought for and occupied Dalmatia we shall have space to refer to in more detail when sailing up the Bocche de Cattaro. As I wandered on in the increasing light I came to another open space, and here rose a tall Corinthian column, certainly of Roman origin; a stray passer-by told me I was in the Piazza de l'Erbe, and showed me that the ancient column used to be a pillory, for there were still the irons hanging by a chain. At its summit was a strange beast, said to be the Lion of St Mark. As I was standing before this column the light seemed suddenly to increase, there passed over the square a curious cold shiver, it was the shiver of the dawn heralding another day that was breaking. I

Austria

passed on in my walk round through narrow streets, past churches that promised much of interest, again through that archway that I learnt was the Porta Marina. Now I could see the Lion of Venice upon it, and the inscription that tells of the battle of Lepanto.

That there are many interests aroused in Zara was evident even in this walk in the dawning light; and afterwards I was able to see the beauty of the work that has been left, and the remains that have been collected in the museum of St Donato, formerly a church built of fragments of Roman work, with narrow Romanesque arches. This church has gone through all kinds of vicissitudes, having been a military magazine and a wine-cellar, but now the building is rescued for an honourable purpose, and the collection within its walls is of great historical value. The learned Monseignor Bulic, of whom we shall hear more at Spalato, suggests that here, or near here, was built a temple to Livia, the spouse of the Emperor Augustus, and part of this temple was used in the ninth century to build this church.

In the cathedral is a vast deal to detain the traveller —architecture, wood-carving, and rich metal shrines for relics. In the church of St Simeon the minutely worked and richly decorated sarcophagus with the bones of Simeon is said to have been brought here from Jerusalem in 1290. St Simeon is the patron Saint of Zara, and on October 8th his feast is kept up, an excellent opportunity to see the population of Zara and the surrounding country.

To show that Zara is by no means to-day given wholly up to antiquity, we once met a party of

POLA

Down the Istrian Coast

British tourists, who, at the short halt of the steamers, entered the town solely to find the Maraschino factory, for which the place has a great renown. As a fact, there are several factories that make this liquor from the fruit and leaves of the local cherry or small plum that here has a peculiar flavour which will not survive the transplantation of the trees. All around Zara are spots of historic charm, and perhaps one of the best routes whereby to explore the interior of Dalmatia and the hill district is to take the route to Benkovac, and on to Kistanje, and then on to Knin. Vineyards and wild barren lands are passed, and there is plenty of work for geologist and historian, and for the lover of picturesque peasantry. Of course the best hotels must not be expected in this district, but the strangeness and freshness of the experience well repays all trouble and inconvenience, and between the towns Kistanje and Knin, is the Roman Arch that tells of a town referred to by Pliny as a fortress, that became a most important commercial town of the Romans in the fourth century, where many gold and silver coins, inscriptions, and fibulae, rings, weapons, statues, etc., have been found.

In the picturesque town of Knin, that lies on the river Krka at the foot of a precipitous crowned rocky hill, there is a good hotel and an interesting house industry of the peasants, and, above all, a museum with finds of the Neolithic and bronze ages, and a remarkable collection of Croatic antiquities, Byzantine coins, and finds of women's ornaments, that are partly like those found in Bosnia, and others as those discovered amongst the Cechs and Wends.

From Knin excursions may be made into the water-

Austria

fall district of the Krka. The Velebit mountains that lie to the north rise to a height of 6000 feet, as do the Dinaric Alps that lie to the north and east. The costume, dances, and folklore of the peasantry is full of matter for the student and artist.

CHAPTER XVIII

DOWN THE DALMATIAN COAST FROM SEBENICO TO CATTARO

FROM Knin the railway can be taken to Sebenico, but we will resume our pleasant sea route between the rocky islands and over the gentle, placid sea, meeting those who come overland from Knin at the port of Sebenico, from whence also excursions can be made to the Krka waterfalls. In this district the peasants wear a gorgeous costume, the women covering themselves with coins and filagree ornaments, and the men have a rich-toned eastern dress.

There is an immense deal to excite the wonders of the traveller in this district, both in the population, the scenery, and the relics of past civilisation. The quaint customs of the peasant folk, and their stern, hard habits, the women still being treated somewhat after the eastern fashion, as creatures of burden and use, but yet with a freedom that is not eastern. To see a group dancing, dressed in all their finery of coin-decked headgear, and bejewelled dresses, is a fascinating sight. The peasants of the inland are called Morlaken, from a combination of More, Sea, and Volacco, Wallacks, say some writers; but to-day they prefer to be called Serbs or Croats, or simply Dalmatians.

Austria

Like all primitive races they are fond of festivals and weddings, christenings, and funerals; and fair or market days give occasion for gatherings, whereat their interesting dresses and customs can well be studied. The scenery of the Krka, with its lakes and waterfalls, reminds one somewhat, of what the Trollhattan district in Sweden was before the falls were despoiled of their beauty by big industrial, ugly buildings; but, of course, colour and vegetation are very different here to the northern growth and colour.

To get a good insight into the history, folklore, population, and antiquities of this district, and, in fact, of the whole of Dalmatia, a work by Reinhard Petermann, issued by the society for developing the kingdom of Dalmatia, is an excellent, learned, and pleasantly written volume, well illustrated by Herr Fischer; we can merely suggest, in our space, all the novel sights and fascinating history that may here be met with and studied, and must wander onwards, southwards to Sebenico, that has been called from its appearance and position a little Genoa. Here in the open space by the Poljana the peasants of the district gather, and in the cathedral they may be seen at the festivals.

To see the very beautiful great doorway of the cathedral, with its rich floreated and figured decoration in pointed Gothic, is alone worth a halt in Sebenico. Begun in the middle of the fifteenth and finished in the middle of the sixteenth century, the building is full of rich details and forms a glorious whole.

Down the Dalmatian Coast

In the civic buildings Venetian influence is quickly seen, as so frequently throughout Dalmatia, and in wandering about the narrow streets, many of them stepped, the jewellers' shops with the local trinkets, and the figures of the passers-by bedecked with these trinkets on their gay costumes, will fascinate the artist and the lover of quaint, picturesque costume.

It is not far from Sebenico to Spalato, but we must make a halt at Trau *en route*, for it is perhaps the quaintest, if not the most important, of these remarkable towns. We coast around the point known as Punta Planka, where the more eastern trend of the coast begins, and soon reach the islet on which the fortified Trau was built, a curiously picturesque scene—the old town with its walls and the beautiful campanile of its cathedral, all seemingly lying in a placid sea of silver-grey, deep blue, or ruddy-gold, according to the lights in which it is seen.

A veritable mediæval Venetian town, a happy hunting ground for the heraldic student, for historian and architect, and especially for the amateur of peasant costume and lore. Herr Petermann regrets that the Venetian occupiers built such terribly strong houses 400 years ago, so that the grandfathers of the present race had not to rebuild, but it is this that makes Trau so deeply valuable to traveller and student. Cathedral and churches, religious houses, and the homes of wealthy burghers, all have rich architectural details, and even carry us far back into Greek pre-Christian days. We shall get a glimpse of the whole line of history of Dalmatia, and the variety of races that have influenced it when we are at Cattaro. But in spite of the enticements of Trau we must sail out again over the placid bay in which Trau lies, and onward round through the channel of Spalato, that imperial city, the home of the Emperor Diocletian.

There are other ways of arriving at Spalato than by steamer, for here is (it seems incongruous) a railway station, and one can drive from Trau to Castle Vitturi, and thence, by boat, to Spalato, thus seeing the Riviera of the Seven Castles, where olive and myrtle, pomegranates and laurel flourish luxuriantly.

As we sail into the harbour of Spalato, at once the long line of palatial buildings that faces the sea front arrests the attention. It is our first glimpse of that marvellous palace built by Diocletian; the grand columns of the façade are still there, with shops half hiding them, but behind this long façade is the little antique town, built literally in the palace of the Emperor; the corridors and courts of the palace, now serving as streets, and open spaces for the town. But modern buildings have stretched beyond this square space, for the town now has almost 70,000 inhabitants.

There is a marvellous bewilderment at first in wandering about Spalato. The tiny streets, with grand tall columns and arches and Latin inscriptions, are so unlike any other town. The crowds of men and women in strangely varied and brilliant costumes, some with turban and fez, speak of the east. The

Down the Dalmatian Coast

passing from the Riva amidst the shifting and active modern café life, into this city of the dead, so filled with busy life, is a sensation that abides in the mind. A Roman palace, and now a town where 3000 dwellers have their homes; of the great columns of the façade thirty-eight remain out of fifty-two. There are also interesting mediæval remains, such as the Venetian Hrvoja Tower, built in the fifteenth century. Many will linger in the two market-places, the fruit and green markets, to study the people, with their produce brought in on gaily-decked asses; but soon we see the portal of the cathedral, and a sphinx resting under a lofty arcade, and we find we are before one of the strangest of ecclesiastical buildings; this was the peristyle of the palace, and is now the entrance to the cathedral, once, according to some writers, the mausoleum of the Emperor. Immediately on entering one sees it is a Roman building, temple or mausoleum, with fine Corinthian columns of Egyptian granite surmounted by lesser columns of porphyry. It is stated by some to have been a temple of Diana—Signor Parisic amongst others; a richly sculptured frieze of chariots and hunting scenes gives weight to this statement.

The arrangement as a Christian Church in this circular building is curious. The pulpit is in good Byzantine style, and the stalls have very remarkable carvings. The antique treasures preserved here are very rich: early crosses and missals, and reliquaries. Near the cathedral is the little Temple of Jupiter, now the Baptistry. The doors of the cathedral, in their rich early carving, remind one of the famous portals at Hildesheim, but these are of wood, not bronze.

We passed onwards from this strange, fascinating building, through the narrow streets, often with good square arches, or round, vaulted arches, through which in the narrow dark streets passed the gay colours of the peasant dresses. On the land side of the town we came to the Porta Aurea, or Golden Gate, a gate long hid in the debris of later buildings, but now laid bare; and as we were fortunate enough to have with us Mons. Bulic, the learned director of the museum, and historian of Spalato, he took us up the narrow steps to above the arch of the gateway, and here to our delight and surprise was a tiny chapel, about the size of that richly bejewelled Carl's chapel, in Carlstein, that we saw in Bohemia. This chapel is of the ninth century, and had been hidden for ages, but the little early windows were still there, and standing by the tiny screen that separated the chapel from the entrance was a sweet-faced nun, thus completing the beautiful picture of this linking of a Roman gateway to early Christian life, and on to our own day.

From this Porta Aurea we passed round to the Porta Argentea, on the east wall of the palace, where is housed the extraordinary rich finds made by Mons. Bulic and others — not only at Spalato but at Salona, the Pompeii of Dalmatia. Here were we indeed blessed in having the Monseignor with us, for he showed us of his best treasures from under lock and key, and most delightful was his explanation of the sites

Down the Dalmatian Coast

of the finds and the history and usage of them, for they included women's ornaments, fibulæ, rings, earrings, trinkets, and curious locks of intricate workmanship. Two inkstands he had found; only four such are known in the world. One gold ring was of complex work. It could be made into a single broad ring, or into three rings, suitable for man or woman. The sarcophagi were exceptionally fine, with expressive sculpture, reminding one in their beauty, almost, of those in the museum of Constantinople, of Alexander and others, but they were not of such great dimensions. Coins, statues, reliefs, inscriptions, altars, vases, urns, domestic utensils, including glass feeding-bottles, in fact, nearly every item of Roman life that the earth has preserved to us can be studied here, though badly housed, to Mons. Bulic's repeated regrets. One of the best books on this and Spalato and Salona is by Prof. Jelic, Mons. Bulic, and Prof. Rutar; the work already referred to by Herr Petermann in German, has also good chapters on this district and the museum. Salona is but a short distance by rail from Spalato, or half an hour's drive; really this is the best way to go, as the view of the city, bay, and mountains tells one of the lovely site the Romans chose for this town, the excavations of which Mons. Bulic has superintended. I was pleased to meet this enthusiastic and learned antiquary, for by a curious sequence of events I have met most of the great explorers of antiquity by the spade — Mr Layard, Dr Schliemann, Comendatore Boni of the Forum excavations, Prof. Salinas of Sicily, the

Austria

Abbé Delattre of Carthage; and Mons. Bulic is as ardent as either of these explorers in his eagerness for the work, but is terribly hampered by the want of a suitable building and lack of funds. Much of the Roman work in Salona has in former days been utilised, and so destroyed, but columns, and pillars, the city gates and walls, the theatre and amphitheatre can be traced, and, as in Pompeii, the streets, pavements, and wheel ruts, vividly bringing back the past.

It is with regret that one leaves Spalato and sails out over the lovely sea, beneath the exquisite blue of the sky, and looking back there rises up that long, noble sea front, that now we can understand.

To visit the smaller towns and the islands down this coast, local Lloyd steamers should be taken, such as the Triest-Metkovic or the Triest-Cattaro route. There are crowds of peasants and merchandise on these boats, and plenty of quaint scenes full of strange beauty that are not so well seen on the larger express boats. There are other lines of steamers with lesser fleets, such as the Hungarian and the Cesare lines, that it is as well to know of, as they also call at the smaller places.

A vast amount of rich hunting ground for the travellers lies on the route between Spalato and Ragusa. On the islands—such as Brazza, Lessina— one can get many a romantic story of bygone days, and relics back into the Greek period, and at Metkovic we are on the river Narenta, that descends through Mostar in Herzegovina. Metkovic was a great Serbian

LESINA

Down the Dalmatian Coast

stronghold; from thence in their galleys the Serbs held the whole district in awe, leaguing with the Saracens and compelling even Venice to pay them tribute. Not only is the history romantic, but the natural beauty of these islands is so varied and beautiful. One morning, in the middle of May, I came on deck at 8 a.m. to find we were just off the steep rocky islet of St Andrea, and on the south-east lay the longer islands of Lissa. We were sailing over the battle sea plain of 1866, when on that summer day in July the Austrian navy, under Admiral Tegetthoff, crushed the Italian navy and made the Adriatic so largely an Austrian sea.

'But we halted not at Lissa, but bore south from St Andrea, for the small island of Busi, where are ten caverns of varied beauty discovered by Baron Ransonnet — one, the Bearshole, being over 160 yards in length; but the most beautiful and wonderful of these is the Blue Grotto, found by the Baron in 1884, and as yet but little known to the world. The island is very rocky, and yet with rich grass upon the fairly high hills. The sea when seen with just a breaking ripple is of a lovely aquamarine. As we near the island the colour changes to a wondrous crystal blue, and as we draw still nearer, beneath the greyish yellow lichen-covered rocks, to an emerald green. A few people were on the rocks, and boats awaited us, and in the very gently heaving sea we passed, sitting low in the boat, under the low arch of the cavern, with just space for the boat to glide in, where all was dark, and then emerged into a wondrous strange shimmer of light. We were in a cavern, with

Austria

the water beneath us full of light and of turquoise or clear crystal tones; then came a narrow passage with rocks on either side, and the colour of the water was of a superb hue. Slowly we emerged into a second cavern, with a yet more intense light far beneath; as the oars slowly lifted, crystal gems of light dropped from them, and looking back we saw a fairy scene of supreme beauty. Beneath us the water, down to the pebbles below, that looked as jewels, was of clear, crystal silvery hue, faintly tinged with a tender blue; farther away it was of deeper blue; and behind us in the strange light came another dark boat, lying on this crystal sea, so full of light. Half hid, half seen, the figures in this boat, lit with the light from beneath, were strangely weird. On looking back as we issued from this natural marvel the effect of the high vault of grey-yellow rock, warm in the sunlight and the different colour of the open sea, was very beautiful.

In comparing afterwards the beauty of this Blue Grotto of Busi, and that of Capri, we found opinions very divided. Some said this cavern was the finer, especially the passage from the first to the second cavern, but that the blue of Capri was more pronounced; others that the blue tone here is the finest; but all agree that we had seen a marvel of nature, and are thankful that the sea had permitted our entry, for with even a little wind the entry is impossible.

We sailed back past the grey stone isle of Lissa, with high hills and little herbage, until on the south side we saw some trees, and then steered onwards

Down the Dalmatian Coast

between Lessina and Curzola, with, on the port side, Sabbioncello, and ahead Meleda.

As night was falling we halted on the coast of Sabbioncello, at the little port of Trstenik, or Terstenik, which lies in a little bay. A tiny hamlet lay under the high hills with a little mole on which gleamed a red light. The people put out a couple of boats to see this strange sight of a big ship all lit up, with music and dancing on board, for we were on one of the finest of the Lloyd fleet, the *Thalia*, with people from twenty-four nations on board for an International Press Congress, and our music re-echoed against the silent, grey, rocky hills, that had never, perchance, before given back such sounds.

The southern point of Sabbioncello is not far from the entrance into Gravosa, the port for Ragusa, that powerful city that dates back to the sixth century B.C., when the Greeks founded here Epidaurus. But before ascending the long incline to the walls of Ragusa there are some nature marvels to hold us for a time at Gravosa, the port for the heavy traffic of Ragusa.

This town stands at the mouth of the Ombla, that here opens out into a lovely bay surrounded by wooded-terraced hills and dotted dwellings, intercepted by groups of tall, dark cypress trees. A peculiar little excursion is to ascend the fiord-like opening of the Ombla, shut in by precipitous high rocks, to where the river flows in pure crystal water over a weir. Beyond this is a building where artificial ice is produced, and rising beyond this we see a great amphitheatre and wall of rock, with, it appears, no

Austria

outlet; but at the very foot of this rock, and from it, as it were, there runs a large body of water, exactly as does the Aire in Yorkshire at Malham Cove, but with a far greater body of water. Near the falls is an old chapel dating from the twelfth century. A quaint little excursion this, leading pleasantly up to the beauty of Ragusa, which we can reach from here by water or road, the way from Gravosa to Ragusa being a gentle ascent of three kilometres, say two miles, that is worth walking, for the gradual opening out of the wonderful view, and the pretty entrance into the antique city, between lovely gardens, and picturesque houses, embowered in cypress and palms, oranges and myrtles, glorious roses and flowers, and every type of southern vegetation.

And yet the entrance to Ragusa should also be made by water to get the view of its walls and towers, and all its picturesque buildings, but we shall see this in returning from Cannosa and Lacroma.

Ragusa itself is full of mediæval charm, both of people and city, with a wealthy population enjoying the twentieth-century amenities of good hotels and social life. The view from the terrace of the Hotel Imperial at once tells how much there is to see in Ragusa, and the palm-shaded gardens, full of glorious flowers, gives rest and quiet after exciting sightseeing.

To descend from these modern surroundings, down the hill to the erstwhile drawbridge and solid round towers and imposing walls of the town, is to leap back in the centuries, while the groups of peasants with bedecked mules and asses, the men in fez and

RAGUSA

Down the Dalmatian Coast

turban, and the women in bright, very varied costume, all aid the sensation, and as we pass on down the long Corso, or Stradone, and come to the open spaces with public buildings and churches, cathedral, and, above all, the rector's beautiful palace, one can picture fifteenth-century life; nay, on a fête day one has it here.

In the small market-place still stands the rich architecture of the old patrician houses. Balconies and portals and coats of arms are all well executed.

Whilst standing here on a soft spring day, the weird wailing notes of music of a funeral procession pierced through the air, and the church bells clanged forth as the funeral procession drew near. On another occasion we were present in Ragusa for Corpus Christi procession, when the roads were strewn with flowers and the scene was indeed rich in mediæval form and tones.

The little Mint, now the Dogana, has some very rich Venetian work in its windows and arches; opposite is the Roland statue, and close by is a lovely Renaissance fountain, where the women in the pretty costumes foregather, forming pretty pictures, while their vases are filling.

The Loggia under the rector's palace, where there is a café, forms a pleasant resting-place, and one can examine the capitals of the pillars and their rich sculpture, of such subjects as the Judgment of Solomon, Æsculapius, etc., the whole reminding one so continuously of Venice. It has suffered much, since first built in 1388, from fire and earthquake. The inner court is most picturesque, with its arcaded arches and fine stairways, and above one sees here and there the iron klamps, or ties, holding the building together after the earthquake.

A building that suffered terribly from the 1667 earthquake was the cathedral, but it has very much within it of interest. The building is said to owe its origin to a vow of Richard Cœur de Lion; it is a fact that he was the guest of the Ragusan Senate in 1192. Especially noteworthy are the treasures of bejewelled reliquaries that are marvels of Byzantine and other schools of the metal-worker's art. The greatest marvel of all is the gold reliquary, that holds the head of St Blasius. Brought from the east in 1206, it is of the old Byzantine Justinian's period, and enriched with twelfth-century medallions, with Longobard inscriptions. Another rich reliquary contains the hand of the Saint, and the whole treasury is nearly equal to that of Santiago for rich work and precious bejewelled metals.

But Ragusa and its surroundings, so fascinating are they, claims too much of our space, but before quitting it we take a boat across to the little isle of Lacroma. We pass out round the harbour, and see well the grim old walls and red roofs of the houses of the town above the lovely blue of the water. A white-robed courteous monk received us, and conducted us up the idyllic little rock landing-place to the monastery. We are where Richard Cœur de Lion is said to have landed on his hapless return from the Crusades, here fulfilling his vow to build a church on the spot whereon he should be saved from the tempest. One tradition says he founded the cathedral

THE WALLS OF RAGUSA

Down the Dalmatian Coast

of Ragusa, *i.e.* Maria Maggiore. A later monarch who lived here was King Maximilian. The gardens are now partly in decay, but are yet very lovely. In the beautiful cloisters the masses of roses are in clusters of hundreds, and aloes, vines, and palms flourish profusely; on the rocky coast the water is so pure and crystal, one longed indeed to linger on this lovely silent isle.

Another remarkable water excursion is to Cannosa, where lives the learned Count Gozze, whose family is one of the oldest in Ragusa, having been patrician in the tenth century. We were favoured with introductions to the present holder of the title, and found him a most charming host and learned historian. We landed at the little port, and were soon in the rich vegetation that formed the gardens of Count Gozze's home—prickly pear, camphor trees, bamboos, oranges, mandarins, great clusters of arum lilies, bread fruit-trees, interspersed with fountains and statues. In one place was an oak 700 years old, but in the village at the top of the hill were two gigantic plane trees, one of which it took eleven persons with outstretched arms to encircle, the trunk being about 66 feet in circumference. The whole place and the people are interesting, and in the count's house are treasures of art and antiquity of great value.

One can quickly reach Herzegovina from Gravosa by rail, but we must steam out of the picturesque bay southward, to enter that strange, beautiful fiord of the Dalmatian coasts, the Bocche di Cattaro. The steamers frequently enter the Bocche, or mouth of Cattaro, very early in the morning, and the entry and sail up the Bocche is one of the most enchanting sights the world has to give. It was at five a.m. on a lovely morning late in May when we had the best entry into the Bocche, and as we made the Punto d'Ostro the sun was just climbing over the grey rocky hills, and ahead were the mist-wreathed mountains of Montenegro. A tiny ruddy-sailed bark lay on the blue bay. Hills were all around us as we glided in; an old Roman fort told of the centuries of life; then we came to a narrow pass with a town ahead, Ercegnovi, or Castelnuovo, as the Venetians named it, the scene of many a fierce struggle, especially between cross and crescent. We can steam close in as there is deep water, and we see the old castle and square tower and lovely woods above. The scene is very like the Bosphorus, and lying here was the yacht given by the Czar of Russia to the Prince, now the King of Montenegro.

We bear nearly east over the sea, now grey in shadow, then turn sharply to the right southwards, and we are in the middle of the narrow Kumbor channel; a black mass lies ahead under the shadow of the mountains—it is an ironclad, and on the other side, at the narrowed point, are other vessels. This narrow pass is very lovely, like one of the beautiful passes on the Danube.

We then bore across the wide, beautiful inland sea towards the island of Stradioti, with the tiny islet and church of Sam Otok before it.

Here was a flat plain land with the hills rising above, grey and wreathed in mists, and all round a

Down the Dalmatian Coast

placid silver sea, a scene like the Italian lakes plus the Bosphorus, and in the grey morning light we saw shoals of fish, of which there were tunny, sardines, and mackerel. But now we turned northward, and made for the Channel of the Chains, the most narrow part of the Bocche, and blocked formerly by chains. It is only 1000 feet across, yet there is twenty fathoms depth of water, and the hills run up to 3000 or 4000 feet.

'As we issue from this pass a superb scene of glory and beauty opens out. Two romantic little islets are ahead, floating in a turquoise sea, St Giorgio and Madonna della Scapella, with churches, and spires, and domes, partly hid by tall cypress trees, and ahead are the towns of Perasto, famous, like Devon, for its seamen, and Risano, the earliest Illyrian settlement, behind which climbs up, in serpentine fashion, the old road to Montenegro.

We now steer eastward, and bearing to the south, are in the spacious Gulf of Cattaro. As we skirt along the southern shore we pass the two townlets of Upper and Lower Stoliva. Green pasture is on the lower slopes and on the grey heights above. All these little townlets have their old churches, with well-built Venetian types of campanile, that o'ertop the tall dark cypress and olive trees. Ahead we could see the snow still on the mountains of Montenegro.

On the opposite shore, that is not far off, is the little town of Dobrota, where the houses have portholes for shooting in case of an attack, and on our port side is the town of Perzagno (Prcanj), where for many years they have been building a cathedral.

Austria

'But ahead is Cattaro, and as we enter the sunlight comes down from between the hills, and lights up the line of mist on the mountains, and the low-lying mist on the lake-like beautiful bay, and this strangely enchanting entry into this land of novel charm is ended. We have given it some space, but how inadequate to even imply all the beauty, and history, and legend that clings around the Bocche di Cattaro.

The quay at which we land is really the promenade and market-place of the town, and is full of brilliant detail of the varied peasant life. The handsome Montenegrin women, in their picturesque little caps and coloured dress, bring their produce here for sale, and the stalwart men, and the men of Cattaro and the hills around, and the peasants wearing the fez and Turkish breeches, all form wondrous groups of form, and colour, and character.

The town, seen from the beautiful harbour, has a most romantic ensemble. The great wall zigzags up the craggy hill, locking the city in beneath the precipitous cliff that entirely overhangs it. By the old zigzag path one can climb up to Montenegro in three and a half hours, and in eight hours to the top of the mountain, and it is worth while to climb up this steep, many-stepped path to above the houses, to look down into the town and out over the beautiful bay. The great cathedral, with its double towers, lies in the square, and the strangely quaint, narrow streets that lead up to this are full of bits of architectural beauty and history. Venice, of course, asserts herself. The Porta Marina, through which we passed

Down the Dalmatian Coast

into the town, has the Lion of St Mark upon it. The cathedral goes back to the eighth century, and enshrines the bones of St Trifon, whose day, the third of February, is held as a festival by the Marinarezza, formerly a guild of seamen of the whole of the Bocche; here alone is a subject for the historian. There is another little church, St Luca, that reminds one of the small old cathedral at Athens; here the Greek rites are observed.

The town of Cattaro is one to slowly wander about in, and watch the strangely varied crowds, and gaze into the quaint shops with the hand workers at their work, especially at the filagree work, and then to go out to the Riva and watch the marketers and people from the coast and mountain towns.

An insight into the history of this district gives a new light on many problems of to-day, and upon the varied races that are united under the Austrian Crown; and at the risk of allowing too much space to Dalmatia, we give a succinct summary of the history of this district.

The languages spoken are chiefly Croatian and Serbian, really a single language with a double alphabet, the Serbians using the Russian letters and alphabet, the Croats the Latin. Rizano claims to be the earliest town on this fiord of the south, dating from 228 B.C., and in 168 B.C. the last old Illyrian king was led in triumph as a prisoner to Rome, and from 138 B.C. the Bocche became part of the Illyrian Roman province. In the ninth century A.D. the Saracens destroyed Cattaro, and in the tenth century we have the first entry of the Slav folk, the Serbians, into this

Austria

local history, and in 1002 the famous Bulgarian Czar Samuel, who figures so prominently in Bulgarian legend and history, captured Rizano and Cattaro.

A romantic and tragic point in this history was when the Norman Princess Jacquinta came here and succeeded in making her son George, king. This period, with the history of the Princess Jacquinta, has been utilised of late in local drama. In the middle of the fourteenth century the Serbians, with the help of the men of Cattaro, seriously defeated the Bulgarians, and for a time held the district; and in 1370 the town placed itself under the protection of Ludwig the First of Hungary; but the rule of Hungary was short-lived, and King Turtko of Bosnia and Serbia stepped in and seized upon this and other territories given up by Elizabeth of Hungary. This reign also was short-lived, and after a victory over the Ragusans, Cattaro remained a free town and a republic for a while, until 1420, when the Venetians, under Pietro Loredano, appeared, and on the 23rd of April agreed that Cattaro should retain its free government, that Venice should not hand it over to a third state, and also that it should retain its right to coin the "Triffoni" coins, with the patron saint St Trifon on them. For a time under Venetian overlordship there was peace; then came the Moslems, and from 1480, in view of this danger, a Venetian commander, with the title of rector, resided in Cattaro, but in 1483 the Turks captured Castelnuovo, and for 200 years the struggle between cross and crescent continued, until in 1687 the Venetians reconquered Castelnuovo and the Bocche became wholly

Down the Dalmatian Coast

under the rule of Venice, a rule that was light, and gave freedom to the people, with but few taxes. In 1797 Austria became overlord of the Bocche in a fairly peaceful fashion, but in 1806 the French fought for the district, and the Russians occupied Cattaro; but in 1807, after the peace of Tilsit, the Bocche was handed over to the French, who held it for six years, until the battle of Leipzig; then the French general held it until December 27th 1813, when he capitulated to the English fleet under Hoste. The English rule only lasted twelve days, when Hoste handed Cattaro over to Montenegro, whose prince held it until June 14, 1814, when again the Austrians marched in, and since that date, with the exception of certain risings in 1840 against taxes, and later on in one or two towns against conscription, risings that Austria has dealt with in a lenient and diplomatic fashion, this, during more than two thousand years most troubled land, has been at peace, in its marvellously beautiful home, where nature has been lavishly prodigal with almost every type of blessing she can bestow.

This curt history will show of what strangely mingled origin are the people of this homeland of Austria, and what volcanic elements she has to lead and control.

The express steamers take one quickly back from Cattaro and Ragusa to Triest, but we must bear up eastward and sail up the ofttimes turbulent Quarnero, to halt awhile at the new resort on these Adriatic shores, the gay, prosperous bathing resort of Abbazia that so rapidly has become a European pleasure resort. Abbazia is a paradise of roses and

Austria

palms. On one palm trunk a rose tree was climbing, that was said to have four thousand blooms upon it, and the sight of it confirmed the statement. Handsome villas and lovely walks skirt the soft languid sea that laps so gently on the pebbly and rocky beach, where numerous bathing resorts are well arranged. There is a palatial Kurhaus, plenty of music and amusements, and the music is peculiarly interesting, because of the proximity of all types of national music, Slav, Magyar, and Italian, and this is given by wandering musicians who play with enthusiasm and brilliancy, and we have as well the choice, effective rendering of great works by good Austrian orchestras, and the excellent orchestra of the Direction.

The view from the promenade, and from between the trees and palms of the gardens of all the bay with its dotted towns, including Fiume, is very lovely; the soft blue sea and grey-brown rocky bays, with idyllic little hamlets, the fashionable resorts, such as **Lovrana**, with their palatial hotels and luxurious southern gardens, all redolent with sweet-smelling flowers and trees, make the whole bay a most enchanting winter and spring resort, and in summer it is not too hot. The Monte Maggiore is a prominent feature in the view, and this shields Abbazia from all chilly winds. Not a quarter of a century old, Abbazia has no old buildings to renovate; all is of the newest, and the curative institutions are scientifically up to date and under careful control of the Administration, and sports, regattas, illuminations, excursions, dances, theatricals, give no chance for ennui; whilst the lover of nature is quickly alone in a deep forest, or on a silent sea beach; and the student of man and history

Down the Dalmatian Coast

will soon discover near by old towns and quaint hamlets to interest him deeply with architecture and folklore.

But we must quit the Adriatic shore, passing up the pretty zigzag road that climbs up to the station of the Southern railway.

CHAPTER XIX

THROUGH KÜSTENLAND, GORIZIA (GORZ), AND CARINTHIA (KÄRNTEN)

TO travel from Abbazia, in the soft gentle air of the Adriatic, to Gorizia, we double back on our route to Triest from Carniola, and running westwards at St Peter's commence the northward trend of our journey at Opcina above Triest, still bearing westward across the Küstenland, *i.e.* coast lands.

There is a town lying somewhat to the south of this route that is of great importance from the historical point of view, the Roman city of Aquileia, that has been so often referred to, and whence come the rich finds of Greek and Roman antiquity which we shall see in the museum at Görz.

But in Aquileia also is a museum, in what is now but a townlet, although of great importance as a Roman city before Attila, in 451 A.D., swept down upon it. The colony was founded 200 B.C. After Attila's vengeance the dwellers in Aquileia fled to the Lagunes and founded Venice. An eleventh-century cathedral proves that the town recovered from this blow of Attila's, and was of importance in mediæval times.

To English travellers Aquileia is interesting as the spot where Richard Cœur de Lion was wrecked on his return from the Holy Land, and afterwards spent

Küstenland, Gorizia, and Carinthia

so many months in prison. We have given the other account of his landing at Lacroma, and his fulfilling his vow in Ragusa. The route from Opcina to Gorizia traverses a great distance of the wild barren Karst mountains; like Dartmoor, a wild waste of rock and heather, but with many parts being reclaimed and afforested, and looking rich and green between the grey, rocky wilderness.

At Gorizia, or Görz, we are still amidst a southern vegetation of palms and magnolias and roses. In the pretty public gardens these flourish, and the hotel garden has seats amidst a wealth of myrtle and oleanders, and in the spring beneath palms in rich golden bloom.

In the Piazza Grande one looks up to the dominant castle, its grey old walls and towers standing out above the wooded slopes that lead up to it from the town. Below in the Piazza, the Jesuit church in Renaissance architecture, with the picturesque onion domes, stands just before the Neptune fountain. The whole town has a peaceful placid look about it, in spite of the great barracks that line the road leading out to the railway.

The chief thing to linger over in Görz, beyond the natural beauty of the vegetation of its surroundings, is the old building in the Piazza Corno, utilised as a museum. This was not in the order and excellent arrangement generally found in the Austrian museum, but the collection is of great value, especially the finds from Aquileia. Early Roman and Greek heads of great beauty and care of workmanship, earlier finds of bronze and iron weapons, and vases and some interesting Egyptian tablets. There is also a collection of coins, and interesting glass, and some fine Etruscan vases.

The town itself is of the Italian type, with narrow arcaded streets, and three languages are spoken—Italian, Slav, and German. The cathedral is hardly worth a visit save for its rich treasury, formerly belonging to the Patriarch of Aquileia.

The district we traverse through Gorizia to enter Carinthia, or Karnten, is through a most wild, strange district of deep mountain ravines and narrow defiles, where mountain torrents of a delicate turquoise hue, varying to creamy white, rush between the fantastically worn grey rocks, and give constant music beside the winding roads. In some places the rivers form little lakelets of this soft hue, surrounded by coral-like rocks in graduated steps. At St Lucia we are nearing Carniola, but we pass through this district which we have already visited, and after passing the long Karawanken tunnel, that opened this country more fully to the world, we pass Rosenbach, and make our halt in Villach, one of the chief towns in Carinthia.

The development of this district through the new railway that since 1897 has made Villach a most important centre for all travellers has been most remarkable. I first visited Villach in that year when there was but one small station and the ordinary inn accommodation. Now there are two important stations and numerous large hotels, although perhaps the old spacious inns hold their own for comfort.

The town has a busy prosperous air, the people here being largely of German stock, as is the whole

IN THE IZONZO VALLEY

Küstenland, Gorizia, and Carinthia

of Carinthia, with, of course, a mixture, about 25 per cent. of the Slav or Slavonian folk, who still wear the picturesque dress on church fêtes and holidays.

The district around Villach is full of opportunity for delightful expeditions and excursions; the town itself has a pleasant, old-world air about it. The charm and even wonder in visiting these towns is to be amidst mediæval surroundings, old churches, old monuments, inns with arched passages and vaulted pillared chambers, and yet to be also in the midst of the latest developments of science and building art.

The view from the bridge over the Drave that here rushes tumultuously through the town is very pleasant, with a good view of the Dobratsch mountain. A stroll up the main street to the fine Gothic church of St Jacob will disclose many historic memorials, such as the house of Theophrastus Paracelsus, where Charles V. stayed in 1552, and some good examples of wood and iron work. The monuments in the church are very remarkable, and the carved figures of value for the dress of the period. The marble pulpit is a fine piece of work, with figures of Adam and David, etc., well executed. It is worth while being here for a service, for the organ is a fine one and the singing good. The history of the district can be studied in the museum; and of present developments one of the most interesting places is the woodwork school, where the very heart of the worth and uses of wood is laid bare to the pupil. Every type of tree is studied and the possibilities of the usage of the wood illustrated. Here indeed the meaning of woodwork (that much-

Austria

belittled word in our English scheme of education) can be understood: what a mass of artistic and useful knowledge and work it comprises. Here was work from the most simple toy cut out with a knife by a child, to the elaborate, artistic articles for the home or the church. Decorative work of every description; designing from nature, leading on to the highest of the woodworkers' art, and sculpture of which we saw some powerful examples, such as figures of Dante, Samson, and the Christ. In chatting with the director, who, like so many of these heads of schools, museums, etc., in Austria, had studied well the work of other countries, whilst speaking of England he said, "Your drawing and painting are good, but you have no idea of house industry, and your poor have no idea of art; here the poorest boy can see, with an artistic eye, and utilise his seeing for the useful."

It is a pretty walk across the fields from Villach to Warmbad, one of the most remarkable bathing resorts in Austria, lying in a scene of great beauty. One can drive, or use the railway that in a few minutes runs to the little station of Warmbad—Villach, as it is called. The little station itself is a beauty spot. Here one can sit on the platform amidst the flowers, with a glorious view around of snowy mountain peak, and green pasture meadows, fir forests and orchards. The station and waiting-rooms are absolutely clean, speckless, and with most artistic pictures of the wonder nature scenes attainable in the district. A gong of a mellow tone tells of the coming of a train, but after the rush and hubbub is over, all is peace again, and the peaks of Mittagskogel and Türkenkopf rise up

Küstenland, Gorizia, and Carinthia

majestically in the sunlight, over the plainland around; and from the station a few minutes' walk through a pretty tree and flower-planted park leads to the bathing establishment of Warmbad, a series of handsome buildings in a lovely garden, with fountains and chestnut avenues leading away to mountain walks.

The pure upland air, the scent of the pines and the flowers, the ripple and rush of the Gail Stream that flows at the foot of the hill, with numerous mountain streamlets rushing down to it, all give a delightful sense of calm, idyllic beauty, and the establishment adds all the delightful pleasures of cultured life. The baths were known to the Romans and also to Napoleon; the height above the building is called Napoleon's Höhe. It is small wonder that these heights have ever been extolled.

After a plunge or two in the crystal swimming-bath, I asked a doctor friend the meaning of the strengthening, exhilarating effect, a "jump over the moon" type of feeling. I was told that a year or two ago they could not decide what caused this effect, in spite of many an analysis. But lately they had tested for radium, and found important radio-activity, and that probably was the cause of this exhilaration: at least it is there; and the bathing arrangements in this bath of many springs is a delightful experience. One feels whilst swimming the continual bubbling of the tepid, crystal, clear water, for, as the name denotes, the baths are warm.

On the opposite side of the road, to the various houses of the establishment, there is, next the post-office, an inn for the peasants, that is an absolutely

Austria

astounding lesson for Britishers. I was here once on a Whitmonday, and, perchance, few things can better illustrate the life of the people in their homelands in Austria, than a word upon the sights I saw on that day.

The inn, with its garden, café, and restaurant is marvellously clean. In the garden are tables with coloured cloths upon them; in the restaurant, of course, the cloths are white. The rooms are white, vaulted, with stencilled decorations. The walls are panelled and wainscoted with good woodwork; the pillars are also panelled with pictures of youth and the seasons, and copies of the procession of Trade Guilds, from the paintings of Hans Makart, so that the workmen can see the glorification of their trades. Between the pillars are boxes of greenery, ivy, etc., and this is trailed round the windows; there are hat and coat pegs between the pillars, and all is spotlessly pure and clean, with flowers on the tables, and the tables set for meals have pink and white cloths. I went into the kitchens, and the copper utensils and everything was polished and pure, and the cooking was excellent. But I asked, "Is this for the peasants, all so prettily arranged?" "Ah, yes," was the reply; "they would not come here if it were not clean and well arranged." On this Whitmonday the garden was full of people, most of whom were doing walks in the mountains, and they stir themselves betimes; at 9.30 I saw a young man and girl come in, of the poor, middle-class type, and have their lunch and light beer. They had walked over the mountains and it was midday to them. The smaller, older inns in Villach on the same day were also full of people in

Küstenland, Gorizia, and Carinthia

the evening, drinking light beer before starting homeward; here the surroundings were not so good, but that such a place as that at Warmbad can be established and supported is an impressive lesson for us in England. And close by is a spacious swimming-bath for the poor. A grand bath with the mountains above one, and a rush of the crystal water over a rocky fall forms a douche in this tepid nature bath. The cost is only 20 heller (two pence), including clean bathing dress, and a large bath towel.

The dress of the peasants in the district is full of colour and quaint effect. A pleasant surprise was arranged on the Napoleonshöhe on a lovely day in June, when the sun was intensely hot. A party of English visitors were enticed in the hot sun up to this height, where a soft, green plateau, with many trees around it and brush-wood, was all that was visible, somewhat to the chagrin of the heated, tired guests, when suddenly there appeared from the bushes groups of young girls in the brilliant costumes bearing, in the Slav tongue, a Zakouska—"five o'clock tea" in English—only, all types of little delicacies were added to the tea. The dress of the young girls was a white head-dress with brilliant coloured neckcloths, with rich needlework; a jacket or vest of many colours, while the sleeves of the chemisette were spotless white; the waist was encircled by a girdle of needlework of varied hues, and the very short, thickly pleated skirt of different tones came down to the knees, below which came very thick, fancy-knitted white stockings, with bright coloured garters and high laced boots.

Austria

All were chatting in an unknown tongue, but it was whispered one was an English girl, whose tongue did not betray her, but her legs did, for they were of a slimmer build, in spite of the thick knitted stockings, than those of the sturdily-built local maidens. Such quaint surprises and almost operatic scenes as this can be met with at many a village festival or church holiday throughout these districts.

There are scores of excursions and mountain climbs around Villach that, with Klagenfurth, the capital of Carinthia, form the two principal centres for mountaineers, fishing, or sport expeditions in the province.

There is ample sport in spring, summer, and autumn in this district, and in the winter they boast of the longest and finest toboggan and ski runs in Europe, and the mountaineer can get most exciting and arduous climbs. Warmbad itself lies at the foot of the Dobratsch Mountain, that rises about 7000 feet above sea-level, and from Villach can be seen the whole range of the Karawanken Alps, and the Mangart group that rises to nearly 9000 feet.

That it is not too hot here for pleasurable enjoyment of mountain excursions in summer, may be illustrated by a day spent on June 9th in a little tour that gives a good insight into the strangely wild romantic scenery of the province.

Travelling first to Tarvis over a lovely country with rich meadows and wooded hills, with a fine view of the Mittagskogel, following in part the valley of the

Küstenland, Gorizia, and Carinthia

Gail that rushes turbulently onward to the Drave, we are just on the frontier of Carinthia and Carniola; and as we journey on we get lovely peeps between the pines of the Mangart Mountains, and beyond the serrated broken-up peaks of the Raible Dolomites. A magnificent scene, the great crags and towering peaks and snowy clefts, and below the green uplands and dark fir forests.

We arrive at Weissenfels, a little smoky, iron, industrial town, but in a few moments we climb above the smoke of the works, that lie in a close little valley, and we follow up a mountain stream, a glorious stream, rushing and tumbling and foaming valley-wards, and are soon at the Weissenfels Lake, with its great falls, and water of a most delicate green, varying to a deeper hue. Above towers up the majestic Mangart, almost perpendicular, to the height of nearly 9000 feet. A soft mist lies in the peaks, and cool, pure snow rests between them. Another ten minutes' walk and we reach the Oberessee, or Upper Lake, a tiny, quiet lake of an emerald green; low down around it are the soft, dark woods and fresh, green pines in shadow, and above in brilliant sunlight the sharp, grey rocks rising up to the mist, and far above in the deep blue sky.

This scene is really in Carniola; the two provinces have so much in common in their lake and mountain scenery, and in their people.

The capital of the province of Carinthia is Klagenfurth, a fine old town lying on a level upland, nearly 1500 feet above sea-level, having a glorious view of the Karawanken chain of mountains; a pleasant place to halt in, with, as everywhere in Austria, a good museum and opportunity for historical studies, that we cannot always obtain in English provincial towns of 25,000 inhabitants.

Here is placed the Diet chamber of the province, and the tree-shaded open spaces make it an agreeable resort whence to sally forth and explore Carinthia. The educationist will visit the well-equipped agricultural and mining schools.

It is but a short distance from **Klagenfurth**, by carriage or tramway, to that gem of the province of Carinthia, the Wörther See, and we are near also that rocky defile with its waterfalls known as the Rotwein Klamm, whence came the peasant singers we heard at Veldes in Carniola.

In both these provinces music abounds, and here on the softly beautiful lake, the Wörther See, we heard a men's choir, who sang the expressive and passionate Carinthian folk-songs, that sounded marvellously sweet and beautiful as the harmonies floated over the mirror-like waters of the lake. Much of their music is not published; it is local work, and like so much of the best work done in Austria, in music, science, literature and art, the authors of really great work seem content with local fame, and there is often a deep reverence shown locally for the author or artists who deal with local subjects, and idealise and elevate local legend and history. Here in music the name of Thomas Koschat is revered, as one who has done much for the Carinthian folk-music.

The little isle of Maria Wörth, in the midst of the lake, adds to the charm of the scene of lake and green pasture-land, forest and surrounding mountains

Küstenland, Gorizia, and Carinthia

rising into the varied cloud forms that veil their summits.

There seems a jovial light-heartedness and joy of living in the dwellers on the lake, and a story is told of the priest on the island of Maria Wörth who laughed so loud he could be heard on the other side of the lake. A party would leave one behind to tell a story, and then row across the lake, and it was soon known when the story was told, by the hearty laugh coming across the water.

Steamboats ply on the lake that is eleven miles long, and there are many pleasant resorts on its shores, one of the favourite ones being Portschach, where the Wahliss establishment and its pretty park, with lovely views, is a most popular resort. Here can be heard the local part-songs and excellent orchestral music, and the music lover, especially of folk-songs, will be carried away by the fire and enthusiasm and pathos thrown into the fine part-songs of Carinthia, and the work of Koschat sung by patriotic enthusiasts with excellent voices and good expression.

The mountaineer and sportsman can have plenty of sport in Carinthia; red buck, and other deer, chamois, ibex, hares, pheasants, partridges, wild duck, are amongst the game. The King of Saxony has a shooting estate here, and the rivers, the Gail and the Drave, and the lesser streams and lakes, give ample sport to the fisherman.

Carinthia has within its borders a stretch of the most beautiful part of that great engineering achievement that has opened up a new delight to European travellers—the Tauern Railway. In journeying

Austria

from Opcina to Villach, through the Küstenland and Gorizia, we have seen some of it, the Karawanken section, and now we shall traverse Carinthia from south to north, from Villach to the Tauern Mountains, that give this part of the railway its name.

CHAPTER XX

THE TAUERN RAILWAY TO BAD GASTEIN

THE southern portion of the new line of the Tauern Railway, known as the Karawanken Railways that we have traversed in travelling northward from Triest, passes through country and scenery that is strangely full of nature wonders. The exquisite colour that delights the eye in the rushing mountain streams, and the southern flora, has by the time we reach Villach undergone a great change; in piercing the vast mass of the Karawanken Alps, between Assling and Rosenbach, before we reach Villach, we leave the southern languid air and warm tones of colour, but by no means quit the strange beauty by which this line fascinates the traveller at every mile along its route.

Geographically the line shortens the distance from Central Europe to the Adriatic by some 250 kilometres; politically it is said to be linking up the German population of Bavaria and those dwelling in the partly Slav provinces of Carinthia and Carniola. German excursions from this district to Munich are arranged; on one occasion a thousand went from Villach alone on such an excursion.

To the ordinary traveller the line has opened up a country full of strange delights, hitherto difficult to approach, and the impetus given to the development of the towns on the route has been most remarkable.

Austria

At Spittal, where hitherto had been the old type of comfortable hostelry, at once were built three large, palatial hotels, so confident are the people of the charm and wonder of the surrounding lake and mountain scenery; and the whole district is full of life and development.

Amidst this life on its outskirts, the old town itself is still very quaint. It lies on a deep plain surrounded with snowy peaks, and in its centre rises the great square mass of its castle, in a pretty park and garden, the residence for centuries of the Princes of Porcia. The walls of the castle are decorated with illustrations in gesso work, and plaques of various princes of this family, that claims a very ancient descent. In the centre court around which the castle rises in three tiers of Renaissance arcading, enriched with medallions, there are the arms of Portia and Porcia, " ex sanguine Regum Troianorum et Sicambroium progenitus." But alas, all this long line of descent has fallen on evil days, and the castle is decaying. All was silent as I stood in this court. A bell in beaten iron was there to summon the retainers and varlets in attendance, but the cord was broken. On the north side of the castle were frescoes in colour, of cupids, and illustrations of hunting and fencing, and above, in black and white, knights and bishops; one name I could read was Sylvius of Padua. In the garden were some palms, but stunted by the northern air, and above the avenues of trees rose up the snow-flecked mountains, but the only life in the gardens were the birds, all else seemed dead, and only echoed the note that emperors had stayed here, and also Wallenstein. It was pleasant to go back again into the little town,

The Tauern Railway to Bad Gastein

through the old gateway, and down the hill past an old house with illustrating gesso work and dial, to the bridge that spans the swift flowing Lieser. The church is a very fine fourteenth-century building, and the fine-toned bells struck out for the midday hour as we looked at the most interesting monuments that are around its outside walls.

The larger river upon which Spittal stands is the Drave or Drau, that joins the Danube at Belgrade; and but 13 kilometres distant is the picturesque Millstatt on the lake of the same name, a most lovely little town lying on a promontory that juts out into the lake, with a wealth of lake, and mountain, and forest-gorge excursions, all around it.

Soon after quitting Spittal we leave the old rail of the Südbahn that leads over the Brenner to Innsbruck, an old engineering marvel, and enter upon this new link with the north; at Mühldorf we are amidst trees, rich fields, and pasture slopes, dotted with grey, shingle-roofed houses amidst fruit orchards. The peasantry still stare and wave hands to this new thing in their lives. We soon begin to climb up to a different vegetation.

This Tauern Railway is by no means one upon which a quiet settling in a corner with a book or paper is likely to satisfy any traveller. The corridors of the train are filled with eager sightseers, to catch the romantic glimpses of castle and valley, waterfall and dizzy viaduct; and one good hint is to travel first-class, but take a slow train, then one can have a carriage to oneself, and move from side to side as the train moves onward.

It is interesting to note the heavy timber barricades on the mountain sides as a protection against avalanches, and the strong stone block-houses for the guardians of the line, and the stone zigzags up the banks to prevent landslides. And when one looks at the powerful engines that are attached for the work of these gradients, and then at a slight fairy-like viaduct, one feels an awesome dread lest we go crashing into the valley, far, far beneath.

From Mühldorf we climb slowly up past the deep Klinzerschlucht or ravine, with a peep at a pretty castle, and slowly and laboriously we attain Kolbnitz, from whence some very delightful excursions can be made, especially to the Danielsberg. As we ascend higher the changes of vegetation are very remarkable; here, in the late spring, are racing, spuming, white-foamed streams rushing down to the valleys; the snow peaks are all around, but the lower slopes are all parti-coloured with flowers. As we go on, ever upward, the scene changes to more terrific grandeur, and at Penk we look far down on the Möllthal. We flash in and out of the tunnels, and get peeps of most romantic mediæval castles perched on rocky peaks, and then wide vistas down into valleys. One glorious view is down into the Möllthal, with the isolated basaltic-like peak, the Danielsberg, upon the summit of which a temple to Hercules formerly stood. Here is a most beautiful view. The peep down into the valley of the Moll, with the castle of Unterfalkenstein, gives a wondrous masterpiece of Nature's composition.

Another romantic spot is on the viaduct that leads to the tunnel that pierces below the great mass of rock on which stands the wide, massive ruins of Oberfalkenstein. It is in this district that great

The Tauern Railway to Bad Gastein

engineering feats of overcoming difficulties were carried out. Viaduct after viaduct, then galleries, then tunnels; every type of obstacle was encountered and overcome. The engines used upon these lines, and upon other of the mountain railways of Austria, are big, powerful machines, full of ingenuity and modern development, and excite the admiration of the engineering expert.

A pleasant halting-spot is Obervellach, lying in a rich upland valley, with innumerable opportunities for excursions, and comfortable inns to which to return. The church is of interest to the lover of Gothic work, and the altarpiece is an example of the Dutch master Jan Scorel of the early sixteenth century. Not far off is the castle of Groppenstein, with its two square towers and embattled walls, that with its surrounding wall and outlying towers, perched on the high-wooded rock, forms so picturesque a scene from the railway.

Between this little town and Mallnitz we pass in a valley the electric works that drive the fans for the air in the Tauern tunnel that we are nearing.

Mallnitz is only a widely scattered village with a quiet beauty around it, contrasting with what we have traversed, and with what we shall see as we travel onward; but all around the valley loom up the grey crags and snowy peaks far above the dark pines.

Now we soon enter the tunnel that opened in 1909, pierces the Tauern Alps and, gave freer access to these picturesque scenes.

It is about five miles in length, and the line ascends to the height of about 4000 feet. By the express trains the time in the tunnel is only about ten minutes.

Austria

Before entering from this south side the view is very imposing. The snow peaks and glaciers, with, on the left hand, the wide valley, and river and streams, all form a glorious picture ere we dive into the darkness, and as we issue, again is there a glorious picture; now, on the right, are the rocky snow peaks and white glaciers, with rushing waterfalls on all sides as we halt at the station of Bockstein, beneath the lofty mountain mass of the Hohe Tauern, that forms the boundary of Carinthia and the Duchy of Salzburg. We descend the pass, noting the heavy work to prevent mountain slides, and enter the beautiful Bockstein valley, wherein lies the picturesquely placed little town of Bockstein, within an easy walk of Bad Gastein, the famous health resort.

There are several hotels and a Kurhaus at Bockstein; mountaineers and nature lovers may prefer exploring the district from here instead of from Gastein.

MALLNITZ

CHAPTER XXI

THE TAUERN RAILWAY TO SALZBURG

IN the Duchy of Salzburg we are in a territory that has been known to English travellers for centuries, the capital Salzburg, early in the eighth century, had already its bishop, and was raised to an Archbishopric in 798 by Charlemagne. But the latest development in this Duchy of the twentieth century, the Tauern Railway, has opened to English travellers districts of natural beauty hitherto unknown to them, and made easy of access spots that before were only reached on foot or by driving.

As we have seen, Dame Nature has been effusively lavish in every division of Austria, almost squandering her glories and beauties with apparently reckless profusion. But she has not in other homelands of Austria exhausted her power of exciting wonder and surprise, and here, at Bad Gastein, as we enter the little station, is a scene, even at its door, of quiet, exquisite beauty. From a little height above the station road is a fine prospect looking up the Bockstein valley, and within a minute or two we are far from all hint of railways, and amidst flowers, and mosses, and leaping brooklets, and tiny waterfalls, in the pure, mountain air.

The town of Wildbad Gastein persistently reminded me of the little town of Lynmouth in Devonshire; but here everything is upon a gigantic scale.

Austria

The little brawling, snow-white falls of the Lyn are multiplied a hundred times, nay more, enlarged into the thundering, foaming, terrific falls of the Ache, that leap down betwixt the narrow, rocky gorge in two mighty falls, one of 200, the other of nearly 300 feet, threatening to overwhelm the villas and hotels that are perched and dotted on rocks and every available plot of level space.

Between the two falls is the bridge with the covered way, to protect the passers from the spray clouds that arise in steam-like vapour, and it is a fairy-like yet titanic scene to stand near these ceaselessly roaring waters and watch them lit up by the coloured light thrown upon them. They are veritably alive, smoking, foaming, thundering and hurtling onward, rushing downward to the valley.

In the church of Gastein is a picture of the legend of the origin of the Spa, the stag finding the water.

Until this new railway was open, the Gastein valley and this noted Spa was only reached by a drive of three or four hours from Lend, but now the station is on the outskirts of the town.

In former days Bad Gastein was widely known from the fact that it was the favourite health resort of the Iron Chancellor, a fact that is commemorated on his residence the Schwaigerhaus, whereon is inscribed :

FÜRST BISMARCK
WOHNTE IN DEN JAHREN
1877, 1878, 1879, 1883, 1886,
IN DIESEM HAUSE.

A delightfully beautiful spot he chose for a peaceful retreat from the fierce turmoil of his iron life, and yet

The Tauern Railway to Salzburg

with a reminder of the tumultous in Nature and man, in the ever thundering, passionate force of the restless falls of the Ache.

One of the best of the many walks in and around Bad Gastein is that known as the Kaiser Promenade, leading to the right up above the church over a little wooden bridge with a veritable little bit of Lynmouth around one. Not far on is a bust of Kaiser William I. with seats around it, and a pleasant garden with the now distant music of the falls still in the ear. The idle promenade of the lounger can be turned into a brisk walk by continuing on to the Schwarzen Liesl Café and Kaiser Wilhelm Institute—a pleasant climb; and at the café is a superb view of the whole Gastein valley to the smaller, older town of Hof Gastein. High up, half hid in mist, tower the snowy peaks that shut in the valley, along which wind river and road, and dotted here and there in the green pastures are the grey chalets and white houses; this view is to the north, whilst to the west are yet higher peaks and the Schareck Glacier. The resort, the Schwarze Liesl, takes its name from the favourite hostess of years ago. Now the place is a retreat for old warriors who are invalided, but the café is still a favourite resort for the public.

Gastein is the starting-point for a score of expeditions, either easy walks or arduous climbs up to 10,000 feet; the Schareck and the Sonnblick are about this height. The latter is perhaps best ascended from Mallnitz in ten hours; it is interesting as being the highest meteorological station of the first class in Europe, and the ascent is easily made.

But from our halting-place at Liesl's we will get

Austria

slowly and pleasantly back to Gastein, along the sweet pine-scented road, with pretty peeps of snow peaks between the dark pines. Even our own footfalls are hushed on the fallen spines of the trees, and do not disturb the song of the birds. At a hamlet we get a view down to the little town of palaces below, and the great white falls rushing between them, and then we pass on to the Höhebrücke over the great fall; a lad who comes up calls it the Schrecks or Fearsome Bridge, and truly fearsome is the mighty leap of the vast mass of rushing, thundering waters; and from this bridge a steep path can be taken, that leads close down by the great fall that deafens with its thunder.

Another easy walk but a healthful climb is to the Windischgratz height, but the walks around are innumerable, and the limited space for promenade where the band plays in the town is thus compensated.

The waters are pleasant drinking, and together with the baths, that are well arranged in the hotels, are good for nerve diseases, rheumatism, and kidney, and other complaints; their radio-activity is very great. The promenade salon, a covered promenade with reading and other rooms, makes a pleasant resort in bad weather, and from it the falls and their ceaseless play can be watched, or the light effects studied when they are illuminated. But perhaps the exhilarating properties of the air, and the endless opportunities for excursions, great or small, makes Wildbad Gastein the health resort that it certainly is.

In quitting this mountain paradise we resume the route of the Tauern railway, and run along a mountain ledge the whole length of the Gastein

The Tauern Railway to Salzburg

valley. The town we have just left looks like a scene on the stage, backed with pines and snowy peaks and feathery waterfalls. We begin to descend and cross the great bridge, the Angerbrücke, which is nearly 300 feet high and more than 300 feet wide. The scene is fearfully grand where the torrent bursts through the rocky cliffs, and rushes forcefully on.

We halt above the town of **Hof-Gastein**, the little town with its black, red, and grey roofs, and tall church spire, lying under the hills; the soft tone of the cow bells ascend in the still air, and tell of the principal occupation of the dwellers in the valley. As we slowly descend, the scene is ever changing and full of strange, wild beauty. Tunnel, and bridge, and viaduct lead us on downwards. At Klammstein, in the deep gorge or Klamm, there is a chill air, and brooks from all sides come leaping down in white cascades. Over the torrent of the Ache rise the bare, rocky snow peaks. We pass the Swiss-like grey chalets, with heavy stones on the roofs; on the rich green uplands the river gets wider, and beyond Mursangerbach we see the old road far below, beside the river, slowly, slowly climbing upwards, with a carpet of flowers and rich vegetation on either hand. Onward we go, ever descending, crossing torrents and viaducts, increasingly excited by the vast variety of strange, beauteous nature, until we join in with the old Salzburg railway, and are soon at the beautifully placed station of Schwarzach St Veit, in the rich upland valley, above which peep the snow peaks and through which runs the river Salzach. The little town of Schwarzach has quite enough interest to beguile an hour or two during a halt. The scene along the banks of the river interests, and

Austria

the old church that is linked with the famous fighting Schwarzenbergers, whose castles we saw in Bohemia, especially at Krumau (Krumlov), calls up the past. Whilst halting here one day for a train connection we strolled up above the church to the little cemetery, where the nuns or sisters of the convent adjoining the church are buried; and whilst I was alone, pondering amidst the simple graves, and looking round at the lovely scenes of mountain and upland, a sister appeared, and with silent, loving care sprinkled holy water on the graves of those sisters lying peacefully below. In the calm evening light, with the soft pink hues just flushing the distant snow peaks, this pious action seemed so tenderly loving, and so in keeping with all nature around; the dead and their deeds were remembered, and nature in it's young forces told of new life and fresh energy sprung from the seed of death; and so I stole quietly away, soon to be again rushing towards Salzburg.

We are now on a part of the road that is well known, but still a road of a beauty that never tires. Especially at St Johann im Pongau is there a great view around of the rocky peaks and pinnacles, snow swept, and yet here and there snow flecked; the eyes seemed glutted with beauty all through this district, and yet the mind is not satiated. Below the peaks are the dark pine-clad heights, and at their feet the swift grey river ever rushing onward, and St Johann makes a pleasant halting-place for mountain expeditions or less adventurous excursions.

The scene increases in almost theatrical effects as we near Salzburg and skirt around the massive block of the Untersberg, with a splendid view of the great

The Tauern Railway to Salzburg

citadel of Salzburg on its high rocky plateau. If this approach is made at sunset, often the upper snow-covered peaks are suffused in the deep red of the Alpine glow, and the scene is surpassingly beautiful, and Salzburg seems to promise a strange charm and glamour—a promise that its history and associations and wondrous setting soon fulfils.

CHAPTER XXII

SALZBURG AND THE SALZKAMMERGUT

THERE is a passage in the Studio volume on the Peasant Art of Austria that says, "Unfortunately there is no open-air museum in Austria where we can wander at will and form a complete picture of how the peasants lived in the past, or how some of them live at the present time." But in Austria we have something better; we can still go in the villages and see the life of the peasants, preserving, in some places, all their brilliant costumes, their ceremonies, and their superstitions, their old-world, at least mediæval, life, and then presto! we are in a scientifically equipped technical school, or a well-managed agricultural or forestry museum, and see these same peasants studying the latest science of their daily work.

Nowhere more heartily entered into and enjoyed is the music, song, and dance of the peasants in their picturesque costume than in the Salzkammergut, and on fête days these peasants come into the capital, and under the shadow of the grim old fortress, and vast church buildings that speak so eloquently of former fierce power, the peasant is as jovial to-day, and as picturesquely artistic, as he was when rack and dungeon threatened him with torture and doom.

On one occasion we heard in Salzburg, from a local choir in their local costume, some excellent music, and

Salzburg and the Salzkammergut

one of the performers on the xylophone was an old lady of about eighty, who was an intense enthusiast, and a wonderfully vivacious performer on that curious instrument. After the music came dancing, entered into with a verve and joviality that was contagious, proving how the joy of life is retained by this love of music and dance, and old patriotic customs.

The population of the province of Salzburg is almost wholly German, the folk of other races numbering only about a thousand, and the religion is almost wholly that of the Roman church, having had its bishopric over a thousand years.

The city, like so many cathedral cities, is a quiet old-world town, but singularly interesting, both from its situation and from the wealth of old buildings that are left in and around it, in spite of the fact that so much has been lost through fire.

A good spot to take a first survey of the lower town is upon the bridge that spans the swift-flowing Salzach. From this bridge the old narrow streets that cluster under the great rock which towers above cathedral and palatial buildings can be seen winding their way up to the great fortress of Higher Salzburg that crowns the rock, and here in the lower town is much to hold the visitor. There is one name that stands out above warrior and ecclesiastic, the name of Mozart. The house where the great musician, the marvellous boy-composer, was born, and the museum that contains the MSS. of those compositions so marvellous in a child, MSS. of his later works, his instruments, portraits, and other objects connected with his wonderful career, that had so sad an ending, are all of intense and pathetic interest. But when they show you the poet's skull, a feeling of horror comes over one; it is too pitiable to see this poor bone that once held the brilliant brain that produced such glorious work handled, and placed here for show. Bury it! put it reverently away! is the exclamation and earnest prayer that at once comes to the mind and to the lips.

The quaint old courts and squares around the cathedral, and the palatial residences of the princes of the State and the Church, give many a fine architectural study; but one of the most quaint and antique bits of Salzburg is the churchyard of St Peter, said to date from the period of the earliest bishops of Salzburg; the graves, following the eastern custom, are hewn out of the rock, and each grave has its own holy water stoup. In the church near by are curious carvings of the Adoration of the Magi and the Resurrection, the Roman soldiers bearing cross-bows. All around there is much of interest, both architectural, monumental, and historical.

This churchyard is near the winding path that ascends to the summit of Higher Salzburg, and although now there is a lift, yet the slow walk up, with the gradual opening out of very varied views, is well worth doing.

There is a fine view from the Festungs Gate. Over each gate are figures of bishops and coats of arms. From the plateau on the summit the view on all sides is superb. The low-lying plain is shut in by mountains some snow-capped, others of bare grey rock, whilst lower down the heights are dark with pines. To the west the plain stretches away in the distance, dotted with white villages and castles amidst the varying

SALZBURG

Salzburg and the Salzkammergut

foliage and bright green pasture meadows, through which wind the grey waters of the Salzach.

On the north side immediately below lies the old town, with its domes and spires, and red-roofed and white buildings, the view being shut in by the dark wooded slope of the Capuzinerberg. Away to the south the plain at the foot of the mountains is varied by charming tiny lakes, with dark woods around them, dotted with country houses.

One of the principal of the mountains that rise over the plain-land is the vast mass of the Untersberg, beneath which Charlemagne is said to be lying, waiting for a united Germany once again to arise and rule. The cloud effects on the mountains are nearly always beautiful, sometimes the Untersberg will be veiled in mist, whilst the height of the Hohe Göll stands out clearly in the sunshine like a white, soft cloud in its pure snow mantle.

The interior of the castle is well worth a visit if only to recall all the brilliant scenes that have been enacted here. Some of the rooms date from 1501 The little library is very quaint, with the old paintings and bookshelves.

The chapel of St George has over its door some good carvings of St Christopher and Archbishop Leonard, who died in 1519.

There are many places of public resort in and around Salzburg, two favourites being the heights of the Mönchberg and the Capuzinerberg; this latter is over 2000 feet above sea level, and in the garden is the little house of Mozart, brought from Vienna, in which he wrote the Zauberflöte. From here a lovely walk leads through the woods;

all is so softly calm, but there comes up from the town the rich boom of the church bells into these silent woods; then we reach an Aussicht, and, as from the fortress, the views are extremely lovely and strangely diversified. Another newer point that a cog railway has made easily accessible is the summit of the Gaisberg that is over 4000 feet above sea level, and whence the view is most extensive.

After looking upon all these great marvels of nature, it is a strange thing to go out into the well-kept Stadtpark, and just beyond to visit the Mirabelle Castle, where the ingenuity of man has been exercised in a strange fashion, in building a house and gardens for the amusement of a mistress of Cardinal Wolf Dietrich in 1606. The gardens are full of quaint devices, such as one sees in the Pallavicini gardens near Genoa, or in the grounds of Linderhof, one of the palaces of King Ludwig II. of Bavaria. Here are surprise fountains that drench the unwary spectator, mechanical working and moving toys of a most elaborate type, grottos, caves, and statuary, with a lovely lake and pretty gardens, and the views around of the town and mountains are full of beauty.

There is history and tragedy, romance and beauty enough, clinging to and around Salzburg to hold one for many a day; set, as Salzburg is, in the midst of a land that is teeming with natural beauty, embodying very diversified scenes. One of the most picturesque and charming little lakes is that of the Zeller See, that lies south of Salzburg, and can be visited on travelling from that town to Innsbruck. Here we get a view of various chains of mountains including the Tauern, and all around the lake are dotted pretty

ZELL AM SEE

Salzburg and the Salzkammergut

villas in pretty gardens, and the little steamer makes it very easy to get to all the parts of the lake for mountain excursions, of which there is a veritable plethora from which to choose. Bathing, boating, and fishing, and in winter, skating, and all kinds of sport can be enjoyed here, and the climber has a very wide selection of varied heights.

CHAPTER XXIII

THE SALZKAMMERGUT

THE curious title of this district has become a word that calls up visions of a strange beauty of lake scenery, but really it is a historic name with great meaning. It is the territory or property of the Chamber governing the salt industry; and of the value of this industry we have had a glimpse when we were at **Prachatic**, the quaint old town in Southern Bohemia that was on the salt path from Bavaria into Bohemia, in which country there is no salt. We are in this territory not far from the frontier of Bavaria, and the district now known as the Salzkammergut includes portions of Upper Austria. The Crownland we shall traverse in descending the Danube, and also a part of Styria (Steiermark). The absurd custom of giving the name "Swiss" to any district that has lakes and mountains, and, as in England, to districts that have hills a few hundred feet high, might well become obsolete.

We have Saxon Switzerland, Bohemian Switzerland, valleys in England with hills, 150 feet high called Swiss valleys, and here an attempt is made to call this lovely gem of Austrian homeland Austrian Switzerland, whereas colour and form are very different to the Swiss lake scenery, and to many eyes the beauty is more varied, more gem-

The Salzkammergut

like in colour and form, although not so colossal in shape or height. Each country has its own peculiar beauty, and the distinctive national name should be given to distinctive national beauty.

Here the name of the Salzkammergut lakes recalls at once, to those who know them, a vision of marvellous beauty. In leaving Salzburg for a tour in this artist's paradise we are quickly in the midst of the lake and mountain scenery. The great barrier of the Drachenwand rises up, and then after Plomberg we come upon the idyllic Mondsee, with green woods and the sun throwing beams of gold upon the low pasture-land, recalling in some measure Loch Lomond in Scotland; then we see the little Eglsee, a lake of dark, slate-blue hue, succeeded as we travel on, by exquisite peeps of the Grottensee, the colour of which is reflected from the woods that surround it. At all these spots one would fain halt, so tempting are the walks and the little hotels dotted along the lakes; but we journey on to St Gilgen that lies so peacefully at the head of the lake Aber, or St Wolfgang. The lake is of a lovely blue, and the houses amidst the foliage are dominated by the tall, white church tower rising to its red dome and little spire.

The view down the lake is gentle and peaceful, the wilder rocky crags being distant, and the lower slopes wooded and green with trees and pasture. White sails float over the lake, and there is ample pleasure on its waters for lovers of sailing or rowing, fishing or bathing, and the lake steamers quickly run to many a beauty spot by its waters. The colour of the water changes according to the surroundings and the tone of the sky, sometimes being of a clear delicate emerald.

Even here in this, to English ideas, remote spot, the system of Austrian education helps the clever but poor scholar; for on the height above Falkenstein Ried, on the opposite shore to St Gilgen, is a summer-holiday resort for the needy pupils of the Vienna Gymnasiums and Real Schools, giving them a vigorous, hearty holiday, with mountain expeditions, and genial sallies amidst these lovely surroundings.

We are close to the principal market town of the lake, St Wolfgang, and in journeying thither by the boat, we pass a rather curious thing upon a lake, the tall lighthouse tower, an old square building, with an octagonal tower, with embattled summit, standing proudly as a sea lighthouse, at the mouth of a frontier river, but here it is only the little Dittelbach that comes down from the Schafberg. If the track of this stream is followed up, a pleasant climb leads to some fine waterfalls.

The little town is so delightfully placed, and is so picturesque in itself, that it makes a most pleasant halting spot, and the peasantry are a kind, jovial, free folk; preserving their old customs, loving music and dancing, and holding their mountain traditions in reverence. Their dress is much of the serviceable Tyrolean type, the men, as the women, loving colour. The dress is suitable for their mountain work, and the men look stalwart, sturdy fellows in their round hats with a feather, their short jackets, and tight breeches and strong boots.

MONDSEE

The Salzkammergut

The hostelries are good, and one gets personal service. The chief historical monument in the town of St Wolfgang is the church, with its tall, square tower and arcaded court around it, through the arches of which such exquisite pictures of lake and mountain are framed. Here also is the well of St Wolfgang, with a statue of the saint, and this quaint inscription, the spelling of which is very curious and phonetic.

" Ich pin zu den Eren Sanct Wolfgang gemacht, Abt Wolfgang Haberl zu mannsee hat mich betracht, zu nutz und zu frumm der armen piligrumb, die nit haben Geld umb zu kaufen Wein, dye sollen pei diesen Wasser frellich seyn. Anno den 1515 jar ist das werk volpraht, Gott sey gelobt."

Within the church is the famous carved altar-piece by Michael Pacher, a veritable triumph of the sculptor's art, of the year 1481. The central group represents God the Father enthroned; before Him is kneeling the Virgin Mary, and above soars the Holy Spirit in dovelike form. The delicate tracery of the Baldachins over these principal figures and over the side figures of St Wolfgang and St Benedict is most artistic in treatment and design, and every detail of the subordinate work shows intense loving care in its execution. The whole of this altar-piece, both before and behind, in painting and in sculpture, is full of beauty and historic value.

Various relics of St Wolfgang, who, in the tenth century, was Bishop of Regensburg, are preserved here; his cell has been enclosed in marble, and around it is built a chapel in Renaissance style, and this chapel is a great resort of pilgrims, who pray here and get small medals and diminutive hatchets blessed by touching with them the Chalice used by St Wolfgang; this is preserved in the Sacristy. The hatchet has become the insignia of the place. Little rosettes decked with silver hatchets are given or sold to visitors. The legend is that St Wolfgang threw his hatchet from the top of the Falkenstein, the mountain we passed by the lakeside, and it fell where the church now stands, and is walled up in the central altar. A very early but good example of throwing the hatchet! But St Wolfgang is also the defensive patron against fire and hail, two great enemies of the peasants' crops and homes in their mountain districts. Viktor von Scheffel brings the Wolfgang pilgrimage into one of his religious songs.

If St Wolfgang for a thousand years has attracted pilgrims to his shrine, to-day another marvel is drawing vast numbers to this lovely spot—a nature and science marvel—the mighty Gibraltar-like cliff of the Schafberg, rising precipitously to the height of nearly 6000 feet. This is ascended by the tooth railway that, alas! does away for so many with the healthful climb, with its halts for the beautiful outlooks betwixt the pines. By the mountain railway also, the peeps to be had as we ascend are strangely lovely. At first we ascend through fruit orchards, then we come to the pines, and, as we rise higher and higher we get peeps of strange beauty. Lakes lie below like gems of turquoise or emerald; others are of a deep green, or of a cobalt blue; and as we still ascend we reach the snow—pure patches lie here and

The Salzkammergut

there by the side of the rail. At the upper station we are in winter; snow lies all around; we have a little walk to reach the peak's summit, and then a vast and glorious panorama is around and beneath us, with a wonderful effect of changing light. Vast ranges and peaks of mountains, all snow-clad; to the east and north those jewel gems of lakes. Well may they say this Schafberg is the pearl of the Salzkammergut. Away to the south-west rises the great Untersberg, and to the north is a vast plain, and far, far away rise up the dark lines of the Bohemian forest, beyond the Danube.

On all sides is a scene of exquisite and marvellous beauty. The sun lights up vast ranges of peaks and ridges, glittering with snow; each detail is a beauty, and the whole holds one spellbound.

Here on this height in the crystalline snow grow Alpine flowers that are eagerly picked, and often unwittingly terrible risks are incurred, for the sheer fall from the strange "Sheep's Head" summit (hence the name) is a drop of some thousands of feet, and the overhanging edge is deceptive.

This panorama of lake and mountain shows how absolutely inexhaustible are the excursions and pleasures to be had in this neighbourhood, and also gives one a slight, and yet bewildering idea of all the sights this part of Austria alone can show the traveller; for not only do lake and mountain, valley, plain, and upland invite us, but a great stretch of the Danube valley is within our sight to the northward; and it is a curious reminiscence that in the little town of St Wolfgang, Kaiser Leopold I.

Austria

took shelter whilst he was permitting John Sobieski, the Pole, to free his capital, Vienna, from the Moslem.

The Schafberg is a vain height, for it mirrors its protruding precipice summit in three lakes. The whole district entices one forcibly to linger amidst its strange beauty and genial folk. As we leave the inn of St Wolfgang the old hostess hands us a souvenir of the Saint, the little silver hatchet tied up with the local colours, red and white; and with a " Grüss Gott " thus bids us warmly farewell.

It is but a very short run by railway from St Wolfgang to Ischl, where we are in different surroundings. Instead of the simple townsfolk and peasantry, we are amidst fashionable, yea, court life, for Ischl is a favourite home of Kaiser Franz Josef I., and great hotels, Kurhaus, fashionable crowds, and great orchestras attract the *beau monde* of Europe to Ischl. These sudden contrasts of life are so frequent in Austria, and add to the charm of travel in her borders.

Ischl may, in spite of its fashion, be said to be a jovial place, the nature around it and the deliciously pure air seeming to have an effect upon the invalids even, and the incursions of the peasants of the district with their music and dances, their popular and wedding feasts, help quickly to drive away depression, or that sense of sadness, which in some health resorts often comes over one.

Here the baths and inhalation establishments, and the springs where the visitors resort for cures, are pleasantly situated, and the Kurhaus and hotels

The Salzkammergut

take care that no ennui intrudes itself amidst patients and visitors, and especially is this good for the convalescents who flock here from the cures of other resorts, such as Marienbad, Carlsbad, etc. Excellent Vienna orchestras and theatrical companies provide alternate amusement to the dances, evening receptions, and excursions on lakes and mountains; and sport, fishing, tennis, rowing or sailing, and mountain explorations fill up the days pleasantly and healthfully. For the invalid not yet strong enough for these undertakings, the tree-shaded promenades by river and mountain, with the superb views all around, ever varying, ever changing, soon makes one forget all ones ills, and soon leads on to strength to take the more exacting expeditions, such as up the valleys of the Traun or Ischl, or to the numerous heights around, where such wide views are to be had, or to the spectacle that Ischl always suggests to visitors, the wonder of the Salt mountain, whose mines when illuminated form so fascinating a spectacle.

The dress of the well-to-do peasants in this district, as at St Wolfgang, lends itself to most picturesque effects of both form and colour, and those who are fortunate enough to see a farmer's wedding, with its accompanying ceremonies and dances, will have a scenic spectacle far more picturesque than many an operatic scene.

They study well in the lake district dramatic and scenic effect, and do not forget the beautiful effects with which nature has endowed them.

· A noteworthy, interesting instance of this useful entwining of nature's handiwork with their own

Austria

plans was given by the authorities of the Salzkammergut, when the men and women of some twenty or more nationalities visited the province after the International Press Congress had been held in Vienna.

\ Ischl was *en fête*. Carriages decorated with flowers and acacias received the guests, who were well entertained, but late in the evening they were taken on to Ebensee, too late, as some guests growled, to see the glorious scenery; and as dusk was approaching two gaily decorated boats received the polyglotic visitors to take them on to Gmunden.

Slowly out over the calm lake, now deep in colour, moved the ships; the dark isolated peaks rose up to the night, and one could yet see the varied colours of the rocks, grey and red, and scored with the water torrents of winter. Still the deep pink of the sunset lit the lake, and on the left rose up a great mass as of a widened sugar cone, but only dimly could the mountains be seen in the half-light. Suddenly the bands were silent, the ships glided on very slowly over the dark waters, and another smaller ship all illuminated was seen emerging from the shadow of a great mountain: then the ships stopped; and from over the lake came a voice from the smaller ship offering a welcome to the strangers who had come from all parts of the world to the Salzkammergut. It was the President of the Province who spoke, and on his ceasing rockets went up, the lake was lit up, and all around on height and in valley the peasants lit bonfires, and slowly the illuminated boats glided into Gmunden, where all along the

The Salzkammergut

esplanade were illuminations and fires greeting the foreign visitors, and welcoming them to a local feast, full of local colour. All the men and girls who attended were in the pretty local costumes, and great beer casks decorated with flowers were being tapped by lusty mountaineers, and local orchestras were giving folk-dance music; joviality reigned supreme. A striking contrast to all this cheery noisiness is the life on the higher alm, amidst the troups of peaceful cattle, browsing in the rich, deep pastures, breaking the silence of the eternal heights above by the mellow tone of the cow bells.

This life is full of charm and strange remoteness to the wandering traveller who crosses the mountains and halts suddenly as he comes out upon an unexpected turn in his thread-like path, that gives him a view down upon some such lake as the Traunsee, at the head of which Gmunden stands — a lake so curiously varied in its beauty, assuming colour so diversified, and with such vast masses of mountain forms around it. Early one morning we sailed across it in the quiet grey light; a soft mist veiled the great height of the Traunstein, a mountain of nearly 6000 feet, that makes a good climb though not a high one.

Below there stood out in the deep, green water the lovely point of Traunkirchen, with the old church perched on the Johannisberg; a point that is exquisite in form and colour, and a quiet resting-place for those who prefer the smaller places to the fashion of Gmunden and Ischl.

The views are everywhere beautiful and full of contrasts, steep, barren, precipitous cliffs alternating with deep, green forests, and little villages in rich pasture-land, and far above the towering crags glittering from snow fields even in late summer. And, although to the casual visitor the population in the summer months may seem wholly given up to the catering for passing visitors, yet there is a great deal of industry carried on in these towns, and developments of industries, as at Ebensee, at the northern end of the lake, where there is a good wood-carving school.

'The network of railways, or carriages, will quickly take the traveller to the other lakes in this inexhaustible district of Nature's beauties. Attersee, which we looked down upon from the Schafberg, the largest of all Austria's lakes, is worth visiting, if only for the wondrous blue of its waters. But it is also lovely for the great variety of its scenery, and the steamboat that sails over its bosom gives every opportunity for reaching the various resorts on its shores, from whence expeditions can be made into the mountains, and combination tours can be arranged with railway and steamers, to include the whole of the lakes in the district. This lake is 20 kilometres long (12 miles) and 3 kilometres broad; it lies in its mountain nest 465 metres above sea-level. One of the pleasantest, and also a fashionable resort on this lake is Weissenbach, where there is a luxurious hotel crouched under the precipitous hills, whence romantic walks and climbs in the deep klamms or gorges can be made, and expeditions to higher points that give good work to the climber. Although one is quickly away from every sign of haunt of man, yet from this lake one can go by electric

The Salzkammergut

railway to the Mondsee, which lake we passed before arriving at St Wolfgang. There are two other gems in this lake district, lying to the south of the larger group of lakes, that also possess peculiar charms, or rather there is a group of some eight or nine lakes, the largest of which are the Hallstätter See, and the Alt-Ausseer See. The former, if only for the pleasure of seeing the quaint old town of Hallstatt, with its Tirolean-like houses, perched one above the other, all with the wide roofs and wooden balconies, and its two churches, one with its tall, thin spire on the level little promontory that juts out into the lake. This is the Protestant Church, whilst the Roman Catholic Church is more massive in form, and is perched above on a rocky ledge beneath the mountains that rise high above it.

Here there is much local life and industry, and a royal technical school for wood industries, by no means to be likened to our own woodwork schools, as we have seen elsewhere. The museum here is of curious interest, especially for its Celtic relics. Hallstatt, although only a quaint, small town, will entice many who wish to study the life of the folk of the district, and also for the immense variety of walks and excursions within easy distance to waterfalls and idyllic little villages, by forest and mountain footpaths. From Hallstatt another group of little lakes, the Gosau lakes, can be reached either by carriage or by foot.

There are so many " most beautiful " points in this district, that it is indeed astounding for the very prodigality of Nature's choicest compositions; one hesitates to quote the local statement that here amidst

Austria

their smaller lake jewels is the finest point in the Salzkammergut, but Gosau, a little town of about 1500 inhabitants, has around it the mountains of Hohen Dachstein, the Donnerkogel, the Zwieselalm, and other heights, and a group of little lakes that are romantically beautiful. The water is of a deep crystal green, and towering above are the glacier-rifted heights of the Dachstein, and other mountains, such as the four domed summits of the Donnerkogel, partly bare rock, partly white with snow and ice, the whole forming a series of views that enchant with their beauty.

Here there is no danger of the terrible crowds from which it is impossible to escape in certain European mountain resorts; but that the force that Nature exercises in this district is no longer to be allowed to be exercised for the production of beauty only, is evidenced by the fact that an electric power station is being built here with 18,000 horse-power machines to utilise the water-power of the district.

A railway runs from Hallstatt to the other group of lakes, the Aussee group. We are still on the Traun, the little tumultous river that gives its name to the Traunsee, emerging from the lake at Gmunden, and we are still in the salt district, for close to Aussee are the works of Kainisch. We have crossed the Styrian frontier in this little journey and are back again in the Steirmark, but still in the old Salzkammergut.

The market-town of Aussee is fairly large, having about 12,000 inhabitants, and possesses a fine Kurhaus and good hotels. It lies on the highway

The Salzkammergut

from Gratz, the capital of Styria, to Salzburg, a grand route to-day for the automobilist through marvellous scenery and quaint towns. The old churches of Aussee tell of an interesting past, and have some relics of their mediæval days still to interest the historian. But it is the delightful nature wonders around Aussee that attract, and in an hour we can be at the lake of Alt-Aussee, with that strange, weird range of mountains around us, the Tote, or dead mountains, or on another road, in still less time we reach the Grundlsee, where a little steamer takes us up this romantic little lake, with vast rock walls, and precipices all around, giving peeps to the higher, gloomy heights of the Totegebirge. At the end of the lake is the little landing-place at Gossl, and from here the trip can be extended to the other smaller lakes, the Toplitz and Kammer Lakes.

Vast rock walls enclose the Toplitz Lake, and in the yet more deeply rock-embedded Kammersee is a romantic waterfall, the source of the Traun, that all along its course so adds to the beauty and wild, forceful charm of the scenery.

One can return again and again to the seductive charm of this lake district of Austria. Every faculty of man is brought to bear in enjoying its nature and its beauty, and all knowledge adds to the pleasure of its wonders of mountain, river, rock, forest, woodland, lake and pastureland; for botanist, and geologist, mountaineer, fisherman, and huntsman all have exciting experiences if they thoroughly explore the district; and in the old towns, and amidst the folk of

Austria

the district, the historian, the ethnologist, the archæologist and antiquary can all add to their knowledge and alight on items of interest that will add to the pure fascination of the scenery around them throughout the Salzkammergut.

CHAPTER XXIV

THE DANUBE—FROM THE BAVARIAN FRONTIER TO LINZ

WE are now again approaching that mighty river that has had through the ages so powerful an influence upon the Danubian Empire.

It is but a short railway run from the lake district to the Bavarian-Austrian frontier on the Danube, just east of Passau. From Gmunden the line runs via Attnang Ried and Schärding on the tributary to the Danube, the Inn; and quickly arrives at Passau in Bavaria, where we take the Danube steamer, and for a short distance float as it were in neutral waters, having Austria on the right hand shore and Bavaria on the left. But immediately this Danubian Empire asserts her romantic spell. The waters of the Inn from the Tirol run side by side with the Danube for some distance without mingling, and on the left hand the waters of the Ilz do the same, so that from the deck of the steamer are seen the three colours—on the left the almost black Ilz, on the right the green Inn, and in the centre the yellowish-green Danube, for the Danube is never blue, save perchance far down near its mouth, where the wide expanse of water under a blue sky then becomes blue.

· In descending and ascending the river many times, I have never seen the wondrous legendary blue that is supposed to be the colour of the water.

Austria

In 1873 falling into poetry, or at least rhyme, I wrote:

> "The schoene blaue Donau is not blue,
> But glitters with a yellow-greenish hue."

That was in August. At other times when the glacier water or mountain floods are pouring in, it is of greyish-yellow hue. In one of the latest books on the Danube by Walter Jerrold, a statement is made by a captain that it is blue in the winter, but in October, down where it is miles in width, below Rustchuk, the water was of a greenish-yellow tinge, so the Blue Danube waltz has much to answer for.

The retrospect to Passau is very beautiful, but soon the first of the Danube castles, Krempelstein, is seen, perched on its rocky height with soft, tree-bedecked hills around it, and this as it were, tunes the mind to the romance, pleasure, and calm enjoyment mixed with intellectual excitement there is in a voyage down the Danube through the two Crown lands of Upper and Lower Austria. Another local name for this castle is Schneiderschlössl, *i.e.*, " The Tailor's Little Castle," and a legend is told of the tailor who cribbed the rich brocade for the Bishop of Passau's suit, and was thrown from this rock by the devil in the shape of a goat.

Sometimes there is more than intellectual excitement such as that aroused by the beauty and charm of historic scenes or peasant grouping, for in times of flood or very low water the Danube can be fierce and turbulent, or tricksy is its behaviour, and the navigation requires extreme skill and caution, but these are rare if exciting events; generally a voyage down this mighty flood is wholly a delightful ex-

The Danube

perience, for the saloon steamers are fine boats, with good living on board.

It is not necessary to sleep on board on this Upper Danube journey. Halt can be made at the picturesque, historic towns, or pretty villages, and a month can well be spent on Austrian soil between the Austrian-Bavarian frontier, that is but a kilometre from Passau, and Pressburg or Posony, the Hungarian frontier below Vienna.

The population of Upper Austria, the Crown land that possesses so much of this romantic lake and river scenery, is almost wholly Teutonic, numbering nearly a million souls, with only about 5000 of various races, Cech, Italian, Slovens, intermixed here and there. And the pretty costume of the peasants on the river banks has almost disappeared. In 1873 one saw now and then the gorgeous black and gold jacket and white sleeves, but to-day on the great Holy Days, at the favourite shrines and pilgrimage churches, still as we shall see, crowds of peasants from various provinces may be seen on the steamboats, and the fore part of the ship is always interesting for the life of the people, be it in their strenuous work-a-day life, or in their holiday moods.

If but very few books have appeared in English during the last century on Austria, there have been many books on the Danube, such as Planche's "Descent of the Danube." One of the best works with highly idealised steel plate engravings is Beattie's "The Danube" illustrated by W. H. Bartlett, and a quite modern book that gives many of the legends is "The Danube" by Walter Jerrold; another modern book, Capt. B. Granville Baker's "The Danube with

Austria

Pen and Pencil," has good illustrations from the author's pencil, but travellers will do well to get the little handbook issued by the Danube Steamboat Company in several languages, including English, that is an excellent key to the whole of the river, and is well illustrated. From source to mouth the Danube is a mighty and glorious stream, full of romance, and strange wild beauty.

The pleasurable excitement in journeying on its waters soon begins, for quickly below Krempelstein we see in the middle of the river the, in old days, dreaded Jochstein, the home of a Danube "Mermaid" of the Loreley type. A dark rock rising in the centre of the stream, with a little shrine upon it, once a stronghold, to-day only a praying shrine, with the arms of Bavaria and Austria cut out upon the rock; and now on either hand villages and hills, churches and castles and monasteries, in ruins, or inhabited, keep the traveller's mind occupied with legend and action.

At Marsbach one sees two old Robber Knight's castles, in sight of each other—Rannariedl and Marsbach—picturesque enough now these castles, in artistic ruins, or renewed, as some are, for modern residences, but fierce evidence of the days gone by, when travellers and merchandise on the river were seized as booty. A heavy raft floating by this castle, with a small house upon it, and ten men guiding its course, tells of the travel of old days. Near here the river doubles back on itself, and the scene is very lovely; lofty, rocky, abrupt, woody heights on the one hand, and on the other, sloped corn or pasture fields, with an old white ruin amidst the hills. Then

The Danube

again the scene changes, and the river is as a lake shut in by abrupt rocky, volcanic-like hills. This part of the river is full of ever changing beauty; even the Austrian books will persist in comparing it to the Rhine, but what a libel on the Danube; the beauty here is far more continuous and more varied than on the Rhine, and I have walked and otherwise journeyed up and down that river over a period of many years.

The names of the villages here nearly all end with Zell, *i.e.* cell, and the suggestion is that this favoured spot by nature was a retreat of many of the early Christian hermits in days of persecution, and the churches with the tall slight towers, and domed summits, sometimes in low toned reds, at others in rich verdigris bronze, keep up the legend of hermit and monk.

This part of the river is full of twists and turns through the varied narrow gorges. The Danube by no means flows ever eastward, but is twisted by the hard rocks and mountain heights to every point of the compass, and the hills continually vary in form. As we near Neuhaus, they become steep and pointed and the rocks stand up in castellated forms from amidst the trees. But at Neuhaus, the hills and woods recede from the river, and the old castle with a romanesque tower, stands proudly out on its granite seat, above the little town, that is surrounded with hop gardens, and piles of timber making up for the rafts.

Great barges with the pointed painted prows lie here for the river traffic, and the river itself is wide and calm after its rush through the narrow passes.

Austria

The stream, however, was not too wide, but that in old days it could be blockaded with chains to stay an enemy's course down the river. In the days of the Turkish terror, the great buildings of the castle were used as a refuge for women and children.

On floating down from Neuhaus there comes a most glorious stretch of the river. One can look ahead now and see the glittering water shining far away between the hills. A steamboat is slowly coming up the stream, and in the distance the view is shut by green sloped hills, and an old ruin on a wooded height. The old rambling ruins of Schaumburg are close to Aschach, and legend and history mix themselves up in tradition. The Schaumburgs were a powerful family here and in France, and their history goes back to the twelfth century. According to the historian, Æneas Sylvius, the name should be Schönberg; in Latin he gives it " De monte pulchrio."

But there are other things besides human history to fascinate one on this river. One of the most interesting things on the Danube to study, is the timber work. The great piles of logs are seen waiting at the out falls of the mountain streams, that have brought them down to the Danube, and a halt at some of these tempting spots gives pleasant opportunity to stroll away up amongst the upland meadows, through which these tributaries run, and there from some rustic bridge to watch the men at work on the logs getting them in their wayward obstinacy to travel on down stream; for as the rushing stream carries them on, they have an almost fiendish habit of piling themselves up, blocking all passage. It is quite exciting work to see the woodsmen, with their long

The Danube

spiked and hooked poles, freeing them and starting the logs again on their journey. One reviewer in writing upon the novel, " John Westacott," noted the point, that in that book, incidentally I told the life of a fir tree from the seed dropped into some rock cranny until the tall pine was floated down the river, and became the high mast of a ship, or of one of the 1000-ton barges one sees lower down the stream; and it was from foresters on the Danube banks that I gleaned my knowledge of this fascinating study.

From fighting baron to forester, and from history to legend, from mediæval robber's nest ruins to modern tourist resorts, are the type of variation and ever changing interest that hold one on the Danube.

The story of Undine has a new charm, and the quaint old phraseology of the Niebelungen Lied suits the stately flow of the river, down the banks of which Kriemhild passed to the Huns.

It was at Passau that she came to the Danube. " Am Donauflusse kamen sie in das Baierland." To her uncle the Prince Bishop of Passau,—as she passed by Aschach the scene that met her eyes must have been much as that which delights the traveller of to-day. She passed the night at Everdingen, which is close to Aschach, and as we leave that town we get a view in the distance of the Alps; their white heights and glaciers glittering amidst the dark towering masses. The river now becomes wide, lined on either side with trees and fields, and the hills recede to a distance, and so give this beauteous view of the Alps.

We are now in the heart of the district where

Austria

the Peasant's war of 1626 took such a hold, and the student of this period will do well to make a halt, and glean the local traditions. The Imperial General was Herbertstorf, and the peasants' leader a hatmaker, Stephen Fadinger, a local Andreas Hofer, who conquered from this point to Linz, where he was wounded and died; he was buried where Kriemhild halted at Eferding. The war was terribly bitter and cruel; and General **Herbertstorf** had the body of the peasants' leader dug up and sunk in a swamp.

The Danube now flows on less swiftly as we descend, and winds between numerous flat islands, herons standing idly on the banks. Sometimes it seems impossible to pass amongst these wooded islands, but suddenly a passage opens out of the lake-like expanse, and the scene changes from rock and pine to corn and pasture and fruit orchard, dotted with dark roofed cottages.

It is interesting to watch the navigation of the river steamboats that draw only four feet of water. Often as we glide through the rapids and over the shallows, those who understand the man (or men) with the lead at the bows, will hear him call out, a depth with only a few inches to spare. The lead is really a sounding pole marked in red and black with the measurements; and on the big saloon boats often there are four men at the wheel, so powerful is the current, and I have seen a man hurled from the wheel on to the lower deck when the current nearly overpowered the men. The river is also well marked out with poles and buoys. The officers of the ships are most courteous and gentlemanly, wearing a quiet handsome uniform, and always ready to give all reasonable information.

The Danube

As we near Ottensheim, we pass another raft with six men tugging at the great sweeps, and two men at the end of the raft with poles, sounding for depth. They have their small hut on board, on which is mounted their flag, and as we slow down to pass them, that the wash of the paddles shall not swamp their piled-up timber raft, the square turretted tower of the Castle of Ottensheim, with the white buildings around it, comes in sight. Clustered amidst trees it stands out upon a rocky point in the river; already in the distance we can see the height of the Postlingberg, that looks down upon Linz. The pretty Château of Ottensheim is of ancient date, being mentioned in the twelfth century; lately it was the residence of Count Coudenhove, with whom, in Prague, when Statthalter (Viceroy) of Bohemia, I had the pleasure of some interesting conversations, especially upon the important regulation of the Moldau and Elbe floods, and shipping development, and the improvements at the junction of these two important rivers. Now, as we float past his Château, again the scene changes. The rocks and wooded heights close in, the fine old Cistercian monastery of Wilhering is passed; still higher rise the hills and clustering rocks, and the two pointed towers of the Castle of Buchenau is seen on the left, and then all seems closed in; but we sweep round a sharp turn, with an old fort on either side and a fort on a height, and suddenly Linz appears, shut in by a sharp promontory with a white chapel on its summit, amidst the dark firs. For a time Linz is lost to sight, but we steam on round another promontory to the left, and the whole beautiful sweep of the river is in view with the bridge of Linz crossing the wide river, now placid, and on the left rises the height of the Postlingberg.

The many spired and domed town lies mostly on the right hand, opposite this height, and with the flat country beyond, stretching away to where the broad glittering Danube flows on to the hills beyond, combines to form a very lovely scene, and tempts to a long halt in this important city, the capital of Upper Austria.

In spite of the importance and beauty of this province, it is but thinly populated, the sum of its inhabitants only reaching about a million, and of these, the city of Linz claims about 70,000, with about 14,000 in its suburb or town of Urfahr, on the left bank of the river. In 1896 both towns only numbered about 55,000 inhabitants, showing the recent developments of the city.

This advance is largely owing to the railway developments already noted, and Linz has become an important railway centre, linking up the great seaports of Hamburg and Triest. An Exchange has also been established, and a great museum developed, whilst the educational establishments are very important. These include a Commercial and a Railway Engineers' School.

The adoption of electric tramways, and the mountain rail up the Postlingberg, have also greatly helped the increased prosperity of this ancient city, known to the Romans under the name of Lentia.

On my second visit to Linz, in the year 1873, it was a very quiet country town, and to show how careless the authorities were of sanitary caution in those days, the first sight I saw as I went up in the

LINZ

The Danube

early morning into the Hauptplatz from the Erzherzog Carl Hotel, was a man being borne in on a litter of tree branches, dying, if not already dead, from cholera. As I was just recovering from an attack of this same scourge, I well remember the shock the sight gave me, but such a thing to-day in Austria is impossible, and medical and sanitary matters are well looked after everywhere.

In spite of the splendid position of Linz on the Danube, and the finding of Roman remains within its borders, history is reticent upon events in its life, and it is not before 1098 that it is mentioned as a walled town; tradition has it that Richard Cœur de Lion was entertained here when coming up the Danube after being liberated from Dürrenstein. A curious glimpse of church history is given in the fact that in 1236 three bishops, and the Patriarch of Acquileia with other nobles, and the King of Bohemia, were besieging the town. Since that date it has suffered greatly from sieges, plague, insurrection, and fire, and in spite of the attention bishops gave it, it was strongly Protestant in 1550. To-day in the whole Crown land of Upper Austria there are only about 20,000 Protestants. It became a Bishopric in 1785, and it was at this time the woollen manufactures of Linz were the most prosperous in Austria.

The words of one of these manufacturers, or rather managers, in 1841 to Herr Kohl, gives a striking contrast to the tone to-day of master and men. " The inmost soul of all art is religion, and the fear of God, and our work is a kind of art. I take no workmen of whose character I am not certain. I pay far more heed to this than to their skill," and this manager, or rather "Imperial and Royal Inspector of Woollen Printing" encouraged pleasant chat whilst the work was going on, and talked of putting up Schiller's words:

> "Wenn gute Reden sie begleiten
> So fliesst die Arbeit munter fort." *

To-day, there are important locomotive works, and also spinning and weaving mills, and breweries, in the town and district.

The modern museum at Linz is one of the finest in Austria, well placed with a garden around it, and with a well executed illustrative frieze running round its exterior, above the windows, and the collections are well arranged and of immense value, educationally and intrinsically.

The prettiest view of Linz is seen in coming across the great bridge and entering the Franz Joseph Platz. In the centre of this, the Grande Place of Linz, rises the roccoco column of the Trinity, erected to celebrate the cessation of two great plagues—the pest, and the Turks, who at last were driven back. Here in the early morning the milk and vegetable sellers still have some characteristic costumes, broad hats and black and white head-dresses, and on fête days, in the old cathedral close by, peasants from the surrounding country may be seen in their costumes.

Like all other cities in Austria, Linz during the last twenty-five years has sprung to new life, and the handsome public buildings, such as the Railway Offices, the General Savings Bank, the Parliament

* "When genial chat with work combines,
Then Labour pleasantly moves on."

The Danube

House for Upper Austria, with its pretty poetical monument to the Kaiserin Elizabeth, the Merchants' Hall, and the various educational buildings, especially the Railway Technical Schools, all speak of modern advancement and eager, intellectual development. Few of these buildings were existing when I first knew Linz, and it is a very different thing to walk in and around Linz to-day and in the seventies of the nineteenth century. The churches have always some fête or Saints' day to celebrate. I was once present at a most solemn service here in memory of Her Majesty the Kaiserin Elizabeth, when the music was most impressive.

An interesting example of development is illustrated by my first ascent of the Postlingberg in the seventies, and again in the twentieth century. Wishing to see the view of Linz by moonlight from this height we strolled up the Danube, and, led by some village lads, in the dusk clambered up a goat's path, coming suddenly to a great slit in the rocks, which we had to leap, and so in a tough scramble, which one man of our party gave up as too stiff, we came out on the summit of the Postlingberg, and a glorious view of Linz was below us. As we stood silently in the moonlight, looking at the calm view, some singing arose in the quiet night, and we found it was some watchers at a lime kiln, passing their time by singing and jodling after the Tyrolean mode. Such was our poetical, interesting experience in the seventies; to-day an electric tram takes us across the Danube to Urfahr, and then a mountain railway quickly lifts us up the 1800 feet, and lo! there is a great hotel and restaurant, with a grand terrace, whereon one can dine and watch

Austria

the sunset effects on the distant Alps and the play of light and colour on the nearer heights. The Salzkammergut and half Upper Austria is in view, and the onward sweep of the Danube into Lower Austria, whilst below, as on a raised map, is the city of Linz. Very often the terrace is occupied by some congress or company, and some good music may be heard, and joviality prevails. If one is lazy enough to ride up to the summit, at least one should walk down the mountain, halting at the old forts, and at the interesting pilgrimage church, before descending, and enjoy the varied views as we descend to the town.

It is interesting that in the Niebelungen Lied no mention is made of Linz, and the dangers of attack and robbery on this part of Kriemhild's journey is vividly depicted. Her next halting-place is beyond where the Traun falls into the Danube, where from her proud castle the fair Gotelinde rides out with a gay company of knights and maidens of high degree and great beauty to welcome Kriemhild, and give her " night quarters."

IN THE STODER VALLEY

CHAPTER XXV

THE DANUBE FROM LINZ TO VIENNA

WE must quit Linz, leaving much of its pleasant excursions and of its history unsaid, and follow on Kriemhild's route, but by boat.

It is always well to study the retrospect as we leave these halting spots on the Danube. Here this is very beautiful, but as we sail on, far over the flat land, on the right comes in the view of the Alps, the white snow glittering in the morning sun. On the left the sloping hills are interspersed with wood and corn. Herons stand on the pebbly beaches, and the river winds on between rich meadows.

We float on past castles, and halt at busy riverside towns, where the peasantry, heavily laden, especially in the autumn, come on board, with the produce of fruit and vegetables.

One of the greatest of the vast monasteries so plentiful in Austria is soon approached. This monastery of St Florian, the arch-protector against fire, is an immense building. The author, Herr Kohl, gives a very full account of this monastery, as he saw it in 1841, and he speaks of this cloistered palace as magnificent, and of the kindly work of the fathers. As we shall halt at a similar vast monastery at Melk, we here can only refer to the fact that it possessed 787 houses and farms in the nineteenth

Austria

century, and has a great collection of MSS. and early printed books, and thus hint at the whole charm of the place and its surroundings. Near by is a castle of Prince Auersperg, who was for some time lately the vigorous, learned, and courteous Minister for Agriculture. A prosperous town and a good halting-place is Mauthausen, where the life of the folk can be studied. As Maut the first syllable of its name implies, it was a taxing border in bygone days, and the Avars established a heavy tax here on the Danube merchants. Later Barbarossa's crusading fleet was stopped for toll, but that led to the burning of the town. On the opposite shore the Enns flows into the Danube. Near here stood the Lauriacum of the Romans, an important river station, whence, legend has it, the Christian faith was spread abroad through Austria. These slight hints of history give suggestions to the student of antiquity or mediæval lore of the vast field for research there is throughout this district; and in many a monastery, and in the archives of the towns and churches, there are probably documents lying *perdu* that would throw valuable light on the past. We have passed St Florian, where there are 70,000 volumes and many MSS., and we shall see at Melk how glorious can be a monastery library, if we had not already learnt it at Prague and elsewhere; it was in such hoards of documents that Palacky found so much for his most fascinating historical work. The Enns forms the boundary of the Crownland of Lower Austria, and we are once again in the province of the capital; but how much there is to see and delight in ere we see again the tall spire of St Stephen.

The Danube from Linz to Vienna

As we pass along onward over the greyish-green waters we get a lovely peep between the trees of the castle of Wallsee, a great castellated palace dominated by its high square tower. A curious evidence of the change come over the life of the district is given by a description of the work and life of the beavers, who built their houses and bred on the river banks in the early half of the seventeenth century. Steam has probably driven them away, as it has driven the crocodiles from the Lower Nile.

It is at Wallsee that the greatest beauty of the Danube commences, so say many writers, but it is very difficult to exactly state which part of the Danube can claim pre-eminence in beauty. " Only in a series of dithyrambics and to the accomplishment of the harp are they worthily to be sung," exclaims one writer as he describes the scenes after leaving Wallsee. Sometimes in the evening the men of the boat, or passengers, sing on the bows the folk songs of the district, and this is a more appropriate accompaniment to the beauty than even the harp.

As we approach Grein the high rocks and wooded hills close in on the river, and there seems no way out. Then the waters open out into a lake-like expanse, and the pretty detached little town of Grein appears on the left. Years ago, when I first saw this spot, it was a village-like town with only its white homely houses and great square castle, and its church, with a red topped roof and tiny tower, but to-day castle and church are there still, but all along the shore are picturesque villas and pretty hotels tempting one desperately, to land and halt here for exploration of all the romantic scenery that seems so poetically and caressingly to envelop Grein. Well may it be called the pearl of the Danube for itself and its surroundings.

An hour's walk from Grein is the little Bath of Kreuzen, and the picturesque Château Clam. Another interesting walk is to the Stillenstein Klamm, the very name inviting one to a stroll up between its romantic cliffs. "The mountains rise steeply on either side as we pass up the Klamm, clothed from the very water's edge with beech and pine and other trees. About the great grey boulders of rock are a profusion of ferns and mosses. The whole is like the beauty of some Devonshire lane and stream: a kind of lyric loveliness, that uplifts and gladdens, where the grandeur of the great river to which the stream is hurrying has something rather of epic sweep and solemnity." So writes Walter Jerrold of this mighty edition of a Devonshire ravine, and we are soon to see, in quitting Grein, how the Danube in old times could be not only epic but tragic in its fierceness.

As we leave the pleasant landing-stage and move out into the wide stream all is placid, and looking back the river is shut in by hills, as if it were a lake. The passengers crowd to the bows of the boat to get the view and the excitement; as we quickly get into the rush of a rapid; steam is shut off, and we move swiftly onwards, borne by the torrent, down the Greiner Schwall, on the surging, boiling waters. Then comes a quiet short stretch of the river, and the rocks narrow in; again we are in the boiling waters; the rocks seem to overhang the river, and ahead there is a little rocky islet with a cross upon it; it seems we must crash into it, but we rush past this

The Danube from Linz to Vienna

isle that divides the river, and are quickly in the boiling, surging Strudel. The boat sways and trembles in the rushing current; ahead is a strong old ruin, the castle of Werfenstein, and we are again in peaceful waters, with the high walls around us; but quickly we are once more in surging waters. On the left we see an inscription telling how the dangers of this, the Wirbel, have been lessened, and we pass on into quieter waters. But let me quote:—

"Agnes watched the scene, but it was beyond her power to take in the sight of rocks and chalets, wood and covert, and rocks piled in fantastic shapes around her. The waters foamed and boiled, the steamer seemed to shake and tremble beneath their feet. The river grew narrower and more narrow, until the leaping, tossing waters seemed to give no room to pass a high-peaked, fir-clad rock ahead. All eyes were strained. It was but a few moments; the ship seemed to leap onward, and they were safely past the old ruin below the cross-capped rock, and the passengers breathed again, as the ship still went swiftly on, now in calm, placid water, with a wider course, and high hills overshadowing them.

"The vicar and his daughter both turned to Ralph with an exclamation of surprise at this exciting scene; but Ralph said: 'Look ahead, we shall soon be in the Wirbel'; and ere many minutes had elapsed again the steamer was rushing through the boiling, surging waters, that whirl round the rock and ruin of Haustein." So I wrote in "John Westacott" many years ago, and to-day the scene has but little altered, and this note describes how rapidly the scenes are passed.

There is much of history and legend clinging round this romantic pass, and the Worth island carries us back into Celtic and Roman days. All river traffic could easily be blocked by the possessor of this islet. The cross has a legend of its own, of a certain Count, who, with his wife, was wrecked in trying to pass the Strudel; he saved himself, and in grief at the loss of his wife became a hermit on this island. The wife too was saved from the stream, and she mourned her husband for twelve years; but hearing of the holy hermit on the island, went to him for pious consolation, and lo! it was her husband, and as a thank-offering for their salvation and reunion they erected this cross.

The speed at which we rush down this most interesting part of the river compels one to visit the spot again and again to understand its beauty; a good way is to come up the river, as, of course, the struggle against the stream compels a slower pace. A cannon is generally fired as we enter the gorge, to halt anything leaving Grein. When this happens at night the effect of the thundering reverberation echoing from rock to rock and hill to hill is very alarming to the passengers sleeping below, a fact I utilise in " John Westacott," that story being dated during the Franco-Prussian War.

The granite rock formation is deeply interesting to the geologist; and the botanist who wanders up the Klamms will find interesting specimens to repay the time, even if the romantic scenery is not sufficient repayment.

As we come from the rush and hurry, and fretting wear of this rocky gorge, we see, as the river widens

The Danube from Linz to Vienna

out a peaceful little village, with white houses, perchance on a fête day hung with flags, that contrast with the dark firs on the over-towering hills, and then we soon come to Sarmingstein, with its old, grey, round ruined tower.

The passenger boats in the old days, before steam, were called the Ordinari, and the rowers and steerers had to be very adept and alert to bring their boats through the rapids, and how the passengers must have rejoiced when they reached Sarbingstein, now called Sarmingstein. The legends, and history, and stories upon this part of the Danube are voluminous — the Devil's Tower, and the Black Monk, magical lights and disasters. The searcher into folklore and legend can have his fill here. By watching rafts rush these and other rapids, one can glean somewhat of the peril of the old days. In some cases the raftsmen have high seats to jump into as they rush a torrent, and it is exciting to see them work their rafts into position, and as they are entering a surging rapid, jump on this raised seat to be out of the rush of the water.

At Sarmingstein the view is wholly changed, and it is very beautiful; on the right are pleasant slopes, with occasional rocks and pines, interspersed with soft green pasture and delicate-tinted birch and other trees, contrasting with the dark fir patches; and here and there are dark wooden, and white chalet-like houses. In the autumn an added colour is given by rich corn plateaus, high up, whence the forests slope to the river.

Calmly we sail on now. A raft is lying on the river with one solitary man upon it. The left bank becomes flat with picturesque bits of dark rock jutting up here and there, backed by richly cultivated hills.

Then the river winds, and ahead on an outjutting bluff we see the white walls of the stately castle of Persenbeug, commanding this upper stretch of the river, and a wide stretch of waters beyond. The corruption of this word from Bosen—Beug or the " evil (dangerous) bend "—is a curious one; formerly it was dangerous, to-day it is a lovely spot, and the royal castle and park are open to the public, and just opposite, on the right bank, is the old town of Ybbs, all combining to make this a delightful halting-place for either modernist or the archæologist, or Nature friend.

This point of the Danube was utilised as an important station by the Romans, as the name Pons Isidis implies, and all through the ages it has been utilised as a military station. Persenbeug became a castle in the ninth century, and later on the Grafschaft or county, linked with it, was a wide and rich one. Fistright and ecclesiastics struggled here for supremacy, as everywhere, and the arrival by water of the Emperor Henry III., with Bishop Bruno, must have formed a stately pageant; but it ended tragically, for the floor of the banqueting hall fell in with Emperor and Bishop and Abbot, and hostess, the Countess Richlinde, all falling into the bathroom below—a proof that they had bathrooms in days of yore in these castles. One account gives it that the Bishop fell on the edge of the bath-tub; and in Austria I have seen a bathroom, with an enormous tub that required many a bucket and much labour to fill it, and anyone who fell on its solid edge would

The Danube from Linz to Vienna

certainly be killed, as were the Countess, Bishop and Abbot, the Emperor escaping.

The gardens and park of the castle are well laid out, and the views, especially from the towers, are superb, embracing the hills and rocks around the great reaches of the Danube, and far-away glimpses of the Alps.

Ybbs has good baths and good inns and delightful walks, and here, where an Englishman would only look for a primary school, is a most important fruit-culture school, and, of course, a good local museum. All down the river it will be seen how carefully the fruit orchards are tended. It was somewhat of a surprise to meet here a torpedo boat flotilla—one scarcely expects to see warships on a river—but the Danube, especially lower down, is carefully patrolled where the river becomes a vast frontier.

From the river across the flat country by Ybbs we get the outline of the Alps, and the whole scene is very peaceful and beautiful as we pass onward by the little town of Sausenstein, with its old castle and church, and then ahead on a high hill we see a great church with two towers and black domes, and soon reach the town of Marbach.

This is one of the most famous spots on the Danube, and if one is here on the great fête days of the church on the hill, the Maria Taferl Church, the crowd of peasants in their various costumes is most interesting and picturesque. It is curious, then, to see the crowds on the steamboats of the pilgrims coming from the festival. The peasants in their bright colours mingling with the acolytes, still wearing their red cassocks and white surplices. All wear medals and flowers,

Austria

and pictures of Maria of the Taferl. The church, so conspicuous from a distance, is about 1500 feet above sea level, and stands upon a plateau that gives a grand prospect for hundreds of miles; and for many a year the people have flocked to the spot as to a local Lourdes, or Lorretto. The origin of the devotion to this "Maria of the little table" is said to have been an image of the Virgin that hung in an oak tree over a stone table, whereon the peasants used to feast after giving thanks for a good harvest. A peasant essayed to cut down this tree, but his axe cut his foot, and looking up he saw the image, and was contrite, whereupon the image immediately cured his foot. This miraculous cure was quickly spread abroad, and the fame of the image has spread even to this day, and vast, and most varied, are the crowds who, for three days now in every September, pray for benefactions at this shrine of Maria Taferl.

The local literature throughout Austria is always interesting, and often learned, and here the legends, and shall we say superstitions, are worth reading, and a local romance of the Middle Ages, entitled "Jesse and Maria," embodies a true picture of life on the Danube shores of that period.

We must not halt too long at these romantic spots, for greater scenes, if not more beautiful, are ahead. There is a fine wide stretch of the river ere we come to the much-sung of Pöchlarn—Great Pöchlarn on the right, and Little Pöchlarn on the left bank. Even the Danube Steamship Company's guide falls into rythmic prose as it approaches Pöchlarn—

"Es rauscht ein Klang von Nibelungen Lied ueber den Strom"—

The Danube from Linz to Vienna

but it also tells of the days when Pöchlarn was the harbour for the Roman river flotilla, and the valuable collection of the stone age found near by, and preserved in the museum.

It was here that the windows of the castle were all freely open, instead of suspiciously closed with shutters, to greet Kriemhild and her retinue. Many a stanza is given to her reception at Bechelaren, as the Lied spells it, by the young daughter and spouse of Rüdiger—

"Die Fenstern an die Mauern sah man geoffnet stehn
Die Veste Bechelaren war auf gethan zu sehn"—

and their entry into the wide halls of the castle, below which ran the Danube, is well described, and a rich exchange of presents was made, ere Kriemhild passed onward to Medeliche, or Mölk (Melk) as we know it now.

Perhaps it is from these stanzas that the name "Blue" Danube has been taken, for Kriemhild was escorted, "Die blaue Donau nieder bis gen Mutakaren hin," *i.e.* "along the banks of the Blue Danube from Mölk to Mautern."

But before we reach Mölk, we pass the picturesque old castle of Weiteneck, a curious romantic old pile on a precipitous rock, with a great square tower, and tower on tower around it, and a little stone balcony above the dark rock. Here, as nearly always near these strongholds, there is broken water and rapids, proving a dangerous passage, and a better chance to pounce on booty or enemy. This was one of the castles of Rüdiger, the husband of Kriemhild's hostess.

And now ahead comes in sight one of the most

vast and important, and most imposing buildings on the whole stretch of the Danube, the great Monastery of Melk. As the great pile of buildings comes in sight, stretching along the rocky wooded ridge, high above the river, the stately domes and towers and long palatial line of the monastery command a halt, and we disembark at the quiet landing stage, and drive up through the quaint old town to the Stoklassa Hotel, in a lovely avenue, from whence we look out on to the great monastery.

The birds are singing, and there comes up the musical ring of hammer on anvil, but again, as everywhere in this Danubian empire, close by, in this little old-world retreat, there are great new school buildings.

\But as in Rome, and Athens, one is at once attracted to the forum and acropolis, here it is the vast dominating Stift or monastery that entices, and we proceed up the Stiftweg, through the first gate, and up the steps to the great gate, with the date 1718 upon it. Roccoco statues are upon it, and as we cross over the drawbridge and enter the first court, we see an old round tower on the right hand, a remnant of twelfth-century work. We pass on through a great Portico, and then enter the inner court, with a great bronze fountain in the centre. The buildings around are of the classical order, and as we halt and look around, we feel as though we were in some great college; but all is silent, and there is no quick young life surging around. We pass on along a corridor, and enter the church. All is in the richest roccoco style and a blaze, but yet an artistic blaze of gold, with rich carving over the stalls, and a Last

The Danube from Linz to Vienna

Supper over the altar. The special Loges or pews for the abbot, or nobles, are above the altar, and are closed in and glazed.

The great bells boom and clang as we stand before the altar, in front of which swings a great artistic lamp in silver and copper. The dome is of great height, and is all illustrated, and the pulpit is a gorgeous mass of rich gold, expressively carved.

At the side altars also there is some most excellent carving, especially one scene of the Circumcision. The relics, skeletons, and bones are decked out in silk and velvet, and jewels and gold, and in the chapels there is very much of artistic worth and quaint interest. As we come out of the west doors of this impressive, vast, gorgeous building, we step out through an archway on to the famous balcony, that with its arch forms so conspicuous a point from the Danube. From it, what a glorious expanse of view, superbly beautiful, we look upon. The glittering broad flood of the river, the hills beyond, and castle and hamlet, forest, woodland and pasture; a view that ever lingers impressively in the mind.

'As we were slowly strolling back through the courts, an old priest appeared—a Friar Tuck-like priest—and we began a chat; but ere long another keen-faced brother appeared, and joined in the talk, and on finding we were interested in history and antiquity, soon told us he knew Egypt and Tunis, and the name of Pere Delattre of Carthage quickly formed a bond of union between us. We were delighted to hear the newcomer was Brother Berthold, known to the world as Dr Hofer, and as he soon had to leave he arranged that Dr Schachinger, the librarian, should meet us at 9 o'clock in the morning and show us what we so longed to see, the library, and also other treasures of the monastery.

But ere Brother Berthold left us, he took us up through the garden to the north side of the monastery to the Loggia, now used as a restaurant for the students, and to the east, up an avenue, that recalled Addison's walk; the whole thing continually reminded one of Oxford. We passed on round to the fish-pond, and to a view outlook, where were seats, and a table, all covered with Latin and German phrases, in praise of the beauty of the spot.

And truly here also was another glorious view of hills and corn and forest, and to the east, the high dark clustering hills of that district we are about to enter by the Danube gate, the Wachau, the much-praised tourist district of the river. All was so still and peaceful, nought but the birds broke the silence, but there was a disturber of the peace, a very tiny, but potent one, the *Gelsoe*!—a very special mosquito, with a very special sting, that breeds in the little stagnant ornamental ponds. But some brothers were strolling to and fro in the arcaded walks unheeding these tormentors. Palms and accacias, and the red Glycena tree, and other botanical varieties were in the gardens, and we had a chat with the gardener, who regretted more was not done here, and as usual with so many Austrian workmen, he tried to get information on English gardening, and asked if we get good orchids, and showed us some plants, like ice plants, he called Portutac flowers. From the gardens we passed on through the terraces, and had a peep at the Skittle Alley, where some students were

MÖLK

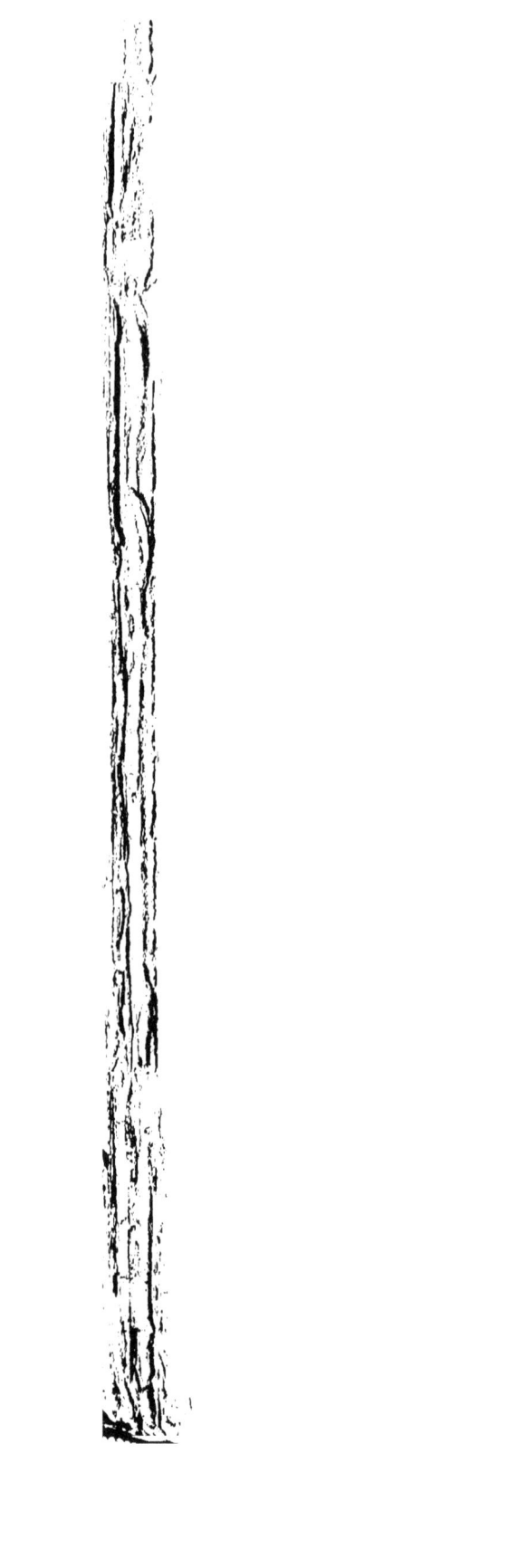

The Danube from Linz to Vienna

amusing themselves; near by were two towers, one round, the other twelve-sided, with great bastions, a remnant of the older buildings, and here we sat and rested again to the song of the birds, accompanied by the sounds of the roll of the balls.

As we passed down to the town all was peacefully still, the quaint old gable roofs leading up to the vast line of the monastery, that with its domes and spires, now lit up by the setting sun, wholly dominated the town.

Then suddenly the town was alert. The firemen were out; they put their hose in the Roland well, ladders were run up to a house; all the, till then, sleeping town came out to see. A little fat captain gave vigorous orders. The hose was rushed up on to a roof, and soon a good jet of water was passing over the house, and landing in the street on the other side of the way, and the brave firemen in red and black brass-bound helmets rescued imaginary fair maidens from imaginary flames, for it was only practice for the Fire Brigade. So we left the pleasant little town and went down to the arm of the Danube, and across the bridges, and enjoyed the picturesque view from below of the majestic pile of the buildings and the famous Loge and its archway before the double towers of the great church.

The next morning we were in the library at 9 a.m., and had just time to drink in all the fascinating charm of this most beautiful home for books ere Prof. Fr. Schachinger arrived, and gave us a hearty greeting. Around us, in good bindings, were about 70,000 to 80,000 volumes. Old globes and charts and folios lay on the tables, and in glass cases were the choicest treasures, and all in such a beauteous home—this stately hall enriched and decorated with carving and inlaid woods, and the ceilings illuminated with paintings. Many a treasure of early printed books we were shown, and Gutenberg's work of 1450-55; a German Bible, 1473; a Mölker Mass Book of 1483 printed in Nuremberg; a "Beda" MS. of the ninth century, and some most lovely missals; a splendid example of the Koran. One could linger in this beau ideal of a library for days, but we passed onward through the Kaiser Zimmer (Emperor's room), where Marie Antoinette amongst others had stayed, and later, Napoleon in 1809, when the French troops drank from the abbey cellars to the tune of 50,000 to 60,000 pints of wine a day. When the Emperor Francis Joseph was married to the Empress Elizabeth, they stayed here. The dining-hall is a stately room; from this we passed out to the great archway to get the view in the morning light; now better understanding the buildings, having the great church behind us, the library on the right, and the dining-hall on the left, then facing about to look upon the impressive scene of nature. But Melk had yet treasures of art wherewith to surprise us, and we were led into the Praelatie, and were shown some interesting portraits of past abbots, and in the house chapel, a fine expressive "Marie" of Albert Dürer. The present abbot is the president of the wine industry of the district, and, said our guide, "he has great possessions." Regret was expressed to us that the abbot was then in Vienna, and our regret was intensified when we learned that we could not see the famous Cross of Melk, for the

The Danube from Linz to Vienna

abbot always held the key, and so we did not see this gem of metal work of the fourteenth century, of gold and silver, and pearls and jewels. But we were taken into the sacristy, and there we saw gems of ecclesiastical art, equal to those in Moscow and Rome —rich vestments and bejewelled mitres; crystal cups for the sacramental wine and water; richly jewelled Bishop's croziers and staves; Mass vestments of the fourteenth century, one having Christ and John and Marie on the one side, and on the other the Crucifix, and sun and moon; other vestments of the sixteenth century — a rich storehouse of mediæval craft and bejewelled needlework, full of beauty of workmanship.

It was with regret we again went down the long slope into the little town, and bade adieu to the great buildings above. But the little church and its quaint monuments around its outer walls soon occupied our attention, and this, with the museum and its historic treasures, gave us further insight into the history of Melk, that dates from Roman days. A Benedictine monastery was established as far back as the eleventh century, and from that day to this Melk has lived in history, and often made history.

We have lingered long in Melk to try and give some idea of the history, art, folklore, and legend there is stored up in so many of these abbeys and monasteries, and also in the castles, throughout Austria, and English visitors who show a respectful interest in any of these subjects, or a love of beauty or antiquity, are always most courteously received even without introductions.

Austria

When Kriemhild halted here at **Medeliche,** as **Melk** was then called, she and her retinue were handed wine in rich cups of gold. We had seen the jewelled cups and had drank in great delights of the beauty of the place and its possessions.

CHAPTER XXVI

THE DANUBE THROUGH THE WACHAU TO KREMS

WE sail away down the broad flood of the Danube, but quickly the river narrows, the hills and rocky heights close in, and we are entering the romantic stretch of the river that is called the Wachau. Monasteries, ruins, and picturesque villages succeed each other. Schönbühl or Schönbichel, with the old round tower and more modern square buildings, lies on a rocky eminence close to the river, the wooded and cultivated hills sloping around and above it. Then come wild, jagged, rocky heights, and high on a terrific height, overhanging a precipice, with apparently no access on either side save up this dizzy height, is perched the strong robber's nest of Aggstein, an astounding point, the castle seems in the sky. Below is a tiny village, crouching on the river's bank under this castle-crowned rock; a wild, fearfully wild spot, yet very beautiful and full of hints of strange romance.

Seen from below the castle seems small, but above, amidst its walls, there is ample room for housing retainers. The local legends do not fail in romance. We have referred to the hunger towers of these castles, as the ingenious device for getting rid of one's enemies; but here, the fiercest robber knight of all, a certain Schreckenwald (Fear of the Forest) or

Austria

Schreck von Wald, was more refined in his revenge. He had his "rose garden," a slit, or ravine, deep in the mountain side, whence was no escape. Into this he lowered or hurled his victims. But one victim escaped even from the rose garden, a brave young knight who had worsted the Baron in war and in love. Having learned the secrets of the castle, he returned when an orgie had slackened the castle watch, and Schreckenwald was hung to a beam in the hall where he had been feasting, and the rose garden was planted with the chief of his retainers.

To the lover of mediæval lore or architecture, the castle is full of points. It dates from the twelfth to the fifteenth century, and the triple bridges and gates from the land side formed a famous defensive work. A monument to Viktor v. Scheffel, the poet, is now erected here. As we journey eastwards, every village and church and ruin has its legend.

A strange geological curiosity, a gigantic wall of rock that seems to be leaping down the mountain, is called the "Teufelsmauer" or devil's wall. Satan meant to flood the whole valley by running this wall across the river, but an alert cock crowed vigorously and disturbed him, and woke the folks around. The cock is commemorated for his alertness, on the church steeple of St Johan.

As we approach Spitz, the view is very romantic on either side. Here the vine is seen more widely cultivated, and Spitz makes a good halting-place for those who prefer a market town to a fashionable resort. There are scores of excursions from this spot, and the fruit industry can well be studied here; in

AGGSTEIN

The Danube to Krems

the spring the cultivated slopes have a wondrous charm of blossom.

The river now is fairly wide, but it soon closes in again with picturesque hills and with jagged rocks as we reach St Michael's, where everyone looks for the hares on the church roof, said to have been placed there to commemorate a great snow fall that allowed the hares to rove over the church.

A turn in the river, and we are in sight of that castle that all English travellers eagerly look for.

The story of disaster to a brave man, and his rescue by a restless faithful friend, through romantic stratagem, has held its sway over folk for 800 years; and so as we approach Dürrenstein all eyes look out to see the walls of the castle where Richard the Lionheart was imprisoned, until he heard the song of the troubadour Blondel.

The remnants of the castle are on a rocky height, and a line of rocks runs down to the river in irregular shapes. Above the castle the rocks are fantastic, so that it is difficult to tell rock from castle, or from the defensive wall that runs down to the little town beneath, with its old houses and pointed church tower. There is not much of the castle left. When I first saw it in 1873, I noted there were four tall corners remaining, but these appear more like the peaked rocks than built walls. Few people disembark here; they are content with the passing glimpse of the castle from the river. On a packed boat, lately, I and my wife were the sole visitors to Dürrenstein.

We passed up through a little tunnel in the rock, on which the town is built, to the " Gasthaus zum

Austria

Richard Löwenherz," literally the guesthouse of Richard the Lionheart. The very name satisfied us; but above was a pleasant platform on the rocks, tables under flowering oleanders, and we found good feeding and excellent wine, and cleanly rooms at this guesthouse.

We climbed to the castle up a rugged path, and we watched the peasants come in from their labour with their patient oxen, much as they did in Richard's time, and we heard the clack of the handloom, and the thud of the flail, as though we were in centuries long flown by.

Part of the Keep, as well as isolated towers, remain. I clambered into the heart of the castle where wall and rock is intermingled, and there are some windows and doors still left, overgrown with bushes. In one chamber, half rock, half dwelling, one might well conceive Richard to have been held in harsh durance. It is now a weird place, but a glorious view is had both up and down the river from this height, and the silence is intense. The great linking wall and watch towers running to the river are in good preservation and should be cared for. The east gate of the town is also intact, with people living over the gate, looking out over the vineyards that produce a famous wine, the Donau Perle (Pearl of the Danube).

The little town itself is still as in the fifteenth or sixteenth century — great gateways to the houses with arms on the walls, vaulted rooms and narrow streets, and as the sun is setting, the deep-toned vesper bells ring out, and we can hear the bells of Rossatz in the distance, far across the river.

DÜRRENSTEIN

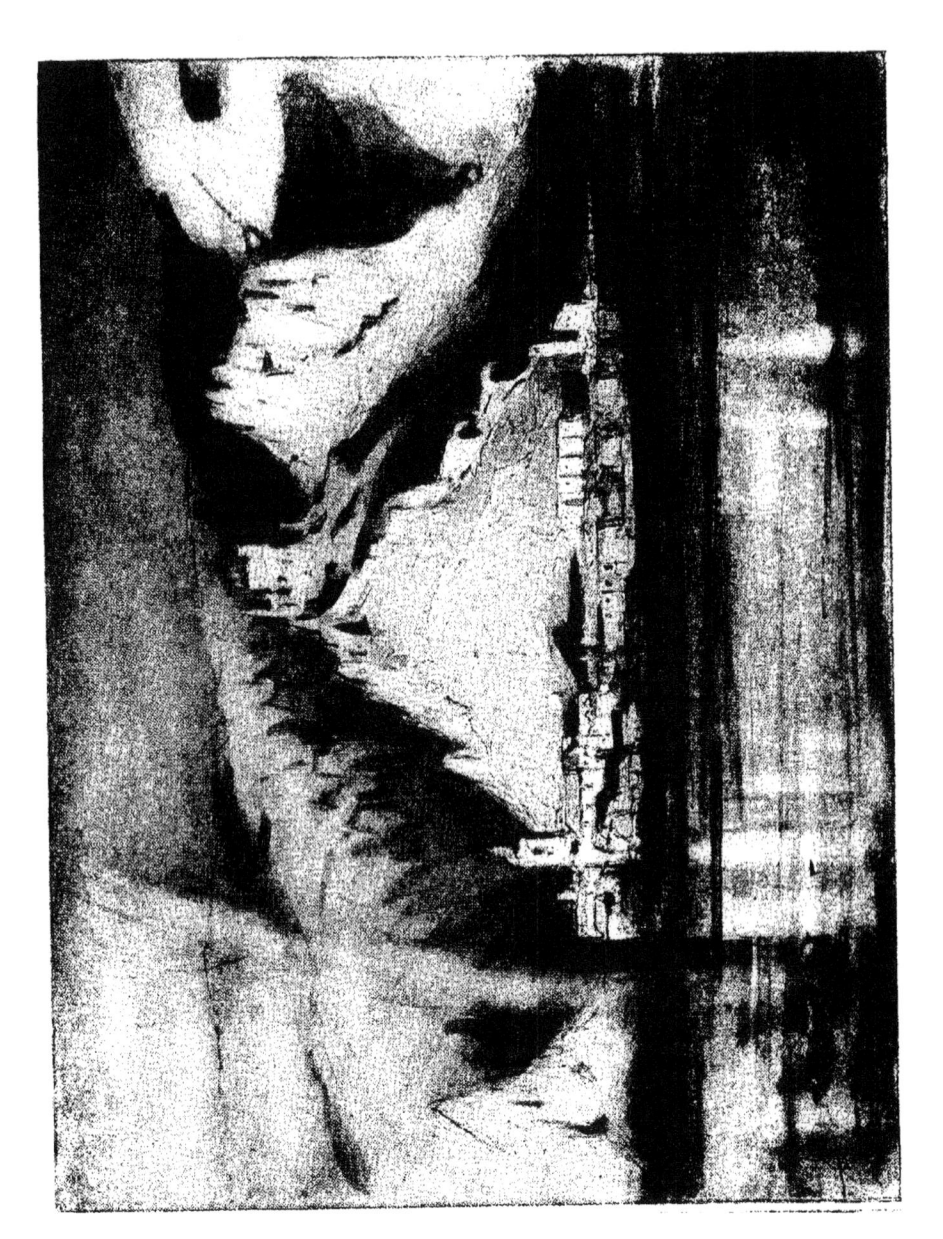

The Danube to Krems

The strong old walls that flank the river side are the once handsome buildings of a château, and a Clarice or St Clara nunnery. Over the door of an Augustinian cloister is an imposing piece of work, with scroll and arabesque ornamentation. Inside the door are quaint carvings of figures in broad hats and bearing spiked clubs; and also of Roman warriors, with spears and feathered helmets, and others in trunk hose—a curious medley. But the doors lead into a lovely little courtyard with trees and flowers, and a passage into the church, where are old frescoes and old doors richly carved.

Many of the houses are mediæval, on one we read the couplet—

> "So lang im Glas noch blinket der Wein
> Brüder lasst uns frohlich sein."

Carpenters and peasants now live where noble and knight and wealthy burgher dwelt in mediæval days. The frescoes in the Augustinian Church of the " Driving out the money changers " and " Christ in the Temple " are good; there is also a fine picture, by Schmidt of Krems, of the beheading of Faustina, and the relics of the Faustina and the Holy Clement are richly enshrined. There is an immense deal in this church to detain the lover of mediæval work; to-day abbot and brothers and priests are gone, and only a Pfarrer serves in this once wealthy and important building, and in the town there are now only four hundred folk, of whom sixty are children. But the whole town breathes of the past, and it was with real regret we quitted our inn, that had been a part of the Augustinian Convent, the walls being seven feet thick, and the great door dates from the fourteenth century. Truly Dürrenstein has far more than the shades of Blondel and his imprisoned master to hold and attract the traveller, and we leave much of its history unsaid. As we sailed on down the Danube flood we had an excellent retrospect of Dürrenstein, with its peak on peak of rock, and its walls that enclose the town.

But the Danube gives but little time for retrospect. Ahead on a high hill is seen another monastery. An enormous mass of buildings, with its red roof and turrets backed by wooded hills. It is the Benedictine Abbey of Gottweig, and we must disembark at Mautern to visit this further treasure-house of books and over a thousand MSS. Engravings, coins, and other art treasures are here also in rich abundance. When I first saw Mautern there was a picturesque old wooden bridge, with a crucifix upon it, linking Mautern with Stein; to-day there is a stiff iron bridge that spans the broad river, but the old square ruined tower and the churches, one with a square tower, the other with an Eastern dome of the onion type, still remain.

Now the scene ahead is totally changed, and all is calm and flat, and thickly wooded islands block the view down stream. But the Eastern domes and high Romanesque towers of Stein, and the continuing houses of the little town of Und linking it to Krems all plead a halt; so we disembark at Krems, from whence to study the district; for all around in streets and buildings are interesting relics of fascinating history. Let us print the old witticism:

STEIN

The Danube to Krems

Stein und Krems are three towns. The catch lies in the name of the little town "Und," really "and" in German. Stein "and" Krems are three towns.

On the Danube, as everywhere, the tourist stream has its special halting-places, but these towns are not tourist-fashionable, so there is no crowd of vehicles or hotel touts to worry the traveller. We found it a hot walk in the month of July from the boat to the town of Krems, but there was a pleasant avenue of trees to give welcome shade. We halted at the "Golden Stag." The names of the inns in these old towns are always reminiscent of old life. We soon found that Krems is a veritable storehouse of bygone life. The streets are bright and clean, and the shops up to date; but the quaint corners, the old gates and towers, make us halt constantly. Modern amenities are not neglected; there is a pretty park with beautiful flowers and fountains, and near this lies the new part of Krems that is rapidly developing. But, alas, some interesting old work has lately been destroyed. When there, in 1908, at the south-east end of the town, one saw some old houses being destroyed that were well illustrated by Sgraffito work—a Star and the I.H.S. with two figures, and above, a crucifix; query was this representing the Trinity; above was the date 1561. Below were scenes from the Prodigal Son. The Prodigal with the pigs in a village; and the next scene, on the right, was a feast, bringing in the jugs and dishes, and the musicians entering. On the left the first scene was gone, the only word left was "Bruder" (brother); of the middle scene some dancing feet only were left, and the upper raised part was just being obliterated with new plaster, but the words were still left, " Vom Verlorenen Sohn." So they were destroying most valuable work that was well worth preserving, and that proved how interesting a town Krems must have been in 1561.

Just below this house was a bridge (iron, alas), over a brook, and from here one could see the site of the old town and the towers and walls; and it was deeply interesting to dive into the centre of the town through its narrow streets with old towers and arches and oriel windows, and many fine old houses.

The Pfarrkirche has much within it of real artistic value; it dates from the eleventh century, but was rebuilt in the seventeenth century. The pulpit is a fine piece of carved work, illustrating the conversion of St Paul; and the frescoes of the virtues are good. A quaint spot surrounded by old houses is the Frauenberg, on which stands the church of this name, older than the present building of the Pfarrkirche; over the door are the words: " Ora pro nobis mater misericordia 1477"; it was rebuilt at this date after the Hussites " profanation " of the older building, but the Jesuits in 1616 restored it.

' There is good work in this church by the famous artist, Kremser Schmidt, whose work we met with at Melk and elsewhere. There is a great deal of excellent work both in painting and carving, and the church is a good example of thirteenth-century work. Outside, between the buttresses, the life of Christ is depicted, the figures being life size, and the painted

The Danube to Krems

background represents Jerusalem. From the church is a fine view of the vineyards all round Krems, and from the tower a wider view of river and landscape. High up in the tower lives the watchman, who strikes a bell every quarter of an hour, and rings a bigger bell, the "Braunglocke," for a quarter of an hour in early morning to call the vineyard workers to their task; in old days he rang also to call them to breakfast and prayer. A day could well be spent in and around this church, so full is it of quaint art and history.

We found that another historic church had succumbed to curious uses, but was now partly rescued for a worthy aim by having one half of it turned into a museum. This was the Dominican Church, the western half, the church of the laity, is the museum; the eastern half, the church of the order, is used as a theatre, and it looked sad to see the tawdry scenery lying about in a noble old religious building, for this church was re-built in 1444, after a fire in 1410. We had to get the key of the western half from the Herr Propst (*i.e.* Prior), Dr Anton Kerschbaumer, who really was the founder of the museum in 1889, and who saved the old church from being a corn warehouse. His own house was most quaint and full of treasures. We found the nave of the church made a noble museum, the collection, although so young, being really fascinating and, historically, of great value, but more space is required to get good organisation.

In 1897 part of a building in the old cloisters was added to the church for the Palæontological section, a collection of real importance; and the Palæo-

Austria

lithic and Neolithic divisions are also most important, containing some remarkable stone weapons. The "Hundsteige" collection alone has 20,000 implements and weapons. This find is said to be the richest Palæolithic find in Lower Austria, and prove these men of primitive days were by no means without culture.

In the bronze exhibit are some very beautiful examples of torques, weapons, etc., and one bronze sword that is a superb gem. When they built the new bridge over the Danube, urns and other prehistoric articles were found, and of later work, especially Roman, there are a crowd of articles, some of peculiar interest.

There is another section in this museum, illustrating the guild life of mediæval days, that is full of charm; the rich banners and insignia of so many trades are here. The cask binders' banner, that is illustrated after a painting by Kremser Schmidt, has Noah planting the vine, a Rubens-like woman treading out the grapes in a tub, and a man at work on the casks; another man is pouring out the new wine, and all is artistically harmonised. There is rich glass, books and MSS., old punishment instruments, and a crowd of objects that will detain the enthusiast for many a day.

From Krems it is but a pleasant walk through Und to Stein. To-day there are houses all the way. And in Stein we again meet with Kremser Schmidt. In spite of his name the people of Stein claim that he was born there, and that the beautiful frescoes in the Rathaus are his work. From Stein we can cross the bridge to Mautern, and so on foot, or by aid of rail

The Danube to Krems

or steamer, explore the whole district, with Krems as headquarters.

Of history Krems has had a surfeit. From prehistoric days on through the days when the Romans came with their swift-moving boats on this Danube frontier. Then came the Slavs, and the Bajuvaren, *i.e.* Bavarians. In 995 Krems is named as a town, so that its claim to be the oldest town in Lower Austria is established, Vienna only being named a town in 1037 and Tuln in 1014. The oldest seal of the town has the Bohemian lion of King Ottakar, with a vine stem and bush; this was succeeded by the Hapsburg seal, the lion being displaced by a helmet with a " bush " of peacock's feathers issuing from it. Husite and Hungarian attacked the town, and the Turkish invasion injured it; and in later days it suffered from the Swedes and its conquest by the French; and, as though war were not sufficient evil, attacks by nature's forces—ice and floods, hail, pest, and fire—have terribly assailed and tried it. To-day it is a picturesque flourishing town, and is doing much to benefit and advance its people under a peaceful rule. Its educational institutions, its trade and commercial and agricultural schools are doing good work, but are not so perfect as in some other parts of the Empire.

Ere leaving Krems we had a hot walk up through vineyards and round the walls that climb up the hillsides, with their watch towers, to find the " Mandl ohne Kopf," the little man without a head. It is a curious headless figure in armour on a wall in a garden near one of the round towers. Like the " Ring " in Nuremberg, those who have not seen the " Mandl "

Austria

have not seen Krems. The figure represents a Swedish major who vented his wrath against holy pictures and images in the Frauenberg church. And on the feast of St Ignatius (July 31), whose statue he split in two, he was reconnoitering near this tower, when a shot from the Austrian forces on the Danube island took off his head, and he is there to this day, headless, on the wall.

CHAPTER XXVII

THE DANUBE FROM KREMS TO THE AUSTRIAN FRONTIER

IT is with regret we leave Krems, for it is the eastern gate out of the pleasant district so full of natural beauty and historic lore, the Wachau.

Now, soon all around is flat; great islands break up the river, which is very wide, and we are quickly looking out over the Tulln plains. Tulln

"Ein Ort am Donau flusse der liegt in Osterland,
   Und ist geheissen Tulme"

So sings the Niebelungen Lied, and it was to "Tulme" that King Ezel rode forth to meet his bride. Small wonder the "Staub der Strasse" (the dust of the route) was never still. For Christian and heathen were with him. Russians, Poles, Greeks, Wallachs, Danes, Thuringians, some with twelve hundred men, others with a thousand. It must have been a brave sight around Kriemhild's spacious tent on this plain of Tulln in the sixth century, if this Lied history is to be credited. In earlier days the Romans had established a camp here, and Tulln as a border town has had an exciting history.

The river becomes shallow and soundings are constant as we steam ahead, but on the right we quickly see a line of low hills; it is the Wiener Wald, the Vienna forest, that the keen sight of the famous

Austria

Burghermeister Lueger has secured for ever as a mighty garden city and pleasure ground for the capital. But there is yet a romantic castle to attract us before we reach Vienna. Greifenstein is seen on the side of a wooded hill. There is plenty of legend and romance clinging to Greifenstein. A mark on the rock of a griffin's claw is said to have given the name to the spot. A more poetical story is told of the unexpected return of the lord of the castle from the Crusades; and behold his wife met him arrayed in her best, and her beautiful hair in long golden plaits decked with ribbons. She was too beautiful; how did she know he was coming? His jealousy was aroused and he called the castle confessor to him, but the confessor gave no satisfactory reply, so the enraged lord hurled him into the Hunger Tower, and his lady's entreaties for mercy confirming his suspicion, he revenged himself upon her by cutting off her long love locks. He swore he would never release the confessor until the stones of the stairway were worn so deep that he could lay the locks of hair in the hole. So all who ascended and descended this stairway out of pity for their priest, said, "Greif an der Stein" (pounce on the stone), and soon a hole was worn, and one day the lord, descending, tripped in this hole, and was picked up dead at the foot of the steps.

As though to sustain an interest in this part of the river until we enter the portals of Vienna, there now comes in sight, on the right hand shore, an immense mass of buildings, with domes and towers, surmounting a high hill. A small town in itself this great building. Bigger, if anything, than Melk is this imposing Augustinian Monastery of Klosterneuburg. Here

The Danube to Austrian Frontier

also are rich collections of art treasures, about 40,000 volumes of books, and no less than 13,000 MSS. Here, as in so many abbeys, the cellars and the gigantic casks, perhaps more noticed than the MSS., are one of the sights for the curious. The wine of the district is a good wine, and the monks know its value.

But we are now again in Vienna, and if we wish to continue our journey through Lower Austria to the Eastern frontier, we can sleep on board and so be ready for the early start in the morning, going on board over night at the Prater Quay.

The commencement of the journey is through a somewhat montonous flat country. Deeply wooded islands of great size break up the volume of water into many channels. As we look back we see the smoke of the great city lying over the plain, and catch glimpses of St Stephen's lofty spire. Soldiers are drilling on the banks. Very soon we are passing the greatest of these islands, Lobau, whence Napoleon in 1809 passed onwards to the crushing defeat of the Austrians at Wagram, on to the peace of Znaim, that pleasant town where we halted in Moravia.

We pass villages in quick succession, the banks of the river still being very flat, and reach the market-town of Fischamend.

In ordinary times the journey down this part of the river is uneventful, but the Danube has its moods and its passions, and in flood time and in drought, even on this part of the voyage, one may be in dubiety as to progress. In the severe drought of 1911 the great saloon steamers could not go up to the Prater Quay, so the smaller boats were utilised, and

Austria

passengers were told that the saloon boats would meet them at Fischamend; but on arriving there, no smoke was seen of the bigger boat, and the soundings gave only just enough water in that great wide river for the lesser craft, and great pebble banks were visible everywhere, and with frequent soundings we crept along and were soon hours behind time.

We are now in a district that would well repay a long halt by the classical student, the province of Pannonia, which Tiberius conquered, so making the Danube the frontier of the Empire.

Vindobona (Vienna) was on the western boundary of this province, and Carnuntum, the capital, influenced the whole of this district, where rich have been the finds of Roman remains.

The fact that it was here that the Stoic Philosopher, Marcus Aurelius, wrote his Meditations, and that Diocletian and other emperors lived, makes the ground deeply interesting. The Vandals settled here in the fourth century, and after the death of Attila in this province in 453, the East Goths occupied the district. At Deutsch-Altenburg, the first important town we come to, the remains of this important occupation can be studied, for in 1904 the Emperor Francis Joseph I. opened the Carnuntum Museum, that contains a rich collection of Roman antiquities, and the amphitheatre and baths, and other remains of the Roman capital have been opened up in recent excavations. At Petronell still stands one of the great Roman gateways, a massive arch with the characteristic brick, or rather tile work, worth halting for in this frontier town. Above it rises a hill with a path to its summit called

The Danube to Austrian Frontier

the Hüttelberg, because the folk made it as they made those hills we saw in Cracow and Lemberg, by carrying up the mould in their hats.

The peasants on board and their dress tell us we are nearing the Hungarian frontier, and soon ahead, down the broad stream, we see rising above the plain-lands a high, flattened, conical hill with a great fortress upon it. A town with a church tower clusters on the river bank beneath this hill, and the great walls and square towers of the castle protect, as it were, the walls of the town that runs down to the river-side. For a time, as we sail on between willow-clad islands, this hill is lost to sight, and over the islands rises a high, crooked peaked mass of hill, all wooded, with a ruin surmounting it, and as we come round a bend in the river we see that this second castle is on a rock some 200 feet high, percipitous to the river, and with a guarding wall with round and octagonal watch-towers ensuring the land side from attack. This is the fortress of Theben; a double castle, its two great bastions at the gateways, with embattled walls connecting them, overlooking the little town beneath. As we go round again we see the other castle of Hainburg, and this castle of Theben on either shore of the Danube command the two bends of the river, having a great view on either side to west and east, and from the north a river falls into the Danube; it is the March that forms the frontier line of Austria and Hungary. At Hainburg we must end our voyage down this romantic, fascinating river, but still romance clings to us, for that ruin on the summit of the broad-capped hill is the Heunenburg or Huns Castle, where Kriemhild and King Etzel halted with all their retinue

Austria

for the night, after staying eighteen days in Vienna for the wedding festivities. Hainburg, on the south shores of the Danube, Heimburg as it is called in the Lied, formed the entry into King Etzel's land, and Hainburg has been fought for throughout the ages. Celt, Huns, German, and Turk have all struggled for its possession, but since 1490 it has been Austrian, and it is a fitting and poetical spot whence to bid adieu to the great river Danube in this book on Austria.

We are in sight again of that great mountain chain the Carpathians, that by its vast line of heights links us up with the Giant Mountains, the northern frontier of the Empire; by the Danube we are linked with the eastern and western frontiers, and if we take the old Roman Danube road we reach the Adriatic, and from this historic ground we take a flying course south-eastwards, and land on the northern shores of Lake Garda, for our tour, through the Tyrol, perhaps to English readers the best known province of Austria.

CHAPTER XXVIII

THROUGH THE TYROL FROM LAKE GARDA TO TRENT (TRIENT OR TRENTO)

AGAIN the scene changes from river and rocky heights, vast monasteries and castled crags, to the shores of a southern lake.

"Kennst du das Land wo die Citronen blühn," wrote Goethe, when he journeyed on the shores of this lovely lake of Garda, and truly this town of Riva inspires poetry, the south-eastern outpost of Austria lying nestled beneath high hills that shadow the soft, turquoise blue crystal waters of the lake. Riva is the southern point of the province of the Tyrol, that has become the pleasure-ground of the world. Innsbruck is the most northerly town; the Engadine bounds the west, and on the east the little town of Toblach is on the confines of Tyrol.

Of the importance of the Tyrol to the health and pleasure-seeking people of the world, one is promptly convinced by a glance at the very long list of health resorts comprised in a schedule arranged according to their heights above sea-level. No less than 351 places are so registered, ranging from 1300 to 9400 feet above the sea, and scores of these hundreds of places are well-known resorts.

But Riva does not appeal to the lover of crisp mountain air, but rather to the lover of soft zephyrs and the lazy life, although close at hand there is ample scope for mountain adventure.

In walking from the Italian frontier to Riva, we pass through some very beautiful scenes. The mighty crags rise crag over crag, high above the lake. In places the hill-sides are walled up in terraces for the lemon gardens. The rocks are of reddish granite hue, and the lake is shut in on either hand by precipitous heights of about 3000 feet; one great peak is isolated, and below this is the pretty fall of the Ponale with the ruins of a castle. The road runs along the ledge of rock, winding round the vast buttresses, one needle of rock springing up at least 3000 feet, and the view of the little town of Riva as we come round is very charming.

We descend from the height to the level of the lake, and enter a hotel with a courtyard surrounded with arches, and a garden with cypress trees and flowers; before us is the mirror-like water of the lake; around, the high, grey-peaked rocks tower up, and just above is the great square tower of the castle of the Scaligers, and half way up a rocky steep is a white castellette, with a round-fronted embattled tower, and other outlying walls and a tourelle.

On the lake the little white-sailed pleasure-boats and the greater fishing-boats with yellow sails glide past, and it is pleasant to sit amidst the flowers and dream, or to take a plunge in the crystal waters of the lake as a revivifier after a warm day's walking. The district between Riva and Trent is a rich district in many ways, both historically and for its southern vegetation. Here, Indian corn, and olives, and vines grow profusely, proving the variety of life there is

A VILLAGE IN GALICIA

Through the Tyrol to Trent

in the Tyrol, when this district is contrasted with the mountain heights we shall shortly traverse.

It was in the autumn of 1880 that I first walked and rode up through this district by the old diligence route. As we approached Arco, the old castle on an isolated black rock seemed to block the route, some 400 feet above the pleasant town, that to-day is a favourite health resort, amidst cypress and olives, orange and lemon gardens, and palms. Here is a school to promote the local olive wood industry. We follow up the course of the river Sarca, passing the village of Dro, most picturesque with its southern type of cottages, and then crossing a bridge beneath which the stream rushes and foams, divided by an islet; beyond on a barren rock we see the castle of Drena, and beyond this we pass through a wild, beautiful district. At one spot there are great blocks of rock, all sliding down into the grey-green waters of the Sarca. Peasants pass by on their asses, or leading patient, meek oxen, with their great wooden yokes, through a rich country of maize and mulberry, olives and vines, that are trailed along from pole to pole. Then the scene changes and we pass through a wild district of stone and cliffs, with a great natural giant wall at the top, through which the road pierces. Then again at the little village of Le Sarche we cross the Sarca that comes rushing in from the mountains that surround us on all sides. We soon arrive at the pretty little lake Toblino, with its picturesque chateau. The road winds round the lake, that on one side lies in the basin of the grey limestone hills, and we get good views of the castle, its round tower, and defensive walls.

Austria

A good halting-spot is on the bridge that spans the stream between the two lakes, to take in the beauty of the scene around. We pass in through the village of Padernione, and then climb the hill-side and look down on the lake below, with its castle in the centre, the rich, luxuriant vegetation all around, and above the barren, craggy heights.

Then comes a piece of road that to the pedestrian is as an oven, between two walls of rock. We are not far from Dante's Inferno, and this is a taste of it; but we get a peep between the rocks, of lake, and castle that tells us paradise here is below; but we press on to Vezzano, where, under the welcome shade of the vine leaves, our host produces an excellent little dinner, especially a soup with Knödeln (dumplings), that a German student with whom we were walking devoured voraciously. The fruit here was exceptionally good, the wine heady as this southern wine is apt to be. The route after Vezzano is very picturesque, it winds on over a village, climbing a height, and then the little lake and village of Terlago is seen far below us; another of these mountain lakes, like a basin with white shores, appears, and ahead is the village of Cadine.

The pass has led us a little north of Trent, and now we bear southward, to the fort built in the rock, that guards the entrance to the valley of Vela, with rocks overhanging and sheltering it, and water running beneath. One great rock mass stands alone, and water forces its way around either side. The view ahead of the grey, cloud-capped peaks is very fine, and below are the white village and waterfalls and caves. It is a district full of charm and of Nature's choicest

THE SCENE WHICH INSPIRED DANTE'S INFERNO, — THE LARINI DI MARCO
NEAR TRIESTE

Through the Tyrol to Trent

compositions. We cross a little bridge beneath which the stream rushes, and then we get a peep of the open view beyond. A waterfall dashes beneath the arched road, and as the view opens out the river Adige comes in sight, and the road winds down between high peaked rocks, and then the rich wide valley of Trent comes into view, and the white town lying under the opposite hills, its white houses climbing here and there the lower-wooded slopes. A mass of castellated rock stands isolated in the valley, surrounded with vines, and blocks the view as we enter the town of Trent (Trento or Trient) and pass on over the bridge to the centre of the city.

This tramp is so exactly the opposite to the usual type of walk one expects to hear of when a tramp in the Tyrol is mentioned, that I have given it somewhat in detail, to show what a strange variety of scenery and surrounding nature one can have in this favourite province. Of mountain climbs over ice and snow, amidst morraines and crevasses, there are thousands in Tyrol—we shall meet with them ere long—but Trent is too interesting and historic a town to rush away from, without a fairly lengthy halt.

The tiny railway that runs from Riva to Mori, and then joins on to the main line to Trent, passes through a district equally interesting as the road we walked, and a digression should be made to visit the castle of Lizzana, where Dante lived for some time. It is said that he gleaned an idea for his Inferno from a savagely wild scene that is near here—a great sea of rocks hurled hither and thither, in most awful, awe-inspiring disorder. The little train crawls and twists

Austria

slowly through one part of this terrible labyrinth, with just space for its passage between the great dark masses of rock. It is in Canto XII. of the Inferno that Dante writes:

> "The place whereto we came to make descent
> Was Alpine rough, and no man's eyes could bear
> The further cause that made me ill content.
>
> "As this side Trent the ruin lieth, where
> Was struck Adiges river in the side
> Through earthquake, or supports that yielded there."

Certainly this pass is supremely savage and worthy of being an aid to the poet's idea of an entrance to Hell; perchance it is the moraine of some mighty glacier, or the fact that a town was buried here in the ninth century by a mountain slide may account for this wild freak of nature.

By this route we pass through Rovereto, where to-day the grape cure is practised under specialists. The position of this town is very romantic, and although in sight of the snow peaks it is a good winter resort.

From the balcony of the Imperial Hotel in Trent, looking out over the pleasant gardens, with the imposing statue of Dante in the foreground embowered in trees and flowers, one can trace most of the principal buildings of the city. The towers and domes and such bits as the jewel-like morsel of the Torre Verde, or Green Tower, all speak of its history that goes back to pre-Roman days.

The epoch that its name at once recalls is that of the sixteenth century, when the great Council of

A BACK STREET IN TRENTO

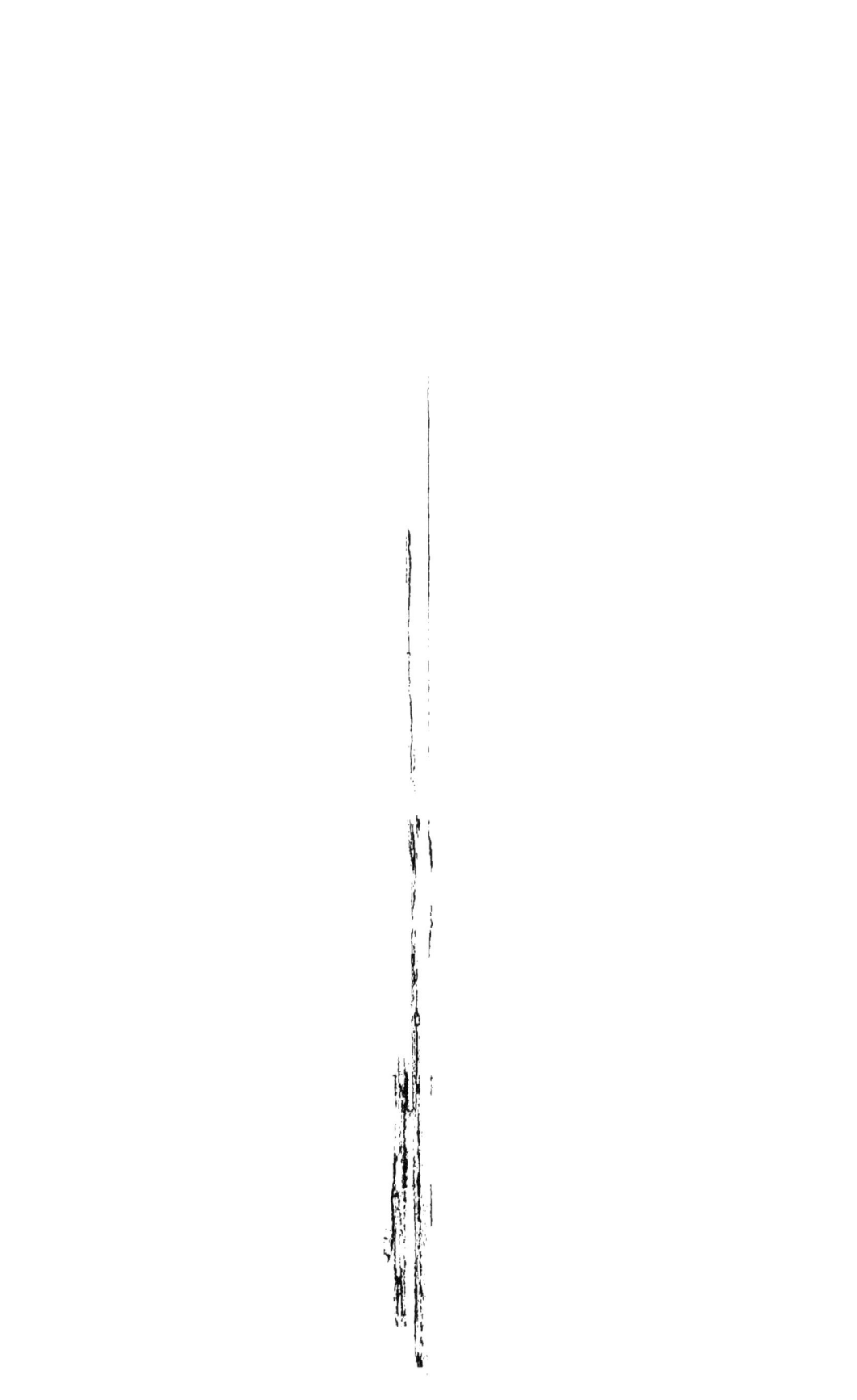

Through the Tyrol to Trent

Trent was held. The church in which the Council sat is much to-day, with very slight alteration, as it was then, and a picture of the Council, preserved in the church, shows the semi-circular arrangement of seats and the general ordering of the Council, that sat intermittently, under three Popes, from 1545 to 1563. Many of the seats bear the arms of the families who occupied them. The cathedral is a fine Romanesque building, with two great lions over the north door that are curious. Many of the streets are delightfully quaint, and full of colour, with the old arches and palaces.

The great Castello Buon Consiglio, formerly a palace of ecclesiastical princes, is most interesting and quaint, and as we emerge from this, that is shown by an under officer, as the building is now used as a barracks, we are in a lovely part of the old town, with the Torre Verde as the central gem. Excellent music can be heard in Trent. On one occasion we were fortunate enough to hear one of the most celebrated bands of the Austrian army, and its rendering of very varied types of music was most masterly, and delicately powerful. Both strings and brass were good, and the men were also good vocalists, singing to their own accompaniment. On another occasion we heard a good rendering of "Aida," with perhaps a little too much forte expression through the entire performance.

In these towns the museums should never be missed. They are never a dull, dusty, collection of heterogeneous articles, and here the Roman remains and MSS., are exceptionally valuable; there are also educational establishments, including

Austria

commercial and industrial schools that are worth visiting.

Innumerable are the excursions that can be made from Trent. The Tourist Information Societies, can be relied upon for useful data for ordinary travellers or climbers.

ROSENGARTEN FROM THETSCHAMINTHAL

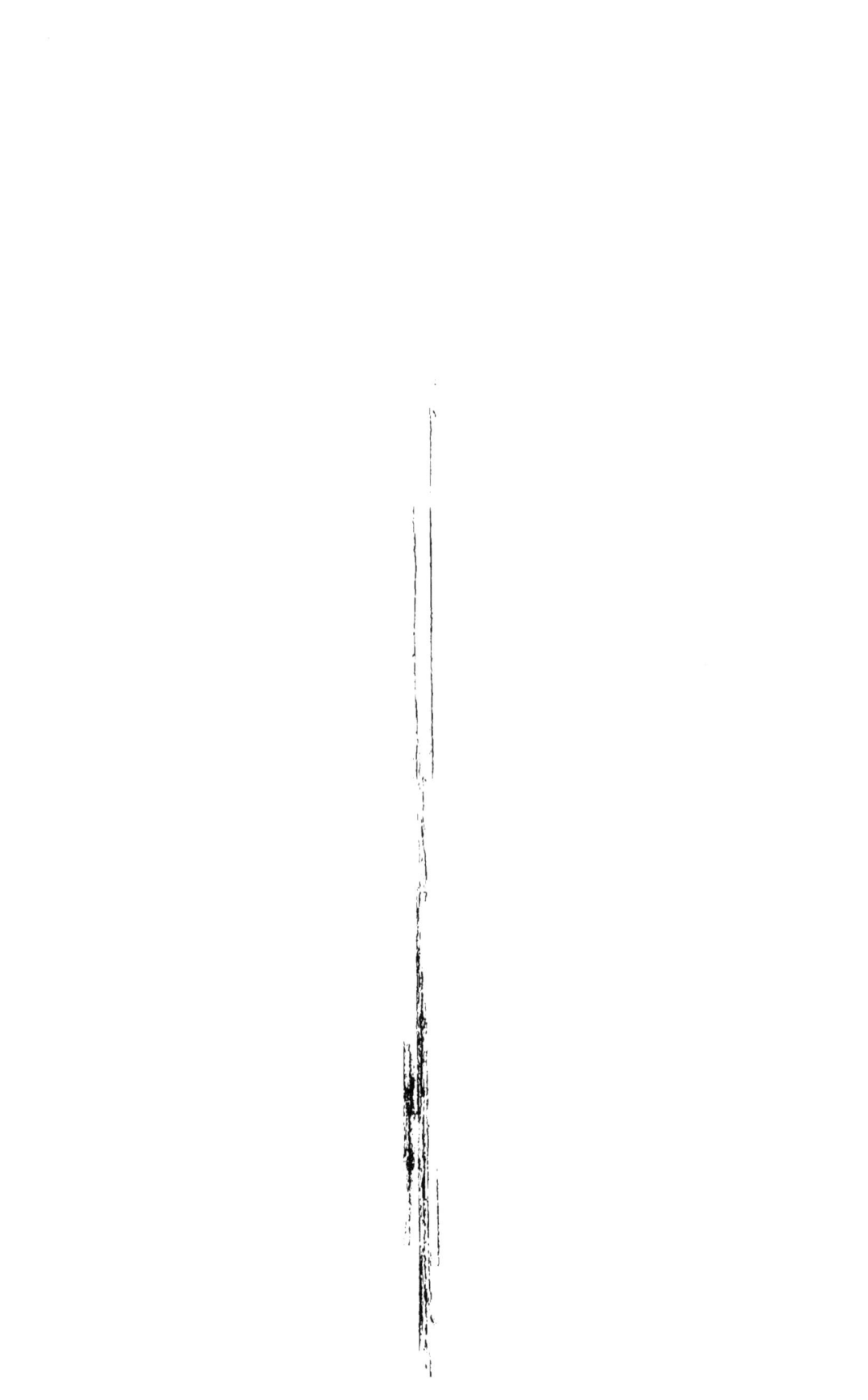

CHAPTER XXIX

THE TYROL FROM TRENT TO MERAN AND CORTINA

TYROL is beyond all the other principalities and provinces of Austria the district for the pedestrian; but the railways to-day quickly bear the walker to the district he chooses for his excursions, and as he travels to reach his destination, snowy peaks and glacier heights plead to him to halt for exploration.

The railway running from Trent to convey us to the enticing spot for Alpinists, Cortina, runs due north to Bozen, where a branch line leads away westward to Meran, the main line passing on northward to Franzensfeste, where the eastern route runs us down to Toblach for Cortina.

But these railway journeys are never monotonous. As we left Trent on one occasion, on crossing the Avisio, that is well described by the guide books as a torrent, we saw where this mountain stream had rushed down and carried away whole houses in its fury. It is but an hour's run to Bozen, and the line passes through cliffs, and then along peaceful fruitful valleys, where little white townlets lie around uprising churches, campaniles, the metal domes of which sparkle in the sunlight. After passing Auer the snow peaks come in sight, and on one point stands out a fine old-walled castle, four square, with four round, towers at each corner, and then Botzen, or Bozen, is seen.

Bozen, the old mediæval town, is now linked across the river Talfer with the rising town of Gries, formerly a village, now a growing health resort; but Bozen has much besides its mere position to attract the traveller and student. To the English-speaking public it is best known as the starting-point for tours amongst the Dolomites.

Although Bozen is in the midst of this ice and crag climbing district yet it is only 850 feet above sea level, and it is the home of a great flower and fruit industry— peaches, apples, pears, walnuts, figs, cherries and roses and violets, and other flowers are here in profusion, and are scientifically cultivated and sent far and wide over Europe. It is gloriously hot in summer, but one can quickly be high up in the mountains to such a resort as Oberbozen, over 4000 feet above sea level, and get the crisp, cool air and magnificently glorious views of the range of the Dolomites, the Oetztaler, and Brenta and other groups.

Nature can give few grander spectacles than to look upon Rosengarten at sunset from Oberbozen, or from Klobenstein, which can also be reached by the same mountain rail that brought us to the Oberbozen. The only drawback to these marvellous, glorious views is the sense of dejection, from the conviction that it is impossible to know even the marvels that nature has to give in this circle around us, of jagged, strange-formed peaks, and vast height masses, mist veiled and ice scored, glowing in such beauteous hues in the waning light; the snow fields tinted with roseate hues, and below the lesser slopes in grey shadow, dark

TRAFOI

The Tyrol to Meran and Cortina

with the pines. There are scores of excursions and mountain expeditions around Bozen, and the journey by road to Toblach and on to Cortina is a glorious one. One of the streets in Bozen is named after Defregger, the artist whose powerful work has so illuminated the history of the Tyrol, and the life of its people; we shall touch upon this life and its history when halting at the capital of the principality, Innsbruck. In Bozen the intellectual life and its business development is aided by schools that assist the special needs of the district, a good new museum and plenty of music, and, of course the hotels are good as throughout the Tyrol; we shall be able, at Innsbruck, to give a reason for this quality in hotel management in the Tyrol.

It is but a short run by rail to Meran, that lies a little higher than Bozen, being nearly 1100 feet above sea level. The former villages of Obermais and Untermais are now joined to Meran, and the beautiful promenades by the slopes of the Passer stream are the resort of the invalids who flock to Meran for lung and other complaints. It is exceptionally an air-cure resort, and everything possible is done to secure quiet pleasure and comfort for the invalid.

The mountains around rise up to 10,000 feet, and these screen Meran from nearly all winds, except the southern, and the register of sunshine for ten years was 197 full sunshine, 32 slight sunshine, and only 10 rainy and 7 snowy days during the autumn season.

For the vigorous Alpinist there is plenty of work near Meran, and throughout Tyrol sport of all sorts can be enjoyed in summer and winter.

There is one interesting spectacular speciality at

Austria

Meran that can be seen on a smaller scale in many towns and villages in Tyrol, but here at Meran is the famous Folk's Theatre with a company of over 300 peasants, performing local plays illustrating Tyrolean life. The historical life that has passed through such noble episodes, and the life of the Alm and villages hid away in the eternal silences beneath the snowy peaks.

The Tyrol is a land of mountain peak often castle crowned as at Sigmundskron, and mountain lake. To look upon a contour map of the principality is to look upon a sea of giant heights and slow moving glaciers, evolving a territory of sublime beauty. And these heights in our days have given tasks to the climber that in former days were deemed impossible. As a writer on mountaineering lately expressed it; this generation " has ascended precipices which our forerunners called perpendicular, and descended gullies which before were deemed death traps."

But we must quit this district of Meran and Bozen, that gives ample scope for pedestrian and climber, and travel up the old railway *en route* for the Brenner Pass to the fortress of Franzensfeste, whence we branch away eastward through the Pusterthal for Toblach and Cortina.

We are traversing Tyrol to give glimpses of its inexhaustible store of mountain resorts and endless variation of scenes. As we leave Bozen we see the grey river rushing between the rich vine-covered hills. The rail twists and winds between rocky cliffs, past wooden mills and wooden bridges, on over mountain torrents that hiss down into the seething river.

At Klausen is a wonderfully picturesque spot, with the white towers of the castle of Sabiona on a

SIGMUNDSKRON

The Tyrol to Meran and Cortina

precipice above the little town, a castle that goes back to Roman days, and the tower has quaint bits of mediæval work to detain the traveller. The river, the Eisack, here is deeper and calmer, having some restful moments in its headlong strenuous career. We cross it ere we arrive at Brixen, lying in a wide upland, the hills receding and opening out wider views. Here the scene begins to change from a southern to a northern aspect. The houses that cluster round the town, that is dominated by the little white double church towers, with dark domes, are of the Northern Tyrol type, with great stones on the roofs, and the vines instead of being trailed along from post to post in pretty southern fashion, are planted in rows as on the Rhine. Pines cover the upper slopes, and beeches and chestnuts the lower banks of the hills. All these towns breathe of bygone ages, the cathedral and the Johannis Church carry us back beyond mediæval days; but there is a most up to date modern curative life carried on here, and for pedestrian work Brixen is a splendid centre.

Franzensfeste is but a couple of miles from Brixen, and as we enter we see the massive old forts that defended this pass in bygone days. We are now 2476 feet above sea level, and we bear away here to the eastward down the famous Pusterthal, that leads down to the Drave or Ober Drau valley, and so links us up again to the romantic district of the Drave and Gail valleys where we halted in Carinthia.

The ramifications and valleys leading from this main valley are simply inexhaustible, and mountain work of every type is plentiful enough to satiate the most determined climber. From Bruneck there is

Austria

now an electric railway that in an hour bears one to Taufers, and from here a score of excursions can be made. The spacious old castle so picturesquely laid out, as it were on a rocky perch, with its round Tourelles and square massive keep, has some excellent architectural work, and is most imposing amidst the mountains.

But the town of Toblach is perhaps the favourite halting-place for the ordinary tourist, or for the mountaineer, the latter going on to Cortina.

This little town of Toblach lies is an upland valley 4133 feet above sea level, and in winter and summer it is full of life.

Cortina, or to give the full name, Cortina d'Ampezzo, is but about nineteen miles south of Toblach, and this has become one of the most favourite resorts, also both in summer and winter, and especially for rock and mountain work. I will let a friend who has climbed most of the difficult heights in Tyrol, Switzerland, and the Pyrenees speak of the work around Cortina.

"The village of Cortina lies at an elevation of about 4000 feet, and is most picturesquely situated in the Ampezzo valley.

"The route from Toblach leads through a wild gorge, passes the light green tinted waters of the little Dürrensee, where the valley opens out, presenting a striking picture of mountains and glacier backed with the huge, jagged, serrated mass of Monte Cristallo.

"The hamlet has a population of only about 800 inhabitants, and yet here lads may be seen painting and drawing from nature, making filagree work, wood-mosaic, and other artistic objects in the cabinet-making school, where the highest art of the wood worker

BRUNECK IN THE PUSTERTHAL

The Tyrol to Meran and Cortina

is taught; and, as at Zakopane, there is also a good lace-working industry of women, and the artistic quality of the work is of a high order.

"Within a radius of five miles are a dozen first-class mountains, ranging in height from 8000 to 10,600 feet, offering climbs unsurpassed in difficulty by any in the Dolomites—noted as it is for the severity of its rock climbs, many presenting the appearance of colossal church spires, pinnacles and towers, which catch the flush of evening light until they glow as burnished copper. The place also affords glorious opportunity for those who enjoy excursions and promenades of less exacting and less exciting character.

"Speaking generally the climbs are only suitable for experts; many of them present no serious difficulty to Alpinists, others are very difficult, such, for instance, as the climb up the north face of the Kleine Zinne, which a few years ago was pronounced by the most expert guides of the district to be unclimbable; and can now only be ascended by those who are satisfied with the scantiest hand and foot hold on the ledges and in the cracks of nearly vertical walls of rock, many hundreds of feet in height. But the rocks are sound and solid.

"The climb to the top of the curious Cinque Torri rocks is unique, inasmuch as seven-eights of the climb is accomplished within the gloomy interior— in the heart of the rocky masses—and it is only when you near the summit that you come out into broad daylight. Then one must climb upon the difficult ledges of the upper fifty feet of these apparently inaccessible rocks, which are split and fissured so sharply from

Austria

each other that a good jump would carry you from one summit to another."

So speaks my friend who has climbed these heights of which he speaks, and he has jotted down the types of climb of the principal of these expeditions—

Name.	Height.	Remarks on the climb.
Monte Cristallo	10,495	Fit only for experts with steady heads.
Piz Popena	10,310	Very difficult.
Kleine Zinne	9,020	North face extremely difficult; impossible to descend by this face.
Cinque Torri rocks	7,750	No serious difficulty.
Sorapis	10,520	Toilsome and difficult.
Nuvolau	8,460	Not difficult.
Monte delle Marmarole	9,620	Not difficult for experts.
Croda da Lago	8,887	Very difficult.
Antelao	10,710	Superb point of view; no difficulty to experts.
Tofana	10,635	Not difficult.
Becco di Mezzodi	8,430	Not difficult.
Croda Rossa	10,330	Toilsome and difficult.

This sketch of mountaineering work at Cortina will suffice to show what vast scope there is in Tyrol for all kinds of mountain work; and we must let this district speak for all, leaving the Alpinists to fill in all the infinite variety, minutiæ, and endless chain of excitement of the work from a variety of experiences throughout Tyrol. We must double back to Franzenfeste for the route over the Brenner to Innsbruck; again following up the rushing Eisack, as we look ahead after leaving Franzensfeste, we see as we approach Sterzing the fields of pure snow lying in the peaked, jagged rocks, and the little town is most picturesque, lying on the lower hills that are cultivated

CRODA DA LAGO

The Tyrol to Meran and Cortina

with care, and with grass and trees to their very summits. On the lower slopes are the brown chalets and grey-green streams, and little white villages climbing the rich green slopes. Then the scene changes to wild savage rocks with hardy fir trees, and with ever-varying scenes we climb on to the summit of the Brenner pass, 4490 feet above sea level. The first of the railway passes over the Alps, opened in 1867, a marvel of engineering work at that period.

As we begin to descend, a solemn little dark green lake varies the scene, and the line winds along a precipice that is so sheer from the carriage windows, that once when passing along it, a young American travelling companion went to the other side of the carriage to give a little extra balance to the train.

The rail winds and twists and curves above lovely valleys, and gradually the streams become wider, and we drop slowly down until we wind on through a fruitful valley, and Innsbruck is reached.

CHAPTER XXX

INNSBRUCK AND THE ARLBERG

INNSBRUCK is very frequently the gate by which travellers enter Austria. In this volume it will be the gate, with the magnificent avenue of the Arlberg, by which we quit this Empire, so munificently blessed by Nature, and so fascinating in its history and its people.

The principality or crownland of the Tyrol with the Vorarlberg has a population of about a million inhabitants; the German element largely predominating, which it does to a greater extent in the north, while, in the south, an Italian element amounts to over 300,000 souls. It has been said that the principal occupation in the Tyrol is hotel keeping, but we have seen how keenly other industries are fostered and developed in various parts of its 10,000 square miles of area, which is over 11,000 square miles if we include Vorarlberg.

The spacious well-built capital has a population of about 60,000 inhabitants, and its buildings and streets are dignified, and not unworthy of the massive nature's handiwork, the snow-clad mountain ranges that literally overshadow the city. I first visited Innsbruck on a hot August day many years ago, and it was indeed hot. But in winter the mountain heights that encircle it, especially on the north, make it a pleasant place to live in, and in the Spring it is a delightful halting-place.

INNSBRUCK

Innsbruck and the Arlberg

There is plenty of history and of historical buildings to interest in Innsbruck, and one can wander up and down its Maria Theresa Street, and under the old arcade, and look up to the mountains high overhead again and again, and then wander on past that gem of house architecture, the Goldenes Dachl (the little gold roof), and study the frescoes and sculpture on it, and stroll on passing some rich examples of mediæval houses, through the Burggraben, to the open spacious Rennweg, with the pretty Hof Gardens and park. But facing this Rennweg is the entrance to the sight of Innsbruck, that is worth travelling very far to see. The Franciscan or Hof Church, with that marvellous monument, one of the grandest, most artistic, and yet strangest that the world has ever seen; the monument to Maximilian, with the exquisitely wrought bronze figures around it; and near by, close to the door, is the simple monument to the daring, indomitable patriot, Andreas Hofer, the noble innkeeper who entered this church to give thanks to God for his second freeing of Innsbruck. The story of Hofer the patriot and martyr, and his heroic struggle that lasted just ten months and ten days, is well told in a local book by Charlotte Coursen, which also gives a good resume of the history of the Tyrol.

There is a very beautiful walk along by the rushing Inn, the Ferdinand's Allee, that gives pretty peeps between the trees of the town, and good views of the mountains along the Inn valley. At the end of this walk is the chain bridge, and the new lift up the Hungerburg; a strange thing this, but an easy way of climbing the height. The Inn, as it rushes on, recalls our start for the tour down the Danube, just below Passau, where it merges itself in the greater flood.

To the economist and the educationalist, one of the most interesting things in Innsbruck of modern life is the Handel's Akademie, or Commercial School. This is a most spacious handsome block of buildings, with every facility for technical classes, and there is one course of instruction given here that is unique. A most elaborate well thought-out course for students studying with a view to the management of hotels. It was, I believe, Herr Karl Landsee, a cultured, far-seeing citizen of Innsbruck, who impressed upon the educational authorities the fact that the chief industry of the Tyrol, and a most important industry throughout the Empire, was hotel-keeping, and whilst courses of education were organised for every trade and profession, there was none for either hotel managers or waiters, and he pointed out the great variety of subjects such men should study to be good managers. At last the courses were arranged, including buying, cooking, glass, linen, furnishing, languages, geography; habits of other nations, sanitation, and the multifarious things a good waiter and a good manager should know. This may account for Innsbruck's boast—they have some of the best hotels in the world.

After studying this modern institution, it is not far to the Karlstrasse, wherein is the great National Museum or Ferdinandeum. Here the history of Innsbruck and of the Tyrol can be studied from prehistoric times down through the ages; and in the picture gallery the life of to-day, as depicted by

IN THE ARLBERG PASS

Innsbruck and the Arlberg

Defregger, will bring back many a scene witnessed on Alm, and in the villages, as well as recalling the fierce struggles of these stalwart mountaineers to preserve their liberty.

All around Innsbruck are excursions innumerable. The quaint old town of Hall is one of the easiest day excursions, and a pleasant way to reach this now is by the tramway, as one gets good views *en route*, and one can stop at will. The grouping of the buildings, especially round the Rathaus at Hall, is full of delightful architectural morsels, and the copper domes of the cathedral, with their ofttimes brilliant colour, add to this charm. The town has a dignified antiquity, and it has preserved a good deal of its mediæval aspect, and to both historian and architect, and more especially to the artist, it has very much of interest. The noble towers of the Stift and Pfarr churches, and the solid Münster Tower form effective bits, and the scene here on a market-day haunts one for a long time. Another excursion now made very easy is to Igls, by carriage, or the route to Berg Isel can be taken, and then passing the massive and beautifully decorated Castle Ambras, which is also a museum of arms, etc., we reach Igls by tramway. The views from this pleasant height, especially if one walks on to Rosenhöhe, on the edge of the pine forests, whose soughing ever speaks of the sea, are always very impressive, even as seen on a rainy day; the cloud gloom over the mountains that now hides and now reveals their glory and vastness is perhaps as beautiful as the effect on a clear sunny day, when the snowy heights glitter in the sun. In the spring these heights are a glory of Alpine flowers, and as we look at the

Austria

peaks around we can see how inexhaustible are the expeditions that can be made from Innsbruck, afoot, in motor, by rail, or by tramway. One list of thirty-four excursions within a ten-mile radius of the town, including some most interesting spots, lies before us, and as in returning from the heights we look down upon the capital of Tyrol, with the grey waters of the Inn rushing through its pleasant tree-bordered gardens, above which rise the historic spires and towers, one gleans faintly how these scenes inspired the patriotism that urged on their national hero, Andreas Hofer, to his heroic actions, and that to-day inspires a glowing love for their country in the hearts of peasants and burghers—a love expressed in their songs and national music.

We quit this gate of the Tyrol ever with regret, but what a glorious avenue have we to pass through ere we quit the confines of Austria! first of all running up the Inn valley, then climbing the giant walls of the Arlberg, and on through the Vorarlberg to the frontier.

As we rise slowly from the Innsbruck level, which is 1880 feet above sea level, we look away to that tremendous wall of rock, the Martinswand, that governs the Inn valley, and soon see peaks of the Dolomite type rising up to 8000 or 9000 feet—such peaks as the great sugar loaf of the Tschirgant. Castles are perched on apparently inaccessible heights, and ever the Inn rushes on, through rocky defiles and dark ravines, whilst the good roads tempt the motorist, and the little footways up through dark pine forests tempt the pedestrian.

. The town of Landeck makes a good halting-spot

HALL IN TIROL

Innsbruck and the Arlberg

in this district, but we climb on upward, and, as we near St Anton, get a striking view of the bluish ice cliffs on the glaciers of the Riffler Mountains that rise over 10,000 feet into the heavens.

At St Anton we are in one of those lovely rich upland valleys, dominated by its dark red church spire that always seem to breathe peace. As it is over 5000 feet in altitude, in winter there is plenty of snow for winter sports. After quitting St Anton we enter the famous Arlberg Tunnel, that is about $6\frac{1}{2}$ miles in length, and has made possible this railway journey through a district so full of beauty. The tunnel passed, we begin to descend, having reached the height of 4300 feet.

We look down into deep *Klamms* and *Schluchts*, gorges and ravines, and then over dark forests to snowy peaks against blue sky and white clouds. The scene is ever changing; we drop slowly down, on through tunnels, over viaducts, that give wondrous peeps into lovely valleys or up to serrated peaks and snow-clad heights. We rush through cuttings and along precipices, until we arrive at Bludenz, where it may be said is the end of this great romance of engineering skill. The groups of mountains we have passed through run up to 12,580 feet, and especially in the Stanzer Valley between St Anton and Landeck are they full of rugged grand beauty, and the expeditions that may be made in this district are endless. From Bludenz we run on along the widening valley of the Ill to Feldkirch, and either quit Austria at the Frontier Station of Buchs, or we may follow along the valley of the Rhine that here skirts the Austrian territory to Bregenz, the capital of the Vorarlberg, where we are on the shores of the Bodensee, or Lake Constance.

Bregenz has suffered the usual fate of frontier towns, and has endured warfare under various nations. In the days of the Romans it was known as Brigantum, a fortified station, and for centuries it was one of the chief fortified southern German towns. It was stormed by the Swedes in 1646, taken by the French in 1796, so that Bregenz has a notable history. To-day it is a small country town little frequented by tourists, but a pleasant place for a halt, with plenty of interesting work for the pedestrian or motorist, and for the historian and archæologist in the near neighbourhood. In winter I have seen good skating on the lake, where in summer, boating, bathing and fishing can be enjoyed, and here on this extreme western point of Austria we conclude our pilgrimage through its homelands.

We have traversed the Empire from the Giant Mountains to the Adriatic and from the Russian frontier to this western frontier by the Rhine, and if the vowels, A, E, I, O, U, adopted by the Emperor Frederick III. in the fifteen century, cannot be used with his words " Alles Erdreich Ist Oesterreich Unterthan," or in Latin, " Austria Est Imperare Orbi Universo," a phrase that no Emperor or monarch has yet ever truthfully been able to adopt; yet if we look at the strangely rich territories and the varied climates, and valuable natural productions of her homelands, if we take the word Erdreich in its literal value of " earth, soil," and to mean Nature's kingdoms, not political kingdoms, the words may be used to-day, for there are few empires possessing so vast

Innsbruck and the Arlberg

a diversity of Nature's riches. And we have been able to give glimpses of the diversity of the people who inhabit this territory—varied, antagonistic, emulous, and yet all working forward in one conglomerate mass, uplifting their homelands and their people, and in so doing advancing the great Empire of Austria, and maintaining her position as the great balancing influence in Central Europe.

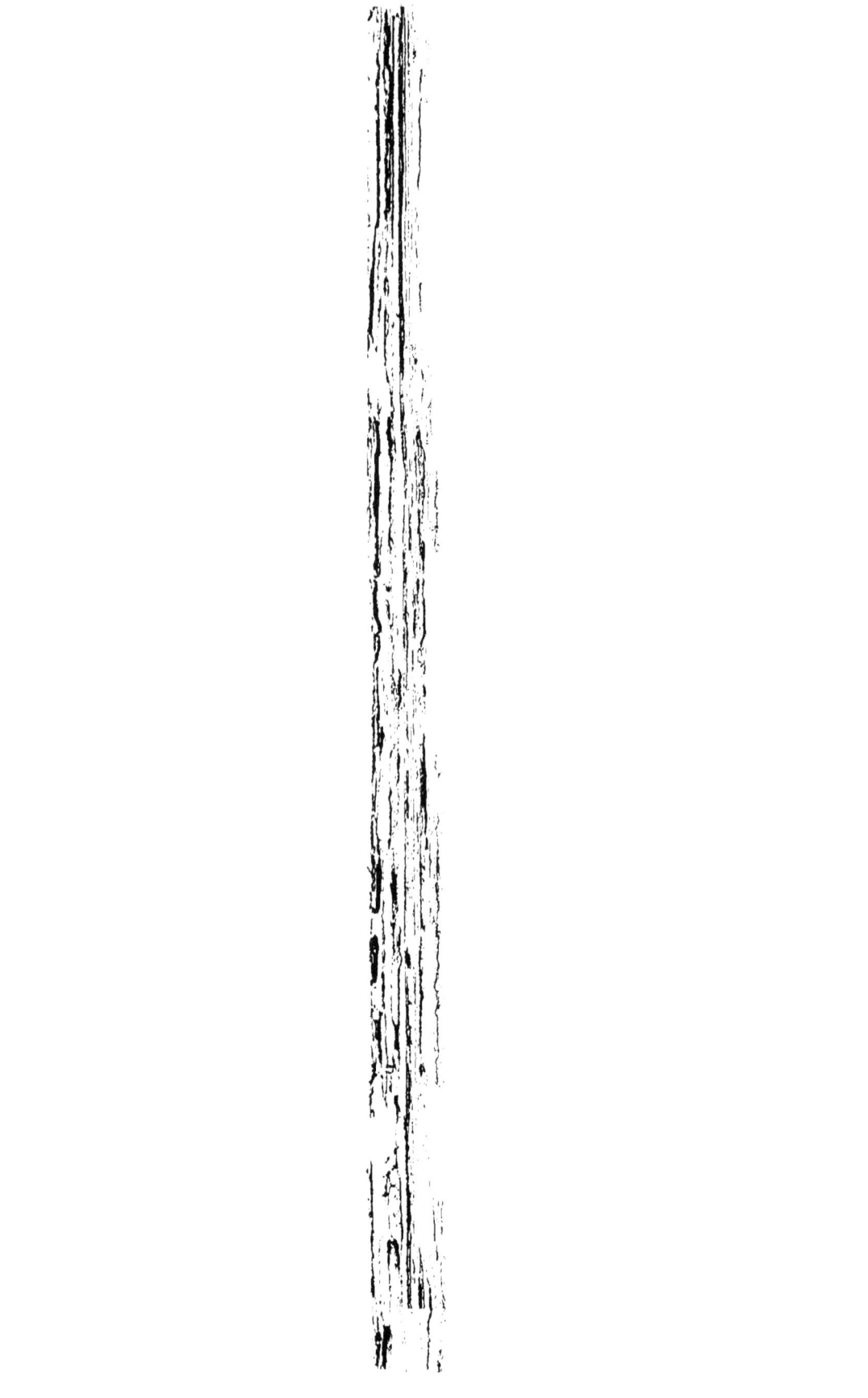

Lutsk
Zamosc
Sandomier
San
Sokal
Brody
Kremenetz
50
Lembérg
Przemysl
Tarnopol
Sambor
Stanislawow
Kaschau
Ungvar
Munkacs
Kolomea
Czernowitz
Marmaros
Bukovina
Khotin
Tokay
Nyiregyhaza
Szathmar
Szigel
Szamos
Debreczin
Bistritz
Grosswardein
Nagy Varad
Kolozsvar
Klausenburg
Bekes
Bekes Csaba
Vásárhely
White Koros
Maros Vasarhely
Marosujvar
Maros
TRANSYLVANIA
Schässburg
Arad
Karlsburg
Mediasch
Fogaras
Kronstadt
Temesvar
Hermannstadt
Red Tow
Lugos
Banat
Versecz
Oravicza
Mehadia
Weisskirchen
Bazias
Orsova
Rimnic
Pitesci
ROMANIA
Walachia
Turnu Severinu
Donau
Pozharevatz
Craiova
Jiu
Oltu (Aluta)
44
Negotin
Widin
Calafatu
Lom
Nicopolis
Timok
Morava
Krushevatz
Nish
Plevna
Vratza
Tirnova
Kopaonik
Pirot
BULGARIA
Mitrovitza
Leskovatz
Yamrukchal
7790
Sofia
Trajans Gate
Pristina
Vitosh
7520
Kazanlik
Vranye
22
24

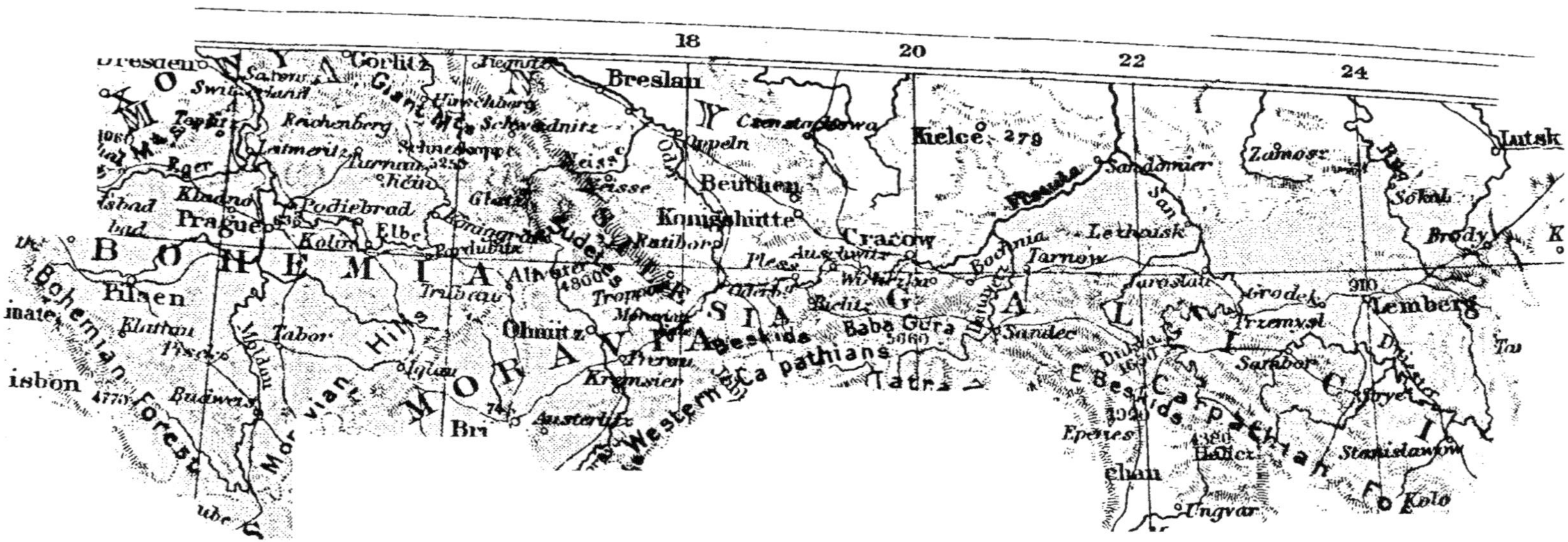

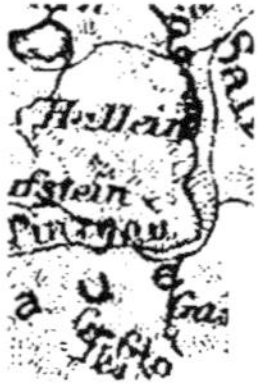

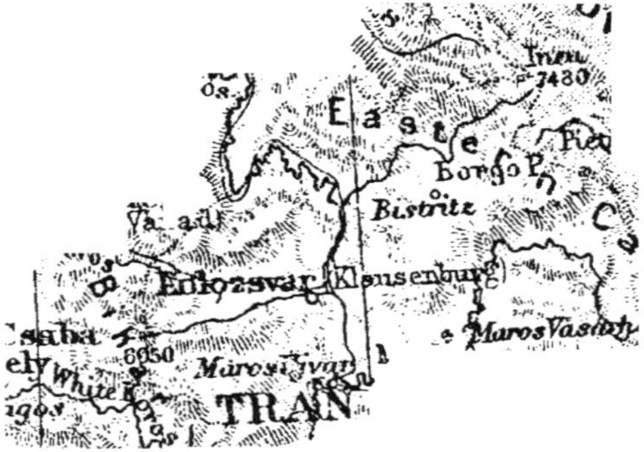

Index

To lessen the number of references, the pages are not cited in which only a casual note is made of a place or person, or where the subject is continued on successive pages.

A

A, E, I, O, U, 300
Abbazia, paradise of roses, 177
Adelsberg, 138
Adelsberg vast caverns, 139
Adersbach, 9
Adige River, 281
Adriatic, 114, 143
Afforestation of the Karst, 146
Aggstein, 259
Agricultural and forestry schools, 99
Alps, the, 241
Alt-Ausseer See, 223
Altvater, 43
Altvater, ascent of, 44
Andreas Hofer, 295, 298
Anne of Bohemia, 17
Anne, Queen, to Richard the Second, 22
Aquileia, 118, 119, 180
Arco, 279
Arlberg, the, 8, 294, 299
Army of the Dual Empire, 104
Arsenal of Graz, 120
Attersee, 222
Attila, 274
Auersperg, Prince, 242
Aussee, 224
Aussig on the Elbe, 39
Austerlitz, 57
Austria, into, *via* the Elbe, 8
Austria, Lower, 108
Austrian Empire, political necessity, 105
Austrian Lloyd's palatial offices, 143
Austrian Lloyd, 149
Avars, the, 119

B

Baden, 110
Bad Gastein, 193, 199
Bajuvaren, the, 119
Beddoes, Dr, 134
Beethoven, 47, 98
Belar, Professor, 135
Benedictine Abbey of Gottweig, 264
Benkovac, 155
Beskiden Mountains, 63
Bezdez, or Bösig, 12, 13
Bismarck, Furst, 200
Black Lake, 35
Blondel, 261
Bludenz, 299
Bocche di Cattaro, 171
Böckstein, 198
Bodenbach, 8
Bodensee, or Lake Constance, 300
Bohemia, 9, 24
Bohemia, Northern and Eastern, 8
Bohemia, Southern and Western, 30
Bohemian glass, 23
Bohemian Paradise, the, 14
Boni, Comendatore, 163
Books on the Danube, 229
Bora, terrific, 144
Bozen, 285, 286
Brazza, 164
Brenner Pass, 293
Brigantum, 300
Brioni, 150
Bristol Castle, 17
British writers and journalists in Carniola, 132
Brixen, 289
Brown, Dr Edward, 133
Bruck, 115
Bruneck, 289
Brünn, centre of cloth and leather trades, 49, 50, 57
Buchs, 299
Budweis, 31, 32
Bukowina, 82, 83

Austria

Bukowina history, 90
Bukowiner Hohe, 74
Bulgarians, settlements of, 87
Bulic, Monseignor, 154, 162, 164
Burghermeister Lueger, 272
Burgstein or Sloup, 11, 12
Busi, Blue Grotto of, 165

C

Calais, 8
Capo d'Istria, 147
"Cardinals' Page," 17, 34
Carinthia (Kärnten), 180
Carlsbad, 8, 38
Carniola history, 130
Carniola, or Krain, 125
Carnuntum, 274
Carnuntum Museum, 274
Carpathians, 63, 72, 89, 98, 276
Carpenter's house, 128
Castle Ambras, 297
Castle Vitturi, 160
Castelnuovo, 176
Cathedral of St Vitus, 23
Cattaro, 157, 174
Cattaro history, 176
Čech students, 27
Celtic tribes, 119
Chabowka, 70
Chains to shut off the Jews, 66
Chambers of Commerce, not as in England, 53
Chamber of Commerce of Lwöw, 79
Charles Bridge, 27
Charles IV., 19
Chods, the, 35
Christianity, early adopted, 119
Cinque Torri, 291
Clementinum, 23
Clifton, 134
Cobenzl, 98
Commerce, Chamber of, 86
Corporate life of small towns, 58
Corpus Christi procession, 127, 129
Cortina d'Ampezzo, 290
Council of Trent, 283
Court of Charles V., 19
Cracow, 63, 67
Croatian and Serbian languages, 175
Cultivation, intense, 21
Curzola, 167
Czernowitz, epitome of Austria, 83

D

Dalmatian coast, 157
Danielsberg, 196
Dante's Inferno 280
Danube, moods and passions, 273
Danube navigation, 234
Danube saloon steamers, 229
Danube Steamship Company, 108
Danube, the, 97, 227
Danube Valley, 217
Davy, Sir Humphry, 132, 133, 134, 136, 138
Defregger, 287
Delattre, Abbe, 164, 253
Deutsch-Altenburg, 274
Diocletian, 119, 160, 274
Dobratsch Mountain, 183, 188
Dolomites, the, 286
Domažlice (Taus), 19, 35
Donnerkogel, the, 224
Dorna Watra, 89
Drage, Geoffrey, Austria Hungary, 102, 103, 104
Drave, 120, 183, 195
Drena, castle of, 279
Dresden, 8
Drought of 1911, 273
Dürrenstein, 261, 264
Dvořàk, 19, 27
Dzieduszycki Museum, 79

E

Eastern Bohemia, 16
Ebensee, 222
Economic situation, 103
Edmunds Klamm, 9, 10
Education, Austrian, 214
Education, Austrian, excellent system, 52
Educational establishments of small Austrian towns, 58
Education, Report on Technical and Commercial (C.D. 419), 104
Edward VII., King, 38
Eger, 8, 39
Eisack, the, 289
Eisenstein, 35
Elbe, 8, 10, 17
Elizabeth, Queen, 22
Emperor Henry III., a stately pageant, 248
Engandine, 277
Engineering feats of overcoming difficulties, 197

Index

English fleet under Hoste, 177
Enns, 109, 120
Epidaurus, 167
Ercegnovi, or Castelnuovo, 172
"Eros and Psyche," remarkable drama, entitled, 80
Ethnographical Museum, 27
Ethnology, 48
Etruscans, the, 118
Etruscan vases, 182

F

Factories, 101
Farmer's house, 128
Fauna and Flora of Carniola, 132
Feistritz, 136
Fête, picturesque, on the Vistula, 66
Fire alarm, ingenious method, 92
Fir tree, life of, 233
Fischamend, 273
Fischer, Herr, 158
Flower Corso, Vienna, 97
Flushing, 8
Folk's Theatre, 288
Folk museums, 122
Folklore and legend, 247
Forestry, 142
"Forgotten Great Englishman, A," 17
Frain, castle of, 60
Francis Joseph I., 93, 111, 274
Franzensbad, 39
Franzensberg, 51
Franzensfeste, 288, 289
Frauenberg, 32
Freedom in Austria, 103
Friedland, 12
Fürstenberg Gardens, 24

G

Galicia, 63, 77
Garda, lake of, 277
Gasthaus zum Richard Löwenherz, 262
Gelsse, the—a very special mosquito, 254
General Radetzky, 130
German population of Bavaria, linking up, 193
German students, 27
Ghega, Karl, 111

Giant Mountains, 11
Giant Mountain excursions, 14
Giewont, the, 71
Gilbert, J., 133
"Gleaming Dawn, The," 17
Gloggnitz, 112
Gmunden, 221
Gorizia (Görz), 180, 181
Gosau, 224
Government credit, 104
Gozze, Count, 171
Gratz or Graz, 114, 115, 116
Gratz, castle of, 47
Gravosa, 167
Greifenstein romance, 272
Grein, town of, 243
Greiner Schwall, 244
Gross and Klein Skal, 14
Gross Skal, 15
Grossen Winterberg, 9
Grottensee, 213
Guild life of mediæval days, 268
Gutenstein, castle of, 37

H

Haida, 12
Hainburg, 275
Hall, 297
Halstätter See, 223
Handel's Akademie, or Commercia School, 296
Hapsburgs, the, 106
Health resorts, Bohemia, 37
Heathen customs, 46
Herrenskretchen, 8, 10
High Tatra Mountains, 69
Historical studies, opportunity for, 190
Hofer, Dr Brother Berthold, 253
Hohenelbe, 14
Hohenfurth, 34
Hohenlohe memoirs, 17
Hohenlohe, Prince, 17, 143
Hook of Holland, 8
Hotel keeping in the Tyrol, 294
"Houses," *i.e.* clubs of the different nationalities, 84
Housewifery school, 72
Hradčany, Royal Palace of the, 23
Hradschin, 22
Hunger tower, 13
Hunger Wall, 27
Hungarian frontier, 275
Hus, canonised as a Saint, 22

Austria

Husinec, 35
Huttelberg, 275

I

Ice-exuding holes, 59
Ilz, the, 227
Industrial life, 104
Inferno, Dante's, 282
Inn, the, 227, 296
Innsbruck, 8
Innsbruck, 277, 294
International Challenge Shield, 20
International Press Congress in Ischl, 220
Ischl, 115, 218
Iser Mountains, 11
Italian frontier to Riva, 278

J

Jacquinta, Norman Princess, 176
Jägerndorf, 44, 45
Jerrold, Walter, 228, 244
Jewish burying ground, 23
Jewish Town Hall, 23
Jews in Galicia, 80
Jičín, 13, 14, 16
Joanneum Museum in Graz, 118, 121
Jochstein, 230
John Hus, birthplace of, 34
Johnsdorf, 10
John Sobieski, overwhelmed Turkish force, 67
John Westacott, 233, 245
Joseph II., Emperor, 52
Julian Alps, 125
Julian Alps, fauna of, 138
Jung Bunzlau, or Mlada Boleslav, 15

K

Kahlenberg, 16, 98
Kalte Rinne, 112
Kamnitz, 10
Kank, 16
Karawanken Alps, 115, 188, 193
Karawanken tunnel, 182
Karlin, 22
Karlov church, 28
Karlsbrunn, 43
Karlstein, 30
Karluv Most, 23
Karst Mountains, 142
King Etzel, 275

Kistanje, 155
Klagenfurt, the capital of Carinthia, 188, 189
Klamm, 112
Klausen, 288
Kleine Zinne, 291
Klosterneuburg, 272
Knight of the Triglav Kingdom, 135
Knin, 155
Kolbnitz, 196
Kohl, Herr J. G., 26, 237
Koschat, Thomas, folk music, 190
Koscieliska Valley, 73
Kosciuszko's tomb, 65
Kosciuszko, 78
Kosciuszko Hill, 67
Krapfenwald, 98
Krempelstein, 228
Krems, 264
Kremser Schmidt, 266, 268
Krems history, 269
Kriemhild, 251, 258, 275
Krka River, 155
Krumau, or Krumlov, 33, 34
Kubelik, 27
Kustenland, the, 141
Kutna Hora, or Kuttenberg, 16, 17

L

"L'Autriche a l'aube de XX Siecle," by Max Marse, 102
Lacroma, isle of, 170
Laibach, 130, 138
Landeck, 298
Landsee, Herr Karl, 296
Lauriacum, 242
Layard, Mr, 163
Leitmeritz, or Litomerice, 11
Legend, land of, Bohemia, 41
Lemberg to the Bukowina, 77
Lessina, 164, 167
Libussa, Princess, 22, 28
Life on the higher alm, 221
Lindtner, Mr, 129
Linz, 32, 109, 235, 236
Lissa, 165, 166
Liszt, 47
Living cheap in Austria, 101
Lizzana, castle of, 281
Ljubljana (Laibach), 125
Lobau, 273
Ludi Horecza, 87
Lussino, 152
Lwów, or Lemberg, 77

Neuhaus, 231, 232
Newspapers, 100
Noric branch of the Celts, 118
Nowy Targ, 70

O

Oberbozen, 286
Oberfalkenstein, 196
Obervellach, 197
Oester-Reich, 94
"Oesterreichisches Statistisches Handbuch," 41, 99
Olmütz, 48
Oman, Professor, 83
Ombla, the, 167
Opcina, 142
Oppa falls, 44
Oppa, Gold, White, Middle, 44
Oppa, the, 43
Ossolinski Museum, 79
Ostend, 8
Ottensheim, 235

P

Pacher, Michael, altar-piece by, 215
Padernione, village of, 280
Palacky, 104
Palacky's History, 17
Palæolithic find, 268
Palm Sunday in Moravia, 46
Pannonia, province of, 274
Paradise for sportsman, fisherman, or mountaineer, botanist, or geologist, 68
Parisio, Signor, 161
Parliament House, 24
Paracelsus, Theophrastus, 183
Pay for peasants, 128
Payne, Peter, the "Forgotten great Englishman," 37
Peasant Art of Austria, 206
Peasant folk, quaint customs, 157
Peasants' peculiar dress, 75
Perasto, famous for its seamen, 173
Perko, Mr, 141
Persenbeug, castle of, 248
Petermann, Reinhard, 158
Petronell, 274
Philanthropic institutions in Vienna, 96
"Pictures from Bohemia," 13
Picturesque dress, women in, 36
Pilsen, 36

Austria

Plants, rarer, 137
Pöchlarn, Great, 250
Pöchlarn, Little, 250
Podiebrad, 17
Pola, 151
Poles free under Austria, 63
Ponale, 278
Population and race, 99
Population of Upper Austria, 229
Poronin, 70, 74
Portshach, 191
Postlingberg, ascent of, in the seventies, 239
Powder Tower, 21
Prachatic, 34
Prague, 16, 19, 21, 28
Prater Quay, 108
Prater, the, 97
Prebischthor, 9
Promysl, 22
Prokov, Rock town of, 16
Prussian campaign of 1866, 16
Pruth, the, 85, 87
Punta Planka, 159
Pusterthal, the, 288, 289

Q

Quarnero, 152, 177
Quarnero and Quarnerolo, 149

R

Race difficulties and aspirations, 105
Ragusa, 164, 168
Raible Dolomites, 189
Railways of Europe, grandmother of, 32
Railways, productive, development by the State, 103
Ransonnet, Baron, 165
Reichenberg, 11
Reichsrath, the, 102
Religious establishments in Czernowitz, 85
Report for the Board of Education on Technical and Commercial Education in Central Europe (C.D. 419), 79
Rex Triglavenses I., 135
Richard Cœur de Lion, 180, 237, 261
Richard Cœur de Lion, guest of the Ragusan Senate, 170
Richard the Second of England, 17
Riva, 277

Riva to Mori, 281
Rivalry of the varied races, 24
Rizano, 175
Rock towns, 9
Roll, the, 12
Römerbad, 123
Rosenbergs, 16, 33, 34
Rosengarten, 286
Rossatz, 262
Rotstein, 15
Rotwein Klamm, 135, 190
Rovensko, 15
Rovereto, 282
Rovigno, 150
Roznik, village of, 127
Rudolphinum, 23
Rupert, Prince, 22
Ruthenians, absolute freedom in Galicia, 82

S

Sabbioncello, 167
Sadagora, 83, 87
Sadowa, 16
St Anton, 299
St Barbara, Church of, 16
St Florian, 241
St Gilgen, 213
St Giorgio and Madonna della Scapella, 173
St Johann, 260
St Johann Pongau, 204
St John's, 28
St Martin, 28
St Martin's, mine of, 16
St Peter and Paul, 28
St Stephen, 106
St Veit, 128
St Wolfgang, 213, 214
Salinas, Professor, 163
Salona, the Pompeii of Dalmatia, 162
Salzburg, 206
Salzburg, Duchy of, 199
Salzkammergut, the, 115, 206, 212
Salzkammergut Lakes, 213
Samuel, Bulgarian Czar, 176
Sann River, 123
Sarca River, 279
Sarcophagi, exceptionally fine, 163
Sarmingstein, 247
Save, 120, 125
Savings Bank, 86, 100
Saxon Switzerland, 8
Schachinger, Dr, 253, 255
Schafberg, the, 216

Index

Schandau, 8
Scheffel, v. Viktor, 260
Schliemann, Dr, 163
Schlossberg, 116, 122
Schneekoppe, 14
Schönbrunn, 93, 97
Schönbühl, or Schönbichel, 259
Schools, excellent, 45
Schreckenstein, castle of, 39
Schreckenwald, the robber knight, 259
Schwarzach, St Veit, 203
Schwarzenberg, Prince, 33
Schwarzenberg territory, Natural History in the, 32
Sebenico, 157, 158
Sedlec, 17
Semmering Pass, 110
Semmering, the, 108, 114
Sevcik, 27, 35
Shaduf wells, 81
Siemiradzki, 67
Sigmundskron, 288
Silesia to Moravia, 43
Silvio Pellico, 52, 144
Skoda establishment, 36
Slav part songs, 135
Slavonian folk, picturesque dress, 183
Slum, town without a, 28
Smetana, 19, 27
Smichov, 22
Sobieski, John, 65, 77, 90, 218
Sokol, 84
Sokol Athletic Society, 36
Southampton, 17
Southern Railway, 109, 113
Spalato, 160
Spielberg, the, 51
Spittal, 111, 194
Spitz, 260
Sports in the forests and mountains, 41
Sport, plenty of, in Carinthia, 191
Stalactite caverns, 74
Statistical Central Commission, Royal and Imperial, 98
"Statistisches Jahrbuch der Autonomen Landesverwaltung," 99
Stein, 264
Stertzing, 292
Stillenstein Klamm, 244
Stradioti, island of, 172
Strahov monastery, the, 27
Styria, the ancient Steiermark of Austria, 113
Styrian Alps, 98

Sudden contrasts of life in Austria, 218
Sudeten, the, 43
Sumava, 35

Т

Tabor, founded by Zizka, 31
Tannenberg, 11
Tarvis, 188
Tatra Mountains, 74, 75
Tauern Mountains, 114, 132
Tauern Railway, 191, 193, 195
Tauern tunnel, 197
Taufers, 290
Taus, 19
Technical Schools, 99
Tegetthoff, Admiral, 165
Teplitz, 39
Tetschen, 11.
Teufelsmauer, 260
Teyn Church, 21
Thaya Valley, 57
Theben, fortress of, 275
Tillage, excellent, 100
Timber work on the Danube, 232
Titian, 19
Tobin, Dr, 133
Toblach, 277, 290
Toblino Lake, 279
Toplitz and Kammer Lakes, 225
Totegebirge, the, 225
Trau, 159
Traunsee, 221
Traunstein, 221
Trautenau, 11, 16
Trent, Trento or Trient, 281
Triest, 142
"Triffoni," coins, 176
Triglav, 130
Triglav Lakes, 135
Troppau, 45, 47
Trosky, 15
Trstenik, 167
Tschirgant, the, 298
Tulln, 271
Turnov (Turnau), 11, 13, 15
Tyrol, 277, 281, 285

U

Und, 264
Undine, 233
Ungarisch-Hradisch, 57
Universal Suffrage, 103

309

Austria

Unterfalkenstein, 196
Untersberg, the, 209

V

Vandals, the, 274
Veit Stoss, 64
Veldes, 136
Velebit Mountains, 152, 156
Vezzano, 280
Vienna, 91
Vienna Flower Corso, 97
Villach, 115
Vindobona (Vienna), 274
Vinohrady, 22, 28
Vistula, 63
Vltava, 23, 27, 33
Vorarlberg, 294
Voslau, 110
Vysehrad, 23, 28

W

Wachau, the, 254, 259, 271
Wages, for men, for women, 52
Wages in factories, 128
Wagner, 19
Wagram, 57, 273
Waldstein, 14, 15, 16
Wallensteins, 12, 15, 45, 61, 194
Wallensteins, palace of, 24
Wallsee, 243
Walpurgis night, 31
Walter Crane, 57
Warmbad bathing resort, 184
Wartberg, 115
Weckelsdorf, 9
Weinzettelwand, 112
Weiteneck, 251
Wenzel's chapel, double church, upper Roman Catholic, lower Protestant, 61
"Whisky's had nae chance," 37
White Dunajec, 71
White Mountain, 22
Whitmonday at Warmbad and Villach, 186
Wiclif period, 17
Wiener Wald, 271
Wochein Lake, 134
Wonder Rabbi Friedmann, 88
Wood-carving and the lace-making schools of Zakopane, 75
Woodwork school, 183, 222
Worther See, 190
Wyclifite wars, 40
Wyscherad, 22

Y

Ybbs, 248

Z

Zakopane, 69, 70, 75
Zara, 153
Zeller See, 210
Zizkov, 22
Znaim, 58, 61, 273
Zwitta River, 55

Lightning Source UK Ltd.
Milton Keynes UK
UKHW021000271118
33302OUK00009B/1056/P